SECURITY ANALYST MULTI-YEAR EARNINGS FORECASTS AND THE CAPITAL MARKET

AMERICAN ACCOUNTING ASSOCIATION

The By-Laws of the American Accounting Association state that the first purpose of the Association shall be "to initiate, encourage, and sponsor research in accounting and to publish or aid in the publication of the results of research." In harmony with this objective, the publication of the Studies in Accounting Research is aimed at encouraging and publishing research. This series is an outgrowth of the research program initiated by the Association in 1965. Under this program research projects and authors are selected by the Director of Research, who is assisted by a Research Advisory Committee.

When the project is commissioned, the author is allowed maximum freedom in conducting research. The author is solely responsible for the procedures followed and the research conclusions.

This project was commissioned by A. Rashad Abdel-khalik during his term as Director of Research. It was completed when Theodore J. Mock was Director of Research. The Research Advisory Committee for this project consisted of:

J. Richard Dietrich	University of Texas at Austin
Robert W. Holthausen	University of Chicago
Dale Morse	Cornell University
Stephen Penman	University of California at Berkeley
Gerald L. Salamon	University of Iowa

SECURITY ANALYST MULTI-YEAR EARNINGS FORECASTS AND THE CAPITAL MARKET

by
Philip Brown, George Foster
and Eric Noreen

AMERICAN ACCOUNTING ASSOCIATION
1985

Library of Congress Catalog Card Number 84-072753
ISBN 0-86539-049-5
Printed in the United States of America

TABLE OF CONTENTS

PREFACE

Financial support for this study came from a grant from the American Accounting Association and from the Stanford Program in Accounting. Much of the research was done when P. Brown and E. Noreen were visiting faculty at Stanford University. The Australian Graduate School of Management provided support for G. Foster in the fall of 1983. Lynch, Jones and Ryan (with the sponsorship of Crocker Investment Management Corp.) and Wells Fargo Investment Advisors provided us with the data bases, without which this research could not have been undertaken. Stan Chamberlin and Gene Hawkins of Lynch, Jones and Ryan, and William Jahnke, William McEwan and Charles Pohl of Wells Fargo provided valued advice on the research.

The monograph was commissioned by A.R. Abdel-khalik in his role as Director of Research for the American Accounting Association. T. Mock was Director of Research at the time publication was approved. We are indebted to both for their support, interest, and encouragement. Our advisory committee, the source of much appreciated comment and criticism, consisted of:

J. Dietrich, The University of Texas at Austin
R. Holthausen, The University of Chicago
D. Morse, Cornell University
S. Penman, The University of California at Berkeley
G. Salamon, The University of Iowa.

During 1983, workshops based on the research were given at The Australian Graduate School of Management, Monash University, N.S.W. Institute of Technology, Stanford University, The University of Arizona, The University of British Columbia, The University of Chicago, The University of Queensland, The University of Washington, and Washington University. We benefited much from the comments of many participants (both verbal and written) and from the discipline of having to explain, justify, or rationalize our research. Assistance from M. Ibrahim, L. Marais, S. Ozler, R. Saenz-Garza, T. Shevlin and D. Then was of considerable help in ensuring that this project came to fruition.

Jeannette Ochoa, Margaret Russ, Yuri Sasaki and Alice Sheehan helped prepare the manuscript. We are indebted to all four, both for their competence and for the good-humored way they handled the numerous revisions of the manuscript. Janet Nuñez's professional editorial work was much appreciated and highly valued.

Philip Brown, University of Western Australia
George Foster, Stanford University
Eric Noreen, University of Washington

CHAPTER 1

INTRODUCTION AND SUMMARY

1.1 Introduction

Research using security analyst or management forecasts of earnings has been undertaken in the following areas:

I. Properties of earnings forecasts by security analysts,

II. Capital markets and security analyst earnings forecasts,

III. Properties of earnings forecasts by management,

IV. Capital markets and management earnings forecasts, and

V. Benchmark comparisons of security analyst, management, and mechanical model earnings forecasts.

Within each of these five areas, a wide variety of topics has been examined. Table 1.1 provides a categorization of topics for each of the above research areas.

The most important research contribution of this monograph is to the IIB category in Table 1.1. In particular, new results are reported on

- the association between security analysts' multi-year earnings forecasts and security returns, and
- the effect of information timeliness on capital market association measures.

In addition, more extensive evidence than exists in the literature is presented on the IA, IB, IC, and ID categories in Table 1.1. The area where this more extensive evidence addresses topics with limited prior coverage is

- the properties of security analysts' multi-year earnings forecasts.

This chapter presents a summary of our major research findings and discusses their importance. The Appendix to the monograph provides a detailed review of prior research on earnings forecasts, with particular attention paid to where our findings extend that research.

Two data bases are used in this monograph:

(1) Historical Institutional Brokers Estimate System (IBES) data base developed by Lynch, Jones and Ryan. Among other items, it contains consensus security analyst earnings per share (EPS) forecasts for each year of a two-fiscal-year forecast horizon; that is, the current fiscal year (termed FY1) and the fiscal year that follows (termed FY2). The data are provided at monthly intervals and cover forecasts assembled during the January 1976 to December 1980 period. This study examines 500 securities included in the IBES data base.

(2) Security Market Line (Plane) data base of Wells Fargo Investment Advisors. Among other items, it contains individual security analyst EPS forecasts for each year of a five-fiscal-year forecast horizon; that is, the current fiscal year (FY1) and the

TABLE 1.1
CATEGORIZATION OF RESEARCH ON EARNINGS FORECASTS

I. Properties of Earnings Forecasts by Security Analysts

A. Security Analyst Forecast Errors: Statistics on Forecast Error Distributions and Their Determinants

B. Security Analyst Forecast Revisions: Statistics on Frequency of Forecast Revisions and Their Determinants

C. Security Analyst Consensus Forecasts: Properties of and Issues in Aggregating Individual Analyst Forecasts

D. Divergence of Security Analyst Forecasts

E. Security Analyst Earnings Forecast Process: Experimental and Survey Research

II. Capital Markets and Security Analyst Earnings Forecasts

A. Announcement Effect of Security Analyst Forecasts

B. Association Between Security Analyst Earnings Forecast Errors or Forecast Revisions and Security Returns

C. Association Between Security Analyst Earnings Forecast-Based Variables and Capital Market Risk or Return

D. Cross-Sectional Valuation: Role of Security Analyst Forecasts in Explaining Price, PE Ratios, or in Active Equity Valuation Analysis

III. Properties of Earnings Forecasts by Management

A. Management Earnings Forecast Errors: Statistics on Forecast Error Distributions and Their Determinants

B. Management Earnings Forecast Process and Disclosure Decisions: Experimental and Survey Research

C. Characteristics of Firms With Voluntarily Disclosed Management Forecasts

IV. Capital Markets and Management Earnings Forecasts

A. Announcement Effect of Management Forecasts

B. Association Between Management Earnings Forecasts and Security Returns

V. Benchmark Comparisons of Security Analyst, Management, and Mechanical Model Earnings Forecasts

A. Forecasts of Security Analysts vs. Forecasts of Mechanical Models

B. Forecasts of Security Analysts vs. Forecasts of Management

C. Forecasts of Management vs. Forecasts of Mechanical Models

D. Composite Forecast Analysis

subsequent four fiscal years (FY2, FY3, FY4, and FY5). The data are updated monthly and cover forecasts made during the January 1977 to June 1980 period. Information on a maximum of 405 securities is included.

Notation

The following notation is used in this monograph:

FY1 = Fiscal Year 1 Earnings (i.e., Earnings for the next-to-be-announced fiscal year)

FY2 = Fiscal Year 2 Earnings

.

.

.

FYN = Fiscal Year N Earnings

Forecast Error for FYN = Actual Earnings for Fiscal Year N – Forecast of Earnings for Fiscal Year N

FYN+ for Forecast Error means Actual FYN > Forecast FYN

FYN− for Forecast Error means Actual FYN < Forecast FYN

Forecast Revision for FYN = Current Forecast of Earnings for Fiscal Year N – Previous Forecast of Earnings for Fiscal Year N

FYN+ for Forecast Revision means Current FYN Forecast > Previous FYN Forecast

FYN− for Forecast Revision means Current FYN Forecast < Previous FYN Forecast

1.2 The Association Between Security Analysts' Multi-Year Earnings Forecasts and Security Returns

A. Summary of Findings

Chapters 4 and 5 focus on the contemporaneous association between earnings forecast errors (revisions) and security returns. Using the IBES data base, we find:

(1) there is a significant association between (i) one year ahead (FY1) earnings forecast errors and (ii) security returns in the period up to and including the month the actual FY1 earnings is announced,

(2) there is a significant association between (i) two year ahead (FY2) earnings forecast errors (revisions) and (ii) security returns in the period up to and including the month the actual FY1 earnings is announced, and

(3) the association for the FY2 earnings forecast variable is significant, even when the research design takes into account the positive correlation between the sign and magnitude of contemporaneous FY1 and FY2 forecast errors (revisions).

Consider a cross-sectional regression in which security returns are measured over the eleven-month period up to and including the announcement of FY1 earnings. The percentage of the variance in security returns that the FY1 earnings forecast error and the FY2 earnings forecast error individually explain are (from Table 5.7):

	1977	**1978**	**1979**	**1980**
FY1	5.7%	12.2%	9.0%	10.6%
FY2	10.7	10.4	9.9	22.3

The above percentages relate to a regression in which the positive correlation between the FY1 and FY2 forecast errors is attributed to FY1. The following percentages relate to a regression in which the positive correlation is attributed to FY2:

	1977	**1978**	**1979**	**1980**
FY2	16.3%	22.5%	18.8%	24.5%
FY1	0.1	0.0	0.1	8.5

These results are consistent with the capital market employing a multi-year earnings forecast horizon rather than a single year ahead forecast horizon.

A related research design was applied to the Wells Fargo data base. Security returns were measured over the eleven-month period up to and including the end of the FY1 fiscal year. The percentages of the variance in security returns that the FY1, FY2, ..., FY5 forecast revisions explain are (from Table 5.16):

	1977	**1978**	**1979**
FY1	35.3%	16.7%	8.7%
FY2	6.8	14.2	12.0
FY3	0.3	14.2	3.3
FY4	0.0	0.2	11.9
FY5	0.0	2.1	0.1

The above percentages relate to a regression in which FY1 enters first, then FY2 enters after having been made orthogonal to FY1, then FY3 enters after having been made orthogonal to FY1 and FY2, etc. The following percentages relate to a regression in which FY5 enters first, then FY4 enters after having been made orthogonal to FY5, etc.

	1977	**1978**	**1979**
FY5	31.3%	45.0%	32.6%
FY4	1.1	0.2	0.5
FY3	5.6	0.9	0.3
FY2	4.1	0.5	2.9
FY1	0.4	0.9	0.1

These results reinforce the IBES data base finding that the capital market has a multi-year earnings forecast horizon rather than a single year ahead forecast horizon.

Evidence supporting the importance of earnings forecasts of years beyond FY1 also comes from other tests in Chapters 4 and 5. For instance, Chapter 5 reports results for an average cumulative abnormal return (ACAR) analysis that focuses on the forecast revision month in the IBES data base. Of particular interest were observations for which the consensus forecast for FY2 was revised up or down from the prior month's forecast, but for which the forecast for FY1 was unchanged. A capital market that focused on only one year ahead (FY1) earnings forecasts would treat all these observations as equivalent. There is strong evidence in Chapter 5 that the capital market revalues downward (upward) the security prices of those companies for which the FY2 earnings forecasts are revised downward (upward), even when the FY1 forecast is unchanged.

B. Importance of Findings

1. The length of the forecast horizon used by the capital market is important to corporate management. Commentators on American business often criticize the alleged short-run focus of management decisions. One rationale offered for this short-run orientation is the capital market's alleged myopic focus or fixation on the current quarter's or the current year's reported income. Rappaport [1983] notes:

> The belief that the stock market has a short time horizon has led many companies to a preoccupation with short-term financial results, particularly current-period reported earnings per share, and as a consequence has discouraged attention to research and development and capital investment with long term payoffs.

Statements made by managers attempting to take publicly listed companies private often refer to the short-run orientation of the capital market — see Grimm [1983]. The results in this monograph are inconsistent with the capital market having a myopic focus, or short-run fixation on the current quarter's or the current year's reported income. Clearlyl stated rationales need not be the underlying motivations of management behavior. For instance, short-run behavior could be motivated by a short-term performance plan based on current reported income. However, at a minimum our results place an increased onus on management to provide support for the allegation that short-run decision making is "necessary" because of the short time horizon used by the capital market.

2. The length of the forecast horizon used by the capital market is important for resource allocation by security analysts. The results noted above suggest that analysts can gain more insight into the determinants of security returns by focusing on how firm, industry, economy, etc. developments will impact the future sequence of earnings than by focusing on just their impact on one year ahead earnings. Survey research by Moizer and Arnold [1982] and Arnold, Moizer and Noreen [1983] indicates that most security analysts claim to have a multi-year horizon. This evidence is provided by the response to a question concerning the forecast horizon used by security analysts in their earnings forecasts:

	American Security Analysts (102 Responses)	British Security Analysts (200 Responses)
Up to 3 Months	1%	1%
4 - 6 Months	0	2
7 - 12 Months	15	22
13 - 24 Months	27	49
2 - 3 Years	36	} 19
4 - 5 Years	12	
Greater than 5 Years	7	4
No Forecast	2	3

Some 84% of American security analysts and 75% of British security analysts reported using a forecast horizon longer than twelve months ahead.

One perspective on reported earnings is that it is comprised of a permanent component (for which the capital market sets a positive multiple in price determination) and a transitory component (for which the capital market places a zero multiple in price determination). Evidence consistent with the FY1 reported earnings figure having a sizeable transitory component is in Beaver and Morse [1978] and Beaver, Lambert and Morse [1980]. The results in this monograph reinforce this finding from a multi-year perspective. Our finding that the FY2 forecast error has a significant association with security returns when its common correlation is attributed to the FY1 forecast error, but that the FY1 forecast error has a relatively small association when its common correlation is attributed to the FY2 forecast error, is consistent with the transitory component of the FY1 forecast error being large relative to the transitory component of the FY2 forecast error. This finding has implications for the evaluation of forecasts by security analysts. If the analyst desires to minimize a criterion function such as mean square error or mean absolute error, the analyst will want to include the permanent and the transitory components in the earnings forecast as both of these will be included in the earnings figure actually reported by the firm. If, however, the analyst desires to explain or to predict security price movements, the analyst will want to focus on the permanent component of earnings.

An important area for future research is operationalizing the permanent and transitory components. One might suspect, for example, that the impact on earnings of employee strikes and plant closures and writedowns should be classified largely as transitory. At this stage, however, we know little about *how* the earnings concept implicit in security price determination differs from either pre- or post-extraordinary item GAAP reported earnings.

3. The finding that earnings forecast years beyond FY1 have significant explanatory power is important to accounting research. Previous studies have probed the hypothesis that there is a mechanistic relation between the current year's reported earnings and security price behavior. Research approaches have included: (a) examining whether an FY1 forecast error based on a non-reported earnings measure has a higher association with security returns than an FY1 forecast error based on reported earnings, and (b) examining the market reaction to voluntary or mandated accounting changes that have cash flow consequences. Foster [1978, pp 220-223, 352-359] provides a discussion of this research and of proposals for corporate disclosure or reporting policies which

assume there is a mechanistic relationship between one year's reported earnings and security returns. The results in this monograph are inconsistent with the mechanistic hypothesis. When it is assessing the security price revaluation implications of earnings signals, the capital market looks beyond just the current year's reported earnings. For example, the capital market revalues a firm with an FY1 + ; FY2+ combination of forecast errors (revisions) differently from a firm with an FY1 + ; FY2– combination of forecast errors (revisions).

The results in this monograph are also relevant to research examining the relative importance of accounting (and other variables) in explaining security price movements. For instance, Gonedes [1974] examined the ability of one year ahead forecast errors for seven accounting variables (e.g., earnings per share, current ratio, and a leverage measure) to explain contemporaneous security returns. The conclusion was that "our results seem to ascribe special importance to the information reflected in the earnings-per-share variable" (p.49). The results in Chapter 5 indicate that a focus on only one year ahead EPS will understate the explanatory power of the EPS variable. An interesting study would be to adopt a multi-year forecast horizon for each of the variables in a multivariate design similar in spirit to that of Gonedes [1974].

1.3 The Effect of Information Timeliness on Capital Market Association Measures

A. Summary of Findings

Much existing research into the association between accounting numbers and security returns has used expectations models based on the past series of reported annual or interim earnings. The use of security analyst forecasts as an expectations model has several appealing properties.

(i) Security analysts can access an information set broader than the past series of reported annual or interim earnings.

(ii) Security analyst forecasts can be updated more frequently than can forecasts from mechanical models based on the past series of reported annual or interim earnings.

The results in Chapter 4 provide strong evidence that use of a more timely expectations model enables a researcher to better approximate the capital market's classification of firms into "bad news" (actual earnings released in month 0 is less than forecasted earnings in month –T) or "good news" (actual earnings released in month 0 exceeds earnings forecasted in month –T) categories. Consider security returns over the [T = –5, 0] month period, i.e., the five months preceding and the month of the actual earnings announcement. The most timely expectations model would use a security analyst forecast available at the start of month –5; less timely expectations models would use analyst forecasts available at the start of month –6, –7, ..., etc. The average cumulative abnormal returns for the [–5, 0] period, using analyst forecasts ranked in terms of timeliness, is:

	Average Cumulative Abnormal Returns	
	"Bad News Forecast" Error Portfolio	"Good News Forecast" Error Portfolio
Month –10 Earnings Forecast (Least Timely)	–5.3%	2.1%
Month – 9 " "	–5.5	2.4
Month – 8 " "	–5.9	2.6
Month – 7 " "	–6.1	2.8
Month – 6 " "	–6.2	2.8
Month – 5 " " (Most Timely)	–6.5	3.0

For both the "bad news" and "good news" categories, the same consistent result is found, i.e., the more timely the expectations model, the stronger the association between average cumulative abnormal returns and earnings forecast errors.

B. Importance of Findings

1. In several areas of capital market research, the choice of a timely expectations model can improve the reliability of inferences drawn from that research. One research area focuses on a single class of signals (e.g., earnings) and makes inferences across firms as to the relative informativeness of that signal. For example, are the earnings releases of small firms more informative than those of large firms? To address this question, it is important that the expectations models used for small vs. large firms be equally well-specified. By selecting security analyst forecasts issued immediately prior to each company's earnings releases, differences across firms in the frequency of their information releases (and thus the timeliness of any one signal such as the prior interim earnings release) could be taken into account in the research.

Another area where the choice of an expectations model is important is research on the relative informativeness of alternative signals, e.g., primary earnings per share vs. extraordinary items per share vs. dividends per share. Unless the expectations model for each signal is equally well specified, misleading inferences about the relative informativeness of each signal may be made. The results in Chapter 4 illustrate how the magnitude of the association measure can be affected by changing the timeliness of the expectations model.

2. In applied areas such as legal litigation, questions arise as to the information content of specific parts of a management press release, e.g., the information content of a management forecast of an 80 percent decline in earnings that is included in a press release also announcing employment cutbacks, senior management changes, and debt rescheduling. An important issue in this context is the market's earnings expectation immediately prior to the press release. Security analysts potentially can incorporate a series of negative developments occurring since the release of the last interim or annual earnings report. Recent security analyst forecasts can thus be used to gain more insight into the information content of the management forecast of an 80 percent decline in earnings compared to the use of an expectations model based on the past interim or annual earnings series.

1.4 The Properties of Security Analysts' Multi-Year Earnings Forecasts

A. Summary of Findings

Chapters 2 to 5 present evidence that:

(i) When security analysts make year by year earnings forecasts for a multi-year horizon, there is a positive correlation between the sign and magnitude of the revisions made across years of that horizon. For instance, in the Wells Fargo (individual analyst) data base, the unconditional relative frequency of an upward revision in the earnings forecast for FY5 is only .073. However, if the earnings forecast for FY4 is revised upward in month t, the relative frequency with which FY5 is also revised upward in month t increases to .928 (from Table 2.12). A similar finding is reported for the IBES consensus forecast data base. For instance, the unconditional relative frequency of a downward revision in the FY2 consensus earnings forecast is .295 (when the consensus forecast is defined to be the median forecast). However, if the FY1 consensus earnings forecast is revised downward in month t, the relative frequency with which the FY2 consensus earnings forecast is also revised downward in month t increases to .533 (from Table 2.6).

(ii) Over the 22-month period prior to the month in which the actual earnings are announced, there is a systematic reduction in the magnitude of consensus forecast errors. For instance, using the following error measure – [(Actual EPS – Forecasted EPS)^2 / (Security Price at End of Forecast Month)] x 100 – the median value of the distribution is (from Table 3.5):

	Month of the Earnings Forecast Relative to the Month of the Actual Earnings Announcement					
	–22	–18	–14	–10	–6	–2
Squared Forecast Error	1.041	0.783	0.564	0.386	0.166	0.049

Over this same period, there is also a systematic reduction in the dispersion of consensus forecast errors. For instance, using the above error measure, the interquartile range (.75 percentile minus .25 percentile) of the distribution of forecast errors is (from Table 3.5):

	Month of the Earnings Forecast Relative to the Month of the Actual Earnings Announcement					
	–22	–18	–14	–10	–6	–2
Interquartile Range	5.951	4.778	3.664	2.346	1.016	0.284

Both of the above results are consistent with prior research that has focused on a one year ahead forecast horizon.

(iii) The sign and magnitude of security returns in the twelve-month period *preceding* a revision in consensus security analyst earnings forecasts is positively associated with the sign of that forecast revision. For instance, the average cumulative abnormal return (ACAR) of one year ahead forecast revisions is (from Figure 4.1):

Period Used to Cumulate Abnormal Returns	Average Cumulative Abnormal Returns: FY1 Revised Down in Month 0	Average Cumulative Abnormal Returns: FY1 Revised Up in Month 0
Months [–12, –10]	–1.25%	0.51%
Months [–9, –7]	–1.58	1.18
Months [–6, –4]	–2.36	1.78
Month [–3]	–1.18	0.85
Month [–2]	–1.54	1.05
Month [–1]	–1.41	1.02
Months [–12, –1]	–9.32	6.39

These patterns are even more marked when the subsample with both FY1 and FY2 revised down or up in month 0 is examined (from Figure 5.1):

Period Used to Cumulate Abnormal Returns	Average Cumulative Abnormal Returns: Both FY1 and FY2 Revised Down in Month 0	Average Cumulative Abnormal Returns: Both FY1 and FY2 Revised Up in Month 0
Months [–12, –10]	–1.56%	0.91%
Months [–9, –7]	–1.75	1.64
Months [–6, –4]	–3.14	2.52
Month [–3]	–1.60	1.19
Month [–2]	–1.98	1.46
Month [–1]	–2.00	1.48
Months [–12, –1]	–12.03	9.20

In *every* single month in the [–12, –1] period, the sign of the average abnormal return for the above FY1 + ; FY2 + and the FY1–; FY2– portfolios is consistent with the sign of the earnings forecast revision in month 0. A similar statement applies to the previously noted returns for the FY1 + and FY1– portfolios.

B. Importance of Findings

1. Over the 22-month period prior to the announcement month of the earnings being forecast, there is a progressive increase in the information about the fiscal year being forecast (e.g., announcements of new sales contracts, the signing of labor agreements, and interim earnings reports). The findings in Chapter 3 that both (a) the magnitude of forecast errors and (b) their dispersion systematically decrease over the –22 to –1 month period are consistent with security analysts incorporating this information in their earnings forecasts. However, the finding in Chapter 4 that security price changes precede analyst forecast revisions raises the possibility that analysts do not incorporate information into their forecasts in a timely fashion. One explanation for the Chapter 4 finding is that security analysts do not report their revised earnings forecasts until they have made capital market transactions based on such information. A second explanation is that security analysts do not consciously ignore information, but that the aggregate capital market is a more efficient processor of publicly available information than any individual security analyst or composite of security analysts. A third explanation is that security prices impound information to which analysts do not yet have access. Insider trading by management is one mechanism by which information internal to the firm is impounded.

A fourth explanation is that severe time lags exist between individual analyst revisions being made public and their inclusion in consensus forecast data bases.

2. The time-series and cross-sectional tests in Chapter 4 of this monograph indicate that while security returns do lead security analyst forecasts revisions, no more than ten percent of the variance of analyst forecast revisions can be explained by prior security returns. These results are consistent with security analysts using a broad information set rather than just the past series of the one variable (i.e., security returns). Clearly, model misspecification could result in the ten percent figure being an underestimate of the amount of information about future earnings that analysts extract from security price movements. However, from an economic survival perspective, the notion that security analysts are simply recoding information already in a publicly observable variable (security returns) is unappealing. The development and expansion of summary forecast services such as IBES by Lynch, Jones and Ryan and ICARUS by Zacks Investment Research would be difficult to explain if analysts simply use security prices as their primary information source when forecasting earnings.

3. The results on the systematic reduction in (a) the magnitude of forecast errors, and (b) the dispersion of forecast errors as the forecast horizon is reduced, are important to research on the relative forecasting abilities of security analysts, management, and mechanical models (see Section A.6 of the Appendix). When the time at which (say) a mechanical model's forecast can be made differs from that of a security analyst's forecast, the Tables in Chapter 3 can be used to gain insight into how that timing difference translates to a difference in mean absolute error, mean square error, etc. (The results in those Tables are sample and time dependent; we are not suggesting they be used in a mechanical way for other firms or time periods.)

4. The results on the properties of multi-year security analyst earnings forecasts noted above are important for the design of capital market studies. For instance, the finding that forecast revisions for different years of a forecast horizon are positively correlated means that research designs need to control for this correlation when examining the incremental information content of any one year's forecast revision in that horizon. (See Chapter 5 for discussion of the orthogonalization approach used to address this research design issue.)

CHAPTER 2

DESCRIPTION OF DATA BASES

2.1 Introduction

This chapter has two objectives: (1) to describe the two data bases used in the research, and (2) to explore aspects of the data bases that have implications either for experimental design or for the drawing of inferences from the research.

The IBES historical data base contains consensus security analyst EPS forecast information for each year of a two-year forecast horizon. The data are available at monthly intervals and cover the January 1976 to December 1980 period. This study examines 500 securities included in this data base.

The Wells Fargo data base contains individual security analyst EPS forecast information for each year of a five-year forecast horizon. It is updated monthly and covers the January 1977 to June 1980 period. Information on a maximum of 405 securities is included.

2.2 The IBES Data Base

IBES was developed by Lynch, Jones and Ryan in the early 1970's to systematically collect and distribute the earnings forecasts of security analysts from "leading Wall Street and Regional brokerage firms." As of 1984, over 2700 companies were covered and over 80 brokerage firms provided earnings forecasts.

A. Company and Data Coverage

The data base in this research is the IBES "Summary History Tape" covering the 60-month period from January 1976 to December 1980. This tape includes the following data items for both a one year ahead (FY1) and a two years ahead (FY2) horizon for up to 500 companies for each of the above 60 months:

- Number of analyst forecasts available.
- Number of forecasts revised down.
- Number of forecasts revised up.
- Highest forecast.
- Lowest forecast.
- Median forecast.
- Mean forecast.
- Standard deviation of forecasts.
- End date of the fiscal year.
- Primary/diluted EPS indicator.
- Adjustment factor for stock splits, etc.
- Latest actual earnings per share.

The "Summary History Tape" does not include information about the individual analysts or the individual forecasts underlying the above data items.

Analysts provide their forecasts to IBES with an indication of whether primary EPS or diluted EPS is being forecast. IBES then makes a judgment call (keyed to the distribution between primary and diluted estimates for each stock) as to what to report in their summary statistics. If primary (diluted) is reported, the forecasts of all individual analysts are restated by IBES to a primary (diluted) basis before calculating summary statistics. For the period examined, most summary statistics are reported on a primary basis:

	Fiscal Year				
	1976	**1977**	**1978**	**1979**	**1980**
Number of Firms IBES Reported on Primary Basis	308	430	435	433	431
Number of Firms IBES Reported on Diluted Basis	18	26	29	54	63
Number of Firms for which Forecast Data Not Available That Year	174	44	36	13	6
Size of Sample	500	500	500	500	500

IBES provides no specific instructions to individual analysts about the treatment of "extraordinary" items. Based on conversations with IBES officials and security analysts, it appears that analysts typically forecast EPS before extraordinary items. IBES passes each individual forecast through a heuristic filter. If the forecast is "flagged" as an outlier, the analyst is contacted. In some cases, IBES will ask the analyst to restate the forecast to an EPS before extraordinary figure if (say) the earlier submitted forecast captures a large item apparently excluded by other analysts.

B. Analysts Represented

Table 2.1 contains a breakdown of the number of analyst forecasts for each company at selected months in the January 1976 to December 1980 period. In January 1976, 433 companies had one year ahead forecasts in the IBES data base – the median number of individual analyst forecasts per company was seven. In December 1980, 498 companies had one year ahead forecasts and the median number of forecasts per company was 12. For two year ahead forecasts, the number of companies represented ranged from 369 in January 1976 to 468 in December 1980; the median number of forecasts per company was six in January 1976 and ten in December 1980.

C. Individual Analyst Forecast Revision Statistics

Individual analyst forecasts in any consecutive two-month period can be placed into one of five categories:

(i) Downward revision: $\hat{EPS}_{i,t+1} < \hat{EPS}_{i,t}$.

(ii) No change: $\hat{EPS}_{i,t+1} = \hat{EPS}_{i,t}$.

(iii) Upward revision: $\hat{EPS}_{i,t+1} > \hat{EPS}_{i,t}$.

(iv) $\hat{EPS}_{i,t+1}$ included in data base but not $\hat{EPS}_{i,t}$.

(v) $\hat{EPS}_{i,t}$ included in data base but not $\hat{EPS}_{i,t+1}$.

TABLE 2.1

IBES: Distribution of Number of Analyst Forecasts Per Company

A. ONE YEAR AHEAD EPS FORECASTS (FY1)

MONTH	NUMBER OF ANALYST FORECASTS PER COMPANY							# OF COMPANIES ACTIVE
	1-4	5-8	9-12	13-16	17-20	21-25	26-30	
January 1976	30.7%	26.6%	20.5%	13.4%	5.8%	3.0%	0.0%	433
December 1976	24.2	23.3	16.9	15.3	10.2	8.2	1.8	450
December 1977	26.0	21.6	19.5	16.7	10.6	4.8	0.9	462
December 1978	16.8	17.4	20.7	20.4	12.1	10.6	2.0	489
December 1979	12.5	19.4	23.2	21.6	13.7	9.3	0.2	495
December 1980	11.8	17.9	22.7	21.7	15.5	9.6	0.8	498

B. TWO YEAR AHEAD EPS FORECASTS (FY2)

MONTH	NUMBER OF ANALYST FORECASTS PER COMPANY							# OF COMPANIES ACTIVE
	1-4	5-8	9-12	13-16	17-20	21-25	26-30	
January 1976	34.7%	25.5%	19.5%	11.1%	7.9%	1.4%	0.0%	369
December 1976	29.4	23.0	16.8	13.1	8.9	7.9	1.0	405
December 1977	30.3	20.9	17.7	16.5	10.0	3.9	0.7	412
December 1978	23.1	15.6	20.6	19.5	11.3	7.7	2.0	441
December 1979	22.1	15.9	22.5	17.7	13.1	8.7	0.0	458
December 1980	21.6	17.5	18.8	19.0	15.2	7.5	0.4	468

where $\hat{EPS}_{i,t}$ is an EPS forecast for firm i in month t. Details on categories (iv) and (v) are not provided in the IBES "Summary History Tape."

Table 2.2 presents the percentages of observations falling into categories (i), (ii), and (iii). For FY1 forecasts, 77.2% (of those in (i), (ii) and (iii)) of analysts reported no change in any one month. The comparable percentage for FY2 forecasts is 83.8%. This high percentage of no forecast revisions could be due to several reasons – e.g., (a) each analyst does not reconsider his or her EPS forecast each and every month, or (b) the information arriving since the last forecast does not cause a revision in that forecast.

Table 2.2 presents revision statistics in a calendar time format. Table 2.3 presents revision statistics in an event time format, where month 0 is the month when the annual EPS is announced by the company (as reported on Standard and Poor's Quarterly Compustat tape).[1] The percent of no-change observations is lowest in the –12 to –1 event time period and highest in the –24 to –18 period. Several explanations could exist for this difference; e.g., (i) there are more revision cues in the –12 to –1 event time period and (ii) there is more demand by investors for forecast revisions with a shorter time horizon.

The focus of this monograph is not on the specific information cues that prompt security analysts to revise their earnings forecasts. At minimal cost, however, we can compute the relative frequencies with which analysts revised their forecasts, and tabulate those frequencies by the number of months until the company announced its interim or annual earnings – see Table 2.4. The data in this table are not suggestive of a major clustering of forecast revisions in the month of or the month subsequent to an interim or annual earnings release. In Section 2.3C, similar data are presented in relation to forecast revisions by Wells Fargo security analysts. Further discussion of research issues in this area is contained in Appendix A of this monograph.

D. Consensus Forecast Revision Statistics

At least three proxies for a "consensus" earnings forecast revision can be derived from the IBES "Summary History Tape":

- Median forecast in month t vis-a-vis median forecast in month t–1.
- Mean forecast in month t vis-a-vis mean forecast in month t–1.

---

[1] The number of FY1 and FY2 forecasts in Table 2.2 is 468,021. When forecasts are presented in event time format, there are 418,081 observations. The reduction in observations (49,940) is due to the following:

a. FY2 forecasts made (reported) less than twelve months before actual earnings announcement.	366
b. FY2 forecasts made (reported) prior to twenty-four months before actual earnings announcement.	7
c. FY1 forecasts made (reported) in or subsequent to the actual earnings announcement.	15,638
d. Missing announcement dates on Standard and Poor's Compustat Tape (FY1 = 21,447; FY2 = 12,482).	33,929
	49,940

TABLE 2.2

IBES: Individual Analyst Monthly Forecast Revision Statistics in Calendar Time

A. ONE YEAR AHEAD EPS FORECASTS (FY1)

TIME PERIOD	INDIVIDUAL ANALYSTS			
	DOWN	NO CHANGE	UP	NOB*
January 1976-December 1976	9.2%	78.3%	12.5%	47,623
January 1977-December 1977	11.3	80.3	8.4	50,117
January 1978-December 1978	9.1	78.5	12.3	61,788
January 1979-December 1979	8.3	75.4	16.3	69,952
January 1980-December 1980	13.0	74.8	12.2	70,772
January 1976-December 1980	10.2	77.2	12.6	300,252

B. TWO YEAR AHEAD EPS FORECASTS (FY2)

TIME PERIOD	INDIVIDUAL ANALYSTS			
	DOWN	NO CHANGE	UP	NOB*
January 1976-December 1976	6.7%	84.6%	8.8%	25,430
January 1977-December 1977	9.2	84.5	6.3	26,352
January 1978-December 1978	5.9	83.9	10.2	33,343
January 1979-December 1979	7.1	83.4	9.6	40,402
January 1980-December 1980	8.4	83.3	8.3	42,242
January 1976-December 1980	7.4	83.8	8.7	167,769

*Number of Observations

TABLE 2.3

IBES: Monthly Forecast Revision Statistics in Event Time

EVENT MONTH	INDIVIDUAL ANALYST FORECAST LEVEL				CONSENSUS (MEDIAN) FORECAST LEVEL			
	% DOWN	% SAME	% UP	NOB	% DOWN	% SAME	% UP	NOB
-1	9.1	81.7	9.2	22,355	22.9	54.4	22.7	1,882
-2	11.1	77.0	12.0	24,440	29.9	38.6	31.5	2,124
-3	13.1	72.4	14.5	24,553	28.8	39.9	31.3	2,166
-4	9.7	80.0	10.3	24,201	24.9	47.7	27.3	2,166
-5	10.6	75.5	13.9	23,988	25.2	39.2	35.6	2,161
-6	10.6	74.8	14.6	23,766	26.6	40.3	33.0	2,159
-7	9.2	79.5	11.3	23,594	25.5	43.4	31.1	2,144
-8	9.6	76.3	14.1	23,030	24.2	41.0	34.8	2,146
-9	10.7	74.4	14.9	22,490	25.2	40.3	34.5	2,133
-10	10.7	76.2	13.1	22,225	25.9	41.8	32.3	2,120
-11	10.6	75.2	14.2	22,153	26.0	40.3	33.7	2,123
-12	8.0	82.9	9.1	21,848	22.4	51.7	25.9	2,091
-13	8.2	83.6	8.2	21,122	23.8	51.2	25.0	1,876
-14	8.7	82.7	8.7	18,955	30.1	40.0	30.0	1,802
-15	10.8	78.3	10.9	17,491	30.2	39.1	30.7	1,772
-16	6.4	84.9	8.6	15,946	24.3	46.8	28.9	1,743
-17	6.7	82.8	10.6	14,443	27.1	38.3	34.6	1,685
-18	6.6	83.6	9.7	11,864	29.7	35.5	34.8	1,614
-19	5.5	87.5	7.1	8,698	32.4	36.8	30.8	1,505
-20	4.4	87.4	8.2	6,150	28.9	33.7	37.4	1,323
-21	3.3	89.4	7.3	3,977	30.1	37.3	32.5	1,079
-22	4.5	89.3	6.2	2,394	31.8	41.8	26.4	780
-23	1.6	97.0	1.4	1,290	23.6	56.4	20.0	165
-24	1.0	99.0	0.0	200	20.0	60.0	20.0	5

MONTH 0 = MONTH IN WHICH ACTUAL EPS IS ANNOUNCED

TABLE 2.4

IBES: Revision Frequency of Analysts Relative to Interim/Annual Earnings Announcement Month (0): Ratio of (i) (#↑) + (#↓) to (ii) Total Number of Analysts Included for Stock in IBES

YEAR FORECASTED	AVERAGE RATIO IN EVENT TIME					AVERAGE RATIO CONDITIONAL ON NO EARNINGS ANNNOUNCEMENT THIS MONTH
	Month -2	Month -1	Month 0	Month +1	Month +2	
FY1	.233	.204	.207	.253	.209	.226
FY2	.146	.130	.129	.149	.139	.145

- Number of individual analyst forecasts revised up (#↑) in month t less number of individual analyst forecasts revised down (#↓) in month t. If (#↑) > (#↓) the consensus forecast is interpreted as being revised up.

All three proxies for consensus forecasts are examined in this monograph. The rationale for these three proxies is pragmatic (availability on "Summary History Tape") rather than any claim that they are optimal aggregators of individual analyst forecasts.

In each month, consensus forecasts can be classified into one of the following four categories for FY1 and one of the following sixteen categories for FY1 and FY2:

Single-Year-Ahead Focus (FY1)

FY1 Consensus Revised Down	= –
FY1 Consensus Not Changed	= 0
FY1 Consensus Revised Up	= +
FY1 Consensus Not Available	= *

Multi-Year-Ahead Focus (FY1 and FY2)

FY1–; FY2–	= ––	FY1+; FY2–	= +–
FY1–; FY20	= –0	FY1+; FY20	= +0
FY1–; FY2+	= –+	FY1+; FY2+	= ++
FY1–; FY2*	= –*	FY1+; FY2*	= +*
FY10; FY2–	= 0–	FY1*; FY2–	= *–
FY10; FY20	= 00	FY1*; FY20	= *0
FY10; FY2+	= 0+	FY1*; FY2+	= *+
FY10; FY2*	= 0*	FY1*; FY2*	= **

Several interesting dependency issues can be explored using the above categories and the three proxies for consensus forecasts:

(i) What is the dependency across categories in a given month using alternate proxies for consensus forecasts?

(ii) What is the dependency between the categorization of FY1 and FY2 forecast revisions in a given month for a given consensus proxy?

(iii) What is the dependency over time for observations in a given earnings forecast revision category?

Tables 2.5 and 2.6 present data that relate to (i) and (ii). Tables 2.7 and 2.8 present data relating to (iii).

Using the data in Table 2.5, it is apparent that the three proxies do not result in the same classification of earnings forecast revisions in a given month. Focusing on the 16 categories for FY1 and FY2 combined, there is agreement in 11,598 instances (38.7%). The frequency with which the consensus forecast proxies agree on a pair-wise comparison basis for FY1 and FY2 combined is:

- Median and Mean Proxies = 60.7%
- Median and [(#↑)–(#↓)] Proxies = 44.5%
- Mean and [(#↑)–(#↓)] Proxies = 55.7%

In subsequent work, the effect of using each of the above proxies for consensus forecast revisions will be examined.

An interesting subset of observations in Table 2.5 is that for which FY1 = 0 but

TABLE 2.5

IBES: Number of Observations in Monthly Forecast Revision Categories for Alternative Proxies for Consensus Forecasts

FY1 AND FY2 REVISIONS (1)	MEDIAN AS PROXY (2)	MEAN AS PROXY (3)	(#↑)-(#↓) AS PROXY (4)	NUMBER OF OCCASIONS ON WHICH (2), (3) AND (4) PROXIES AGREE (5)
FY1 ONLY				
-	7104	10540	8905	3013
0	11981	4371	8345	3206
+	8651	12825	11035	3664
*	2264	2264	1715	1715
FY2 ONLY				
-	6086	8095	4983	1996
0	8170	3867	12471	2473
+	6365	8659	5999	2385
*	9379	9379	6547	4744
FY1 AND FY2				
FY1-;FY2-	2869	5195	3644	1758
FY1-;FY20	1634	1008	3460	423
FY1-;FY2+	885	1894	644	112
FY1-;FY2*	1716	2443	1157	720
FY10;FY2-	2011	470	589	68
FY10;FY20	4700	1759	4822	1651
FY10;FY2+	1998	458	678	79
FY10;FY2*	3272	1684	2256	1408
FY1+;FY2-	1206	2430	750	170
FY1+;FY20	1836	1100	4189	399
FY1+;FY2+	3482	6307	4677	2194
FY1+;FY2*	2127	2988	1419	901
FY1*;FY2-	0	0	0	0
FY1*;FY20	0	0	0	0
FY1*;FY2+	0	0	0	0
FY1*;FY2*	2264	2264	1715	1715
	30,000	30,000	30,000	11,598

KEY:
- \- = Consensus Revised Down
- 0 = Consensus Has No Change
- \+ = Consensus Revised Up
- * = No Observation Available

FY2 $\neq$ 0. For instance, using the median as a proxy, 2,011 observations fall in the FY1 = 0; FY2 = – category while 1,998 observations fall in the FY1 = 0; FY2 = + category. These observations represent an especially interesting data base for examining the null hypothesis that the capital market has a myopic focus on FY1.

There is considerable evidence in Table 2.5 that the signs of FY1 and FY2 forecast revisions in a given month for a given consensus proxy are positively correlated. One way to document this positive correlation is to compare (i) the unconditional relative frequency of each FY2 forecast revision category with (ii) the conditional relative frequency of that same FY2 forecast revision category given a specific FY1 forecast revision. Table 2.6 presents these data, for all observations in a given month for which both FY1 and FY2 forecast revisions of –, + or 0 were coded. Consider the FY2 = – category using the median consensus proxy. The unconditional frequency of FY2 = – is .295. However, if FY1 = – in a given month, the conditional frequency of FY2 = – increases to .533. This positive correlation raises important research design issues explored in Chapter 5.

Tables 2.7 and 2.8 present data on the dependency over time for the sign and magnitude of successive consensus forecast revisions. Table 2.7 compares:

(i) $\phi(i,t)$ – the unconditional relative frequency of being in consensus forecast category i in month t, and

(ii) $\phi(i,t \mid i,t-j)$ – the conditional relative frequency of being in consensus forecast category i in month t given membership in category i in month t–j where j = 1 to N.

Only observations for which both FY1 and FY2 forecast revisions are available were included in the computation of (i) and (ii). With very few exceptions in Table 2.7,

$$\phi(i,t \mid i,t-j) > \phi(i,t) \qquad \text{when } j = 1, 2, 4 \text{ or } 6.$$

For instance, if a FY1 consensus (median as proxy) forecast was revised down in month t–1, on 49.3% of occasions it was also revised down in month t. In contrast, only 26.1% of all forecasts are revised down. There are several possible explanations for this persistence – e.g., (i) individual analysts "spread" a given revision over several forecast announcements, or (ii) each individual analyst fully adjusts his or her forecast, but this adjustment across analysts is not simultaneous, with the result that the aggregation process used to compute consensus forecasts induces serial correlation over time in the assignment of firms to earnings change categories.

The computations underlying Table 2.7 utilize only the sign of the consensus forecast revision. To further explore the dependency issue, autocorrelation coefficients for lags 1 to 6 were computed for each firm. Table 2.8 presents the .25, .50, and .75 percentiles of $r_1, r_2, \ldots, r_6$ for firms in the IBES data base. Focusing on FY1 and using the mean as the proxy for consensus forecasts, the median (.50 percentile) for each lag from r_1 to r_6 is positive; e.g., $r_1 = .27$, $r_2 = .21$, and $r_3 = .17$. An r_1 of .27 indicates that the sign and magnitude of the forecast revision in month t–1 explain only 7.29% of the variance of forecast revisions in month t. Using the median as the proxy for consensus forecasts, the comparable percentage for r_1 is only 2.56%. Focusing on FY2, the median is close to zero across all autocorrelations when either the median or mean forecast is used as the proxy for consensus forecasts, e.g., $r_1 = .05$, $r_2 = .06$ and $r_3 = .08$ using the mean.

TABLE 2.6

IBES: Contemporaneous Monthly Revision Frequency Over Forecast Horizon for Observations with Both FY1 and FY2 Available

A. UNCONDITIONAL RELATIVE FREQUENCY OF FY1 FORECAST REVISION CATEGORY

FORECAST REVISION CATEGORY	MEDIAN AS PROXY	MEAN AS PROXY	(#↑)-(#↓) AS PROXY
-	.256	.380	.315
0	.432	.158	.295
+	.312	.462	.390

B. UNCONDITIONAL RELATIVE FREQUENCY OF FY2 FORECAST REVISION CATEGORY

FORECAST REVISION CATEGORY	MEDIAN AS PROXY	MEAN AS PROXY	(#↑)-(#↓) AS PROXY
-	.295	.393	.212
0	.396	.187	.532
+	.309	.420	.256

C. CONDITIONAL RELATIVE FREQUENCY OF FY2 FORECAST REVISION CATEGORY GIVEN FY1 FORECAST REVISION CATEGORY

	MEDIAN AS PROXY	MEAN AS PROXY	(#↑)-(#↓) AS PROXY
FY2- FY1-	.533	.641	.470
FY20 FY1-	.303	.125	.447
FY2+ FY1-	.164	.234	.083
FY2- FY10	.231	.175	.097
FY20 FY10	.540	.655	.792
FY2+ FY10	.229	.170	.111
FY2- FY1+	.185	.247	.078
FY20 FY1+	.281	.112	.436
FY2+ FY1+	.534	.641	.486

TABLE 2.7

IBES: Unconditional and Conditional Relative Frequencies for Membership of Consensus Earnings Forecast Revision Categories

	MEDIAN AS CONSENSUS PROXY				
	$\phi(i,t)$	$\phi(i,t\|i,t-1)$	$\phi(i,t\|i,t-2)$	$\phi(i,t\|i,t-4)$	$\phi(i,t\|i,t-6)$
A. SINGLE YEAR (FY1)					
-	.261	.493	.450	.404	.384
0	.422	.538	.489	.463	.475
+	.316	.500	.465	.416	.396
B. MULTI-YEAR (FY1 AND FY2)					
--	.139	.341	.305	.257	.220
-0	.079	.168	.135	.099	.093
-+	.043	.080	.068	.037	.050
0-	.098	.154	.133	.104	.102
00	.228	.349	.308	.282	.270
0+	.097	.130	.124	.111	.104
+-	.058	.106	.078	.069	.078
+0	.089	.146	.120	.109	.087
++	.169	.340	.305	.267	.237

	MEAN AS CONSENSUS PROXY				
	$\phi(i,t)$	$\phi(i,t\|i,t-1)$	$\phi(i,t\|i,t-2)$	$\phi(i,t\|i,t-4)$	$\phi(i,t\|i,t-6)$
A. SINGLE YEAR (FY1)					
-	.393	.635	.605	.553	.519
0	.130	.283	.271	.243	.240
+	.477	.681	.646	.598	.569
B. MULTI-YEAR (FY1 AND FY2)					
--	.252	.526	.496	.412	.362
-0	.049	.113	.097	.052	.047
-+	.092	.143	.144	.118	.104
0-	.023	.045	.045	.034	.024
00	.085	.275	.266	.249	.213
0+	.022	.039	.039	.017	.011
+-	.118	.200	.166	.145	.143
+0	.053	.097	.074	.059	.053
++	.306	.546	.510	.452	.390

	(#↑)-(#↓) AS CONSENSUS PROXY				
	$\phi(i,t)$	$\phi(i,t\|i,t-1)$	$\phi(i,t\|i,t-2)$	$\phi(i,t\|i,t-4)$	$\phi(i,t\|i,t-6)$
A. SINGLE YEAR (FY1)					
-	.330	.612	.566	.502	.475
0	.260	.375	.364	.323	.323
+	.410	.644	.608	.543	.517
B. MULTI-YEAR (FY1 AND FY2)					
--	.155	.460	.422	.279	.219
-0	.148	.285	.226	.176	.161
-+	.027	.075	.046	.047	.032
0-	.025	.051	.053	.038	.007
00	.206	.336	.342	.279	.287
0+	.029	.072	.031	.024	.030
+-	.032	.098	.060	.071	.042
+0	.179	.308	.247	.169	.154
++	.199	.502	.432	.311	.256

TABLE 2.8

IBES: Cross-Sectional Distribution Statistics for Autocorrelation Coefficients for Monthly Consensus EPS Forecast Revision Series of Each Firm Over the January 1976 to December 1980 Period

DISTRIBUTION STATISTICS	AUTOCORRELATION COEFFICIENTS					
	r_1	r_2	r_3	r_4	r_5	r_6
A. FY1-MEDIAN AS PROXY						
.25 Percentile	.01	.01	-.01	-.03	-.07	-.07
.50 Percentile	.16	.14	.13	.07	.07	.08
.75 Percentile	.33	.29	.27	.20	.19	.23
B. FY2-MEDIAN AS PROXY						
.25 Percentile	-.16	-.12	-.12	-.08	-.12	-.17
.50 Percentile	-.02	.02	.05	.04	.03	.01
.75 Percentile	.12	.19	.19	.20	.18	.18
C. FY1-MEAN AS PROXY						
.25 Percentile	.05	.03	.02	-.03	-.07	-.08
.50 Percentile	.27	.21	.17	.10	.09	.07
.75 Percentile	.48	.38	.35	.25	.24	.25
D. FY2-MEAN AS PROXY						
.25 Percentile	-.07	-.10	-.09	-.08	-.14	-.14
.50 Percentile	.05	.06	.08	.06	.03	.01
.75 Percentile	.22	.23	.22	.22	.19	.22

Thus, when both the magnitude and sign of earnings forecast revisions are considered, on average there is only weak, albeit positive, serial correlation in both the mean and median consensus forecast revision series for FY1 or FY2.

E. Strengths and Limitations of Data Base

The complete IBES data base has several important strengths or advantages (in addition to it being in machine-readable form) from a research viewpoint:

1. A sizeable number of stocks are included, with many industries represented over an extended time period.

2. The names of the individual analysts and details of their forecasts (e.g., amount and time reported to IBES) are available to all subscribers to the IBES system. The ready accessibility of this information serves to increase the incentives that individual analysts have to revise and report their forecasts in an unbiased fashion. The existence of IBES facilitates studies of the relative *timeliness* and *accuracy* of individual analysts, both attributes that are perceived to be of value to the analyst community.

3. IBES devotes resources to increasing consistency across analysts in the variable being forecast; e.g., primary or diluted earnings, before or after extraordinary items. The result is less measurement error in the consensus forecast measures.

4. Over time, IBES has expanded considerably the number of stocks covered, analysts represented, and firms subscribing to its service. This expansion is consistent with the earnings forecast information IBES provides being of value to the analyst community. The IBES service is frequently referenced in general business periodicals.

The main limitations of the data base relate to (i) the lack of information demonstrating its representativeness, and (ii) the existence of possible reporting lags in the system. Although IBES collects forecasts from a broad cross-section of analysts (over 80 brokerage firms), not all security analysts making earnings forecasts for a given company in our sample are represented. For instance, the research departments of some insurance companies and mutual funds develop forecasts for internal consumption but do not circulate them externally in any formal manner. The result is that what we call "consensus" earnings forecasts may not be the same number that would be derived if we had access to all forecasts made for each firm in the sample. Note, however, that if the analysts included in IBES have "private access" to the forecasts made by analysts of insurance companies, mutual funds, etc., the IBES analysts may encode that information in developing their own forecasts.

Reporting Lags

Reporting lags can exist in several areas of the IBES data base:

(i) Lags between an analyst making a forecast revision and when it is reported as a revision by IBES. This lag can arise for several reasons, e.g., (a) an analyst reports forecasts first to clients and only then to IBES, (b) the reporting pattern of analysts is not synchronized with the month-end reporting pattern of IBES (their end of the month being defined as the third Thursday of that month), and (c) IBES does not instantaneously adjust its files when revisions are reported by analysts. IBES officials are of the opinion that (c) is a minimal source of reporting lag in their system. A related problem is that analysts may choose not to report (even to their clients) small revisions in their earnings forecasts.

(ii) Lags between a company announcing its most recent EPS and when IBES updates its most recent EPS for the firm.

Using the annual earnings announcement date information contained on Compustat quarterly tapes, approximately 98 percent of the IBES observations could be classified into one of two categories:

- IBES reports a change in the most recent actual fiscal year in the same calendar month as Compustat records an annual earnings announcement.
- IBES lags Compustat by one month in reporting the announcement of the actual EPS.

Firms that announce their earnings early (late) in the month typically are updated by IBES in the same (next) month – see Table 2.9.

Based on conversations with security analysts and IBES officials, the more severe problem is the lag between an analyst making a forecast revision and when it is reported in the IBES system. It is not possible to identify an announcement date for each consensus earnings forecast in the same way that many event studies of earnings releases, takeover announcements, etc., interpret day 0 (i.e., the day the information cue first became publicly released to the capital market). This reporting lag problem influences the research procedures we employ in several ways, e.g., (a) in many of our association tests we use –12 to –2 months as the pre-announcement period and –1 to 0 months as the period when the earnings forecast is publicly released, and (b) when we include a market consensus forecast measure, we use an approach that aims to capture non-synchronous adjustments of observed variables to continous changes in the underlying information set – see Section 4.4C.

2.3 The Wells Fargo Data Base

The Wells Fargo data base we use contains individual security analyst earnings per share forecasts for one to five years ahead (FY1, FY2, ..., FY5) on a monthly basis from January 1977 to June 1980. The data base underlies a dividend discount model that, when combined with a capital asset pricing model, aims to detect under- or over-valued securities. The data base was developed for use by the clients of Wells Fargo Investment Advisors.

A. Background to Wells Fargo Security Analysis Approach

The Wells Fargo approach has several components: (i) an estimate of the internal rate of return (IRR) of a security derived using a dividend discount model, and (ii) an estimate of the expected return on the security derived using an asset pricing model. Fouse [1976, 1977, 1978] describes the development of the system. Subsequent developments are documented in the monthly issues of the *Security Market Line* (pre-September 1978) and the *Security Market Plane* (post-September 1978).

The estimated IRR is calculated with the following dividend discount model:

$$P_{i0} = \frac{D_{i1}}{(1 + R)} + \frac{D_{i2}}{(1 + R)^2} + \frac{D_{i3}}{(1 + R)^3} + \ldots + \frac{D_{in}}{(1 + R)^n} \tag{2.1}$$

TABLE 2.9

IBES: Lags Between Announcement of Actual EPS by Companies (as Reported by Compustat) and Its Adjustment by IBES

TIMES IBES UPDATES FY2 AS THE NEW FY1 IN THE SAME MONTH AS THE COMPANY RELEASES ITS ANNUAL EARNINGS	= 1685
TIMES IBES LAGS COMPANY RELEASE DATE BY ONE MONTH IN ITS UPDATE OF FY2 AS NEW FY1	= 387

RELEASE DATE OF ANNUAL EARNINGS RELATIVE TO IBES END OF MONTH, FOR 387 ONE MONTH LAG OBSERVATIONS

EARNINGS RELEASED ON DAY	# OF OBSERVATIONS
-10	1
- 9	8
- 8	29
- 7	30
- 6	40
- 5	0
- 4	2
- 3	24
- 2	42
- 1	90
0	121
	387

where P_{i0} = current security price of company i at time 0,
D_{it} = dividend of company i in period t, and
R = internal rate of return of company i.

Analysts input annual dividend predictions for the first five years of the forecast horizon. Subsequent to that year they input:

- A fifth-year normalized EPS growth rate and normalized dividend payout ratio.
- The number of years before a steady-state growth and payout are to be assumed, which is the beginning of the terminal period, or maturity.
- The pattern of growth to be expected between the fifth year and the year of "maturity," the choices being
  - a) a slow decay in the growth rate,
  - b) a linear decay, or
  - c) a rapid decay.
- A terminal growth rate, payout ratio, and implied return on equity [Fouse, 1976, p. 38].

The only specific earnings variable to enter the estimation of IRR is the fifth-year normalized EPS growth rate. However, as part of their activities, individual analysts employed by Wells Fargo in the January 1977 to June 1980 period provided earnings per share forecasts for FY1, FY2, ..., FY5 and entered these in the data base.

B. Analyst and Company Coverage

Individual analysts at Wells Fargo Investment Advisors in the January 1977 to June 1980 period were each assigned a set of securities to follow and were required to provide on a monthly basis estimates to be used as inputs into the Wells Fargo security analysis system. Typically, all securities in the same industry were covered by the same analyst. Summary statistics on the number of individual securities followed by these analysts are:

Number of Securities Followed by Each Analyst

	Median	Lowest	Highest
January 1977	28	8	39
January 1978	35	8	40
January 1979	37	10	40
January 1980	36	13	45

A total of 405 securities were included in the data base, but not every security was covered every month. The number of securities at selected specific months is:

Month	Additions	Deletions	Active Securities
January 1977	—	—	343
January 1978	33	6	370
January 1979	17	16	371
January 1980	8	17	362

Most deletions arise from acquisitions, mergers, and take-overs.

C. Individual Analyst Forecast Revision Statistics

The percentage of revisions over the January 1977 to June 1980 period for each year of the FY1 to FY5 horizon is presented in Table 2.10. By far the most frequent outcome is that the analyst makes no forecast revision for a given month. Note that the individual year EPS forecasts available in the data base play no direct role in the Wells Fargo security analyst approach. For this reason, the motivation for individual analysts to update their forecasts continually as new information becomes available is unclear.

Wells Fargo analysts are more likely to revise their EPS forecasts in the month that interim or annual earnings are announced vis-a-vis months with no earnings announcement. Table 2.11 presents evidence on this issue using a format equivalent to Table 2.4. Over each year of the forecast horizon, month 0 has a higher frequency of revision than months –2, –1, +1, or +2. The data in Table 2.11 do not test whether the earnings release is the information cue prompting the revision. To explore this issue, more details about the release pattern of other cues (e.g., dividend announcements) would need to be examined.

Dependency of Earnings Forecast Revisions Across the FY1 to FY5 Horizon for a Given Forecast Month

Table 2.6 presents evidence that the signs of FY1 and FY2 forecast revisions in the IBES data base in a given month are positively correlated. A similar result is found for the Wells Fargo data base. Table 2.12 presents (i) the unconditional relative frequency of – and + revision codings for each FYT, and (ii) the relative frequency of a revision coding in each FYT (where T = 2 to 5) conditional on the same revision coding occurring in FYT-1. Not only is there a positive correlation in the categorizations of FYT and FYT-1 in a given month, there is also strong evidence that this positive correlation increases in successive years of the forecast horizon. For instance, the unconditional relative frequency of FY3 (FY5) having a + forecast revision is .076 (.073). However, the relative frequency of FY3 (FY5) having a + forecast revision, given that FY2 (FY4) in the same month has a + forecast revision, is .755 (.928). The results in Table 2.12 are consistent with analysts perceiving that the underlying events that cause them to revise their forecasts in FY1, FY2, etc., are also expected to persist in subsequent years of the forecast horizon.

Dependency of Earnings Forecast Revisions Across the FY1 to FY5 Horizon Over Time

Table 2.13 presents summary statistics pertaining to dependencies over time for forecast revisions across the FY1 to FY5 horizon. The basic procedure underlying Table 2.13 is:

1. For each firm, compute the time series of EPS forecast revisions for each horizon year FY1, ..., FY5.

   (a) $[FY1_{t+1}-FY1_t]$, $[FY1_{t+2}-FY1_{t+1}]$, ..., $[FY1_{t+n}-FY1_{t+n-1}]$

   (b) $[FY2_{t+1}-FY2_t]$, $[FY2_{t+2}-FY2_{t+1}]$, ..., $[FY2_{t+n}-FY2_{t+n-1}]$

   •

   •

   •

TABLE 2.10
Wells Fargo: Individual Analyst Monthly Revision Percentages Over January 1977 to June 1980 Period

FORECAST REVISION CATEGORY	FY1	FY2	FY3	FY4	FY5
-	9.3%	7.6%	5.4%	4.6%	4.1%
0	79.4%	83.8%	87.0%	87.6%	88.6%
+	11.3%	8.6%	7.6%	7.8%	7.3%

TABLE 2.11

Wells Fargo: Revision Frequency of Analysts' Forecasts Relative to Interim/Annual Earnings Announcement Month (0)

YEAR FORECASTED	FREQUENCY OF MONTHLY REVISION IN EVENT TIME					FREQUENCY OF MONTHLY REVISION CONDITIONAL ON NO EARNINGS ANNOUNCEMENT
	MONTH -2	MONTH -1	MONTH 0	MONTH +1	MONTH +2	
FY1	.198	.125	.335	.170	.137	.146
FY2	.157	.111	.235	.142	.123	.127
FY3	.123	.094	.188	.112	.099	.103
FY4	.117	.089	.181	.108	.092	.098
FY5	.114	.079	.162	.103	.089	.092

TABLE 2.12

Wells Fargo: Contemporaneous Monthly Revision Over Forecast Horizon

A. UNCONDITIONAL RELATIVE FREQUENCY OF REVISION OF YEAR T IN MONTH J

FORECAST REVISION CATEGORY	T=1	T=2	T=3	T=4	T=5
FYT-	.093	.076	.054	.046	.041
FYT0	.794	.838	.870	.876	.886
FYT+	.113	.086	.076	.078	.073

B. CONDITIONAL RELATIVE FREQUENCY OF REVISION OF YEAR T IN MONTH J GIVEN ANOTHER YEAR'S REVISION IN MONTH J

FORECAST REVISION CATEGORY	T=1	T=2	T=3	T=4	T=5
FYT-|FY1-	1.000	.574	.412	.350	.321
FYT-|FY2-	-	1.000	.645	.522	.462
FYT-|FY3-	-	-	1.000	.783	.691
FYT-|FY4-	-	-	-	1.000	.872
FYT+|FY1+	1.000	.616	.503	.484	.454
FYT+|FY2+	-	1.000	.755	.721	.691
FYT+|FY3+	-	-	1.000	.914	.872
FYT+|FY4+	-	-	-	1.000	.928

TABLE 2.13

Wells Fargo: Median Across Firms for Correlation Between Changes in Successive Monthly Earnings Forecasts of EPS in FYT and FYT + J for Each Firm

HORIZON YEARS CORRELATED	SPEARMAN RANK CORRELATION		PEARSONIAN CORRELATION	
	ALL OBSERVATIONS INCLUDED	OMIT IF BOTH UNCHANGED	ALL OBSERVATIONS INCLUDED	OMIT IF BOTH UNCHANGED
FY1 AND FY2	.68	.65	.70	.66
FY1 AND FY3	.57	.53	.58	.57
FY1 AND FY4	.51	.43	.51	.47
FY1 AND FY5	.50	.42	.45	.39
FY2 AND FY3	.83	.82	.87	.87
FY2 AND FY4	.74	.74	.78	.76
FY2 AND FY5	.72	.67	.73	.74
FY3 AND FY4	.93	.95	.97	.96
FY3 AND FY5	.89	.89	.91	.92
FY4 AND FY5	1.00	.96	.98	.98

(e) $[FY5_{t+1}-FY5_t]$, $[FY5_{t+2}-FY5_{t+1}]$, ..., $[FY5_{t+n}-FY5_{t+n-1}]$

2. For each firm, compute the correlation between pairs of horizon year forecast revisions – e.g., (a) and (b) = FY1/FY2, ..., (d) and (e) = FY4/FY5.

3. For each pair from 2, rank the correlations across all firms and compute the median.

Due to the relatively high frequency of no-change observations in each series (see Table 2.10), the above procedure was employed with two different data sets in 1:

(i) All observations included, and

(ii) Omit an observation from the series of the two forecast horizon years being compared if both were zero.

Both (i) and (ii) yield similar inferences. Spearman rank and Pearsonian correlation coefficients are reported in Table 2.13.

The basic pattern in Table 2.13 is one of positive dependency of forecast revisions across the FY1 to FY5 horizon over time. Note especially that in the latter years of the forecast horizon, the correlation over time is very high. For instance, the median correlation (Pearsonian) between contemporaneous revisions over time in the FY4 and FY5 series is .98. This finding and the related finding in Table 2.12 are both consistent with relatively little *incremental* information in the latter years of the forecast horizon.

Dependency of Earnings Forecast Revisions Over Time for a Given Horizon Year

The final dependency issue examined is whether successive forecast revisions for a given year of the horizon are correlated. For each firm, autocorrelations ($r_1, r_2, \ldots, r_6$) of the forecast revision series for each of FY1, FY2, FY3, FY4, and FY5 were computed. Then each firm's autocorrelation for a given r_n/FYT pair was ranked and the .25, .50, and .75 percentiles calculated. Table 2.14 presents these results. The overwhelming picture is one of essentially zero serial correlation in forecast revisions over time for all of the five years in the forecast horizon. This result is not surprising given the large percentage of zero forecast revisions in the Wells Fargo data base.

D. Strengths and Limitations of Data Base

The Wells Fargo data base has several important strengths from a research viewpoint:

1. A sizeable number of stocks is included, with many industries represented over an extended time period.

2. There is consistency across analysts in what is reported, e.g., all forecasts are for earnings per share before extraordinary items.

3. There is no reporting lag of the primary/secondary distribution kind found with IBES. The clients of Wells Fargo Investment Advisors are the first to receive the earnings forecast and other information produced by the Wells Fargo analysts.

The main limitation of the Wells Fargo data base from a research viewpoint is the relative infrequency of earnings forecast revisions. As noted earlier, individual year EPS forecasts play no direct role in the Wells Fargo security analyst approach and thus the motivation for analysts to update their EPS forecasts continually as new information becomes available is unclear. In 1982, the senior management of Wells Fargo Invest-

TABLE 2.14

Wells Fargo: Percentiles of the Distribution, Across Firms, of Six Coefficients of Autocorrelation in the EPS Forecast Revision Series: Estimated Over the January 1977 to June 1980 Period

FORECAST YEAR	AUTOCORRELATION COEFFICIENTS					
	r_1	r_2	r_3	r_4	r_5	r_6
FY1						
.25 Percentile	-.08	-.06	-.06	-.08	-.10	-.08
.50 Percentile	-.02	-.02	.00	-.02	-.04	.00
.75 Percentile	.01	.08	.09	.06	.07	.14
FY2						
.25 Percentile	-.08	-.06	-.08	-.07	-.10	-.08
.50 Percentile	-.02	-.01	-.01	-.02	-.03	-.01
.75 Percentile	.00	.06	.04	.04	.05	.09
FY3						
.25 Percentile	-.07	-.06	-.08	-.08	-.09	-.06
.50 Percentile	-.03	-.02	-.02	-.03	-.05	-.03
.75 Percentile	.00	.04	.03	.03	.04	.03
FY4						
.25 Percentile	-.06	-.06	-.07	-.08	-.07	-.08
.50 Percentile	-.03	-.02	-.03	-.03	-.04	-.04
.75 Percentile	.00	.02	.05	.03	.04	.05
FY5						
.25 Percentile	-.07	-.07	-.07	-.08	-.08	-.10
.50 Percentile	-.04	-.03	-.03	-.03	-.03	-.04
.75 Percentile	.00	.02	.03	.03	.07	.08

ment Advisors decided to discontinue using their own security analysts to provide inputs into their security valuation model and to use outside services (including IBES). This decision meant that individual year EPS forecasts were no longer produced in a systematic manner by Wells Fargo security analysts.

2.4 Other Data Issues

Two data bases, in addition to IBES and Wells Fargo, are used in the research. The Compustat data base is used for company earnings announcement dates and the reported EPS of each firm in the post-1980 period. The CRSP daily security return file was used to compute monthly security returns.

Market capitalization data from the CRSP monthly file were used to derive statistics on firm size. For the first and last months of the IBES and Wells Fargo data bases, the market capitalization cut-offs of the deciles of all firms on the NYSE were calculated. Then the percentage of IBES and Wells Fargo firms in each decile was determined – see Table 2.15. Not surprisingly, firms with larger market capitalizations are heavily represented in both the IBES and Wells Fargo data bases.

A breakdown of the data base membership of the 500 IBES and 405 Wells Fargo firms is presented in Table 2.16. At subsequent stages in this research, the maximum number of firms available to address a specific issue is used. For instance, Chapter 3 focuses on the properties of consensus earnings forecast error measures. All available firms on the IBES data base are used in Chapter 3, irrespective of whether they are or are not included in the Wells Fargo data base.

TABLE 2.15

Membership of Firms in NYSE Market Capitalization Size Categories

NYSE SIZE CATEGORY	IBES		WELLS FARGO	
	Jan. 1976	Dec. 1980	Jan. 1977	June 1980
0 - .1 (Smallest)	0.9%	0.8%	0.0%	0.3%
.1 - .2	1.1	1.3	0.3	1.1
.2 - .3	1.7	3.8	1.5	1.4
.3 - .4	3.0	2.9	2.9	3.1
.4 - .5	4.3	5.0	3.5	4.6
.5 - .6	6.5	7.7	5.3	5.2
.6 - .7	11.5	12.2	8.2	10.0
.7 - .8	16.5	17.0	17.2	15.8
.8 - .9	24.5	21.8	23.1	23.8
.9 - 1.0 (Largest)	30.0	27.5	38.0	34.7

TABLE 2.16

Representation of Firms in Data Bases Used

FIRM INCLUDED IN	IBES FIRMS	WELLS FARGO FIRMS
Compustat, CRSP, IBES, Wells Fargo	246	246
Compustat, CRSP, IBES only	205	-
Compustat, CRSP, Wells Fargo only	-	82
Compustat, IBES, Wells Fargo only	9	9
Compustat, IBES only	3	-
Compustat, Wells Fargo only	-	4
CRSP, IBES, Wells Fargo only	13	13
CRSP, IBES only	15	-
CRSP, Wells Fargo only	-	28
IBES, Wells Fargo only	5	5
IBES only	4	-
Wells Fargo only	-	18
	500	405

CHAPTER 3

DESCRIPTIVE STATISTICS ON CONSENSUS SECURITY ANALYST EARNINGS FORECASTS

3.1 Overview of Issues Examined and Results

This chapter presents evidence on properties of consensus earnings forecasts using the IBES data base. The evidence presented is in event time format, where time 0 is the month the company reports its actual EPS.[1] Use of this format facilitates analysis of the behavior of forecast errors as the time to announcement of the variable being forecast is reduced. The results presented relate to topics well-researched in the existing literature; as such, they document that the data base is well-behaved relative to results reported in prior studies. However, there are several distinctive features of the analysis in this chapter vis-a-vis the prior literature. *First*, the focus is on a multi-year horizon and not just a single-year horizon; statistics relating to event months –22 to –1 are presented.[2] This focus provides evidence that reinforces the results obtained in Chapter 5 (Security Analyst Multi-Year Earnings Forecast Revisions and Security Price Changes). *Second*, emphasis is placed on distributional statistics such as the fractiles of the distribution and the interquartile ranges. In part due to smaller data bases, much of the prior literature has presented only measures such as the mean or standard deviation. *Third*, more explicit analysis is made of extreme forecast errors and their effect on summary statistics and inferences drawn from those statistics.

The following results are documented in this chapter:

1. The dispersion and accuracy of consensus forecasts. Over the –22 to –1 event month period, there is a systematic reduction in the distribution of forecast errors as the month of the release of the actual EPS is approached. Over this same time period, there is a systematic increase in forecast accuracy. Both results are intuitive. Over the –22 to –1 month period, analysts can access an increasing amount of information about the fiscal period being forecast.

2. The bias of consensus forecasts. Over the 1976 to 1980 period, the percentage of positive forecast errors (i.e., analysts underestimated actual EPS) ranges between 53 percent to 56 percent. However, the average magnitude of forecast overestimates exceeds the average magnitude of forecast underestimates.

3. The effect of extreme observations on inferences drawn from forecast error measures. Deleting the ten most extreme observations in each tail of the forecast error distribution does not change the conclusions noted above.

4. The agreement among security analysts in their forecasts of earnings for the one company over the forecast horizon. As the time to the announcement of actual earnings is reduced, security analysts increase their agreement on the EPS that each firm will announce.

---

[1] Announcement dates of actual earnings are taken from Standard & Poor's Quarterly Compustat file.

[2] Months –22 to –1 were selected, since each of these months has at least 1000 observations. Months –23 and –24, by contrast, had 764 and 161 observations, respectively (for Table 3.1).

3.2 Distribution Evidence Using Alternative Forecast Error Measures

A. Evidence on Dispersion and Accuracy

Distribution evidence for the following three forecast error measures is presented in Tables 3.1 to 3.3 and Figures 3.1 to 3.3:

Table 3.1 and Figure 3.1

$$\text{Actual EPS} - \text{Forecast EPS} \tag{3.1}$$

Table 3.2 and Figure 3.2

$$\frac{\text{Actual EPS} - \text{Forecast EPS}}{\text{Average Absolute Change in Actual EPS (1976-1980)}} \tag{3.2}$$

Table 3.3 and Figure 3.3

$$\frac{\text{Actual EPS} - \text{Forecast EPS}}{\text{Security Price at End of Forecast Month}} \times 100 \tag{3.3}$$

When aggregating (3.1) across firms or over time, differences in the level of earnings can result in a small subset of observations "dominating" the summary measures.[3] Both (3.2) and (3.3) include denominators that attempt to standardize observations across firms or over time. The denominators chosen are always positive (for the sample) and hence problems arising from the treatment of negative denominators are avoided – see Section 3.3 for further discussion.

For each event month T (where T = –22 to –1), (3.1) is calculated for each firm/year observation and all observations are ranked from the most negative to the most positive. This procedure is repeated for (3.2) and (3.3). Tables 3.1, 3.2, and 3.3 report for each event month the mean, the nine deciles of the distribution, the interquartile range (.75 fractile – .25 fractile), the number of observations, and the percentage of observations with positive forecast errors. Figures 3.1 to 3.3 present time-series plots of the interquartile range in Panel A and the .1, .3, .5, .7, and .9 deciles in Panel B.

All three measures report a similar pattern regarding the distribution of forecast errors over the –22 to –1 event month period. There is a systematic reduction in the dispersion of forecast errors as the month of the release of the actual EPS is approached. The interquartile range (IQR) statistic captures this reduction in dispersion as reflected in the .75 and .25 percentiles of the distribution. The IQR for month T is less than the IQR for the prior month in 20 out of 21 comparisons using (3.3) and 21 out of 21 comparisons using (3.1) and (3.2). The systematic reduction in the distribution of forecast errors is also apparent from the time-series plots of the .1, .3, .7, and .9 deciles in Panel B of Figures 3.1 to 3.3. Relative to the prior literature, the added insight from the above analysis is that the systematic reduction occurs for forecasts made in the –22 to –12 period as well as for the –11 to –1 period.

The IQR measure captures the dispersion of the distribution, but is insensitive to whether forecasts become more or less accurate as event month 0 is approached. Two

---

[3] Because (3.1) is based on earnings per share and not earnings, scale differences across firms may be partially controlled for, as (i) firm size and (ii) the number of shares outstanding are positively correlated.

TABLE 3.1

Distribution Statistics for [Actual EPS–Forecast EPS]: Median Forecast as Proxy for the Consensus Forecast

month	mean	deciles									inter-quartile range	N	%>0
		.1	.2	.3	.4	.5	.6	.7	.8	.9			
- 1	-0.017	-0.245	-0.100	-0.045	-0.010	0.010	0.036	0.075	0.140	0.270	0.170	2120	54.3
- 2	-0.028	-0.300	-0.120	-0.051	-0.010	0.010	0.043	0.080	0.160	0.315	0.207	2186	54.3
- 3	-0.041	-0.390	-0.169	-0.080	-0.020	0.010	0.050	0.100	0.199	0.387	0.255	2181	53.8
- 4	-0.053	-0.501	-0.220	-0.100	-0.029	0.010	0.058	0.119	0.220	0.460	0.308	2171	53.3
- 5	-0.057	-0.566	-0.243	-0.102	-0.030	0.020	0.070	0.140	0.263	0.520	0.341	2162	53.5
- 6	-0.053	-0.670	-0.260	-0.110	-0.025	0.027	0.080	0.155	0.300	0.583	0.380	2150	54.9
- 7	-0.053	-0.735	-0.290	-0.112	-0.025	0.025	0.093	0.188	0.350	0.680	0.433	2145	55.2
- 8	-0.062	-0.820	-0.315	-0.125	-0.030	0.030	0.100	0.191	0.375	0.730	0.480	2140	55.5
- 9	-0.056	-0.850	-0.350	-0.140	-0.025	0.040	0.120	0.220	0.420	0.810	0.518	2128	56.2
-10	-0.057	-0.930	-0.380	-0.150	-0.025	0.040	0.130	0.240	0.470	0.885	0.579	2116	56.3
-11	-0.053	-1.020	-0.384	-0.158	-0.030	0.050	0.140	0.263	0.500	0.970	0.610	2119	56.7
-12	-0.041	-1.040	-0.390	-0.160	-0.030	0.059	0.150	0.300	0.536	1.030	0.675	2107	56.6
-13	-0.039	-1.100	-0.415	-0.170	-0.035	0.060	0.157	0.300	0.570	1.060	0.700	2062	56.2
-14	-0.051	-1.180	-0.430	-0.197	-0.050	0.060	0.165	0.315	0.602	1.110	0.735	1849	55.6
-15	-0.075	-1.230	-0.485	-0.210	-0.050	0.055	0.173	0.330	0.610	1.150	0.773	1775	55.0
-16	-0.095	-1.360	-0.535	-0.240	-0.065	0.050	0.165	0.340	0.610	1.220	0.800	1743	54.2
-17	-0.070	-1.370	-0.560	-0.230	-0.060	0.059	0.185	0.355	0.645	1.295	0.845	1715	54.6
-18	-0.081	-1.400	-0.560	-0.260	-0.070	0.050	0.186	0.351	0.662	1.325	0.864	1655	54.2
-19	-0.068	-1.420	-0.590	-0.270	-0.068	0.070	0.192	0.375	0.680	1.385	0.891	1587	54.9
-20	-0.083	-1.507	-0.601	-0.275	-0.065	0.055	0.190	0.357	0.700	1.380	0.900	1478	55.2
-21	-0.088	-1.530	-0.620	-0.255	-0.060	0.070	0.210	0.400	0.735	1.480	0.920	1303	55.7
-22	-0.094	-1.613	-0.665	-0.255	-0.050	0.085	0.210	0.410	0.750	1.518	0.930	1059	56.4

MONTH 0 = MONTH IN WHICH ACTUAL EPS IS ANNOUNCED

TABLE 3.2

Distribution Statistics for [(Actual EPS–Forecast EPS)/Average Absolute Change in EPS]: Median Forecast as Proxy for the Consensus Forecast

month	mean	deciles .1	.2	.3	.4	.5	.6	.7	.8	.9	inter-quartile range	N	%>0
- 1	0.006	-0.347	-0.158	-0.071	-0.016	0.020	0.060	0.112	0.192	0.342	0.250	2119	54.3
- 2	-0.003	-0.420	-0.191	-0.084	-0.018	0.023	0.070	0.127	0.214	0.394	0.295	2185	54.3
- 3	-0.009	-0.549	-0.254	-0.116	-0.038	0.024	0.087	0.161	0.262	0.472	0.386	2180	53.9
- 4	-0.023	-0.675	-0.337	-0.158	-0.049	0.028	0.106	0.195	0.310	0.538	0.483	2170	53.4
- 5	-0.028	-0.752	-0.390	-0.166	-0.045	0.038	0.121	0.216	0.354	0.602	0.541	2161	53.5
- 6	-0.019	-0.846	-0.441	-0.183	-0.039	0.053	0.144	0.260	0.421	0.695	0.608	2149	55.0
- 7	-0.016	-0.932	-0.481	-0.192	-0.045	0.056	0.163	0.292	0.471	0.762	0.707	2144	55.2
- 8	-0.025	-1.011	-0.526	-0.206	-0.049	0.055	0.173	0.322	0.509	0.798	0.759	2139	55.4
- 9	-0.014	-1.109	-0.585	-0.233	-0.045	0.069	0.214	0.374	0.573	0.881	0.858	2128	56.2
-10	-0.012	-1.193	-0.651	-0.255	-0.058	0.075	0.229	0.412	0.618	0.953	0.922	2116	56.3
-11	-0.012	-1.268	-0.678	-0.267	-0.057	0.099	0.250	0.448	0.668	1.016	0.994	2119	56.7
-12	-0.002	-1.396	-0.737	-0.279	-0.054	0.114	0.277	0.492	0.731	1.086	1.097	2107	56.6
-13	0.000	-1.449	-0.763	-0.305	-0.058	0.124	0.286	0.516	0.767	1.139	1.135	2062	56.2
-14	-0.009	-1.550	-0.777	-0.353	-0.093	0.125	0.299	0.538	0.799	1.206	1.208	1849	55.6
-15	-0.027	-1.654	-0.865	-0.389	-0.104	0.114	0.317	0.578	0.842	1.264	1.300	1775	55.0
-16	-0.045	-1.732	-0.893	-0.442	-0.139	0.093	0.307	0.568	0.884	1.336	1.355	1743	54.2
-17	-0.034	-1.762	-0.958	-0.460	-0.116	0.123	0.335	0.579	0.923	1.368	1.434	1715	54.6
-18	-0.042	-1.817	-0.973	-0.493	-0.133	0.119	0.340	0.586	0.924	1.434	1.472	1655	54.2
-19	-0.032	-1.883	-1.009	-0.504	-0.133	0.140	0.359	0.646	1.002	1.523	1.514	1587	54.9
-20	-0.051	-1.945	-1.104	-0.535	-0.120	0.122	0.352	0.647	1.005	1.551	1.571	1478	55.2
-21	-0.025	-2.007	-1.093	-0.508	-0.108	0.146	0.408	0.688	1.077	1.647	1.669	1303	55.7
-22	-0.011	-2.064	-1.168	-0.497	-0.094	0.176	0.410	0.721	1.114	1.684	1.750	1059	56.4

MONTH 0 = MONTH IN WHICH ACTUAL EPS IS ANNOUNCED

TABLE 3.3

Distribution Statistics for [(Actual EPS–Forecast EPS)/Security Price at End of Forecast Month] x 100: Median Forecast as Proxy for the Consensus Forecast

month	mean	deciles									inter-quartile range	N	%>0
		.1	.2	.3	.4	.5	.6	.7	.8	.9			
- 1	-0.387	-1.174	-0.458	-0.173	-0.040	0.050	0.167	0.318	0.633	1.271	0.743	2043	54.4
- 2	-0.414	-1.391	-0.519	-0.219	-0.045	0.052	0.176	0.375	0.670	1.403	0.848	2110	54.4
- 3	-0.580	-1.872	-0.726	-0.306	-0.079	0.053	0.198	0.448	0.809	1.695	1.074	2102	53.9
- 4	-0.683	-2.538	-0.971	-0.376	-0.109	0.056	0.235	0.514	0.923	2.019	1.300	2094	53.2
- 5	-0.683	-2.680	-1.031	-0.403	-0.114	0.069	0.269	0.569	1.096	2.161	1.421	2084	53.4
- 6	-0.673	-2.963	-1.103	-0.434	-0.099	0.104	0.334	0.670	1.237	2.504	1.587	2071	54.9
- 7	-0.622	-3.340	-1.274	-0.473	-0.098	0.105	0.379	0.746	1.442	2.960	1.833	2066	55.4
- 8	-0.677	-3.620	-1.345	-0.505	-0.111	0.115	0.405	0.802	1.680	3.214	1.968	2062	55.6
- 9	-0.601	-3.989	-1.502	-0.543	-0.111	0.166	0.490	0.964	1.958	3.709	2.277	2051	56.1
-10	-0.610	-4.408	-1.663	-0.636	-0.111	0.165	0.548	1.113	2.111	4.142	2.616	2037	56.4
-11	-0.477	-4.655	-1.736	-0.682	-0.126	0.205	0.609	1.242	2.293	4.778	2.795	2038	56.7
-12	-0.363	-4.773	-1.756	-0.700	-0.133	0.243	0.641	1.302	2.527	5.195	2.915	2028	56.6
-13	-0.236	-4.873	-1.851	-0.755	-0.151	0.263	0.646	1.360	2.667	5.444	3.102	1985	56.1
-14	-0.282	-5.510	-1.879	-0.845	-0.199	0.267	0.678	1.411	2.753	5.809	3.228	1784	55.5
-15	-0.456	-5.933	-2.172	-0.908	-0.218	0.227	0.724	1.481	2.857	5.720	3.459	1709	55.0
-16	-0.490	-6.300	-2.314	-1.054	-0.270	0.196	0.711	1.485	2.777	5.690	3.604	1678	54.2
-17	-0.206	-6.197	-2.296	-1.053	-0.235	0.211	0.778	1.533	2.857	5.930	3.494	1649	54.6
-18	-0.212	-5.931	-2.331	-1.000	-0.268	0.194	0.756	1.480	2.827	6.147	3.531	1590	54.3
-19	-0.096	-6.287	-2.548	-1.102	-0.236	0.270	0.800	1.603	3.027	6.345	3.763	1524	54.9
-20	-0.019	-6.372	-2.587	-1.104	-0.226	0.229	0.735	1.594	2.844	6.222	3.863	1413	55.2
-21	-0.115	-6.211	-2.582	-1.128	-0.231	0.298	0.768	1.723	3.113	6.443	3.960	1251	55.8
-22	-0.039	-6.386	-2.586	-1.014	-0.203	0.333	0.867	1.727	3.127	6.977	3.996	1021	56.7

MONTH 0 = MONTH IN WHICH ACTUAL EPS IS ANNOUNCED

FIGURE 3.1

Distribution Statistics for [Actual EPS – Forecast EPS]

PANEL A: INTERQUARTILE RANGE

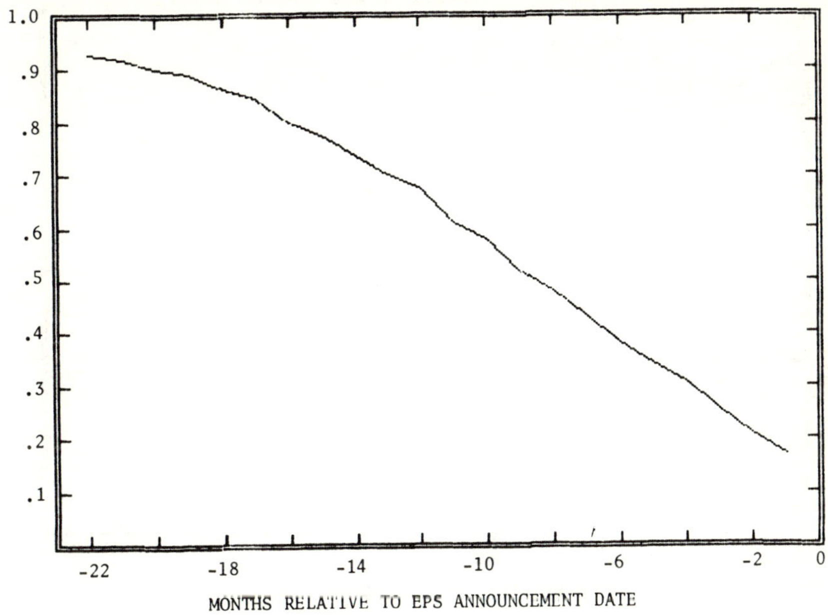

PANEL B: DECILES OF DISTRIBUTION

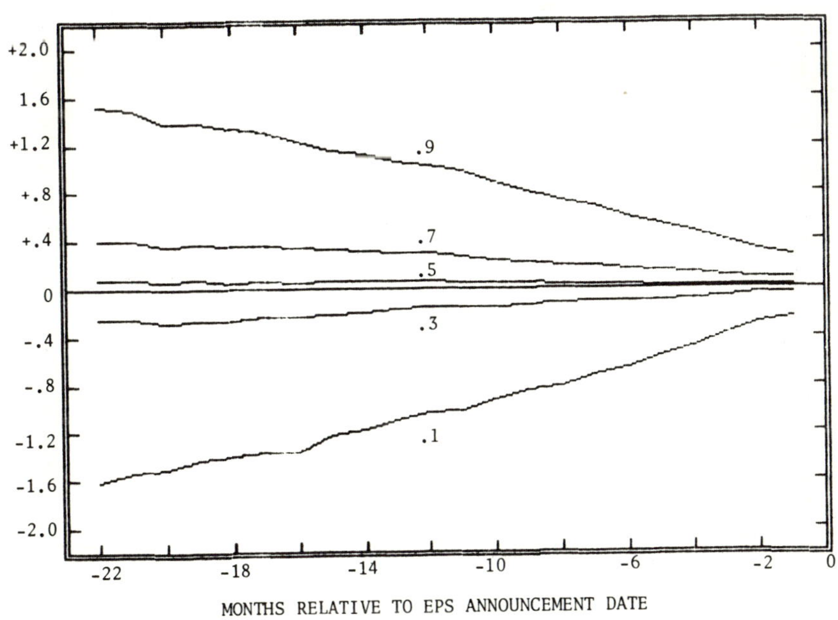

FIGURE 3.2

Distribution Statistics for [(Actual EPS – Forecast EPS)/Average Absolute Change in EPS]

PANEL A: INTERQUARTILE RANGE

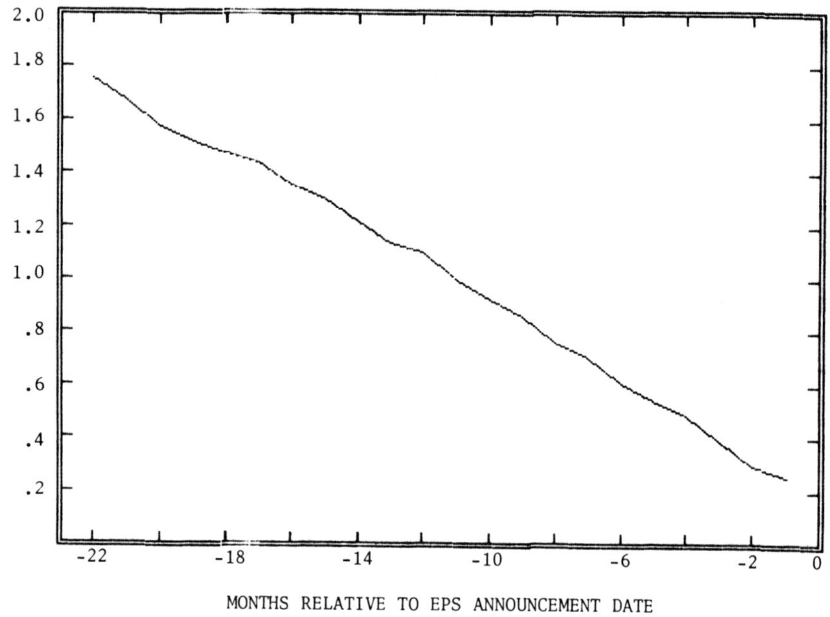

PANEL B: DECILES OF DISTRIBUTION

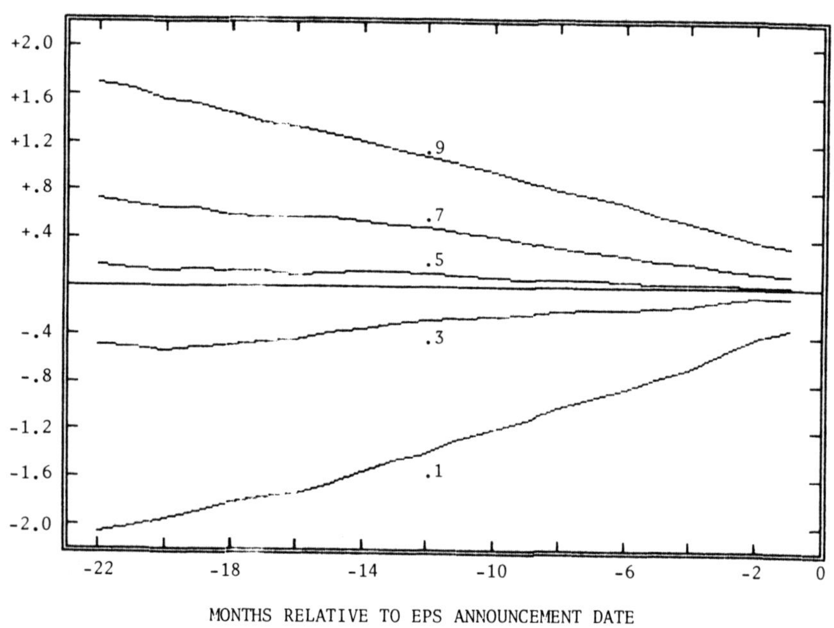

FIGURE 3

Distribution Statistics for [(Actual EPS – Forecast EPS)/Security Price at End of Forecast Month] x 100

PANEL A: INTERQUARTILE RANGE

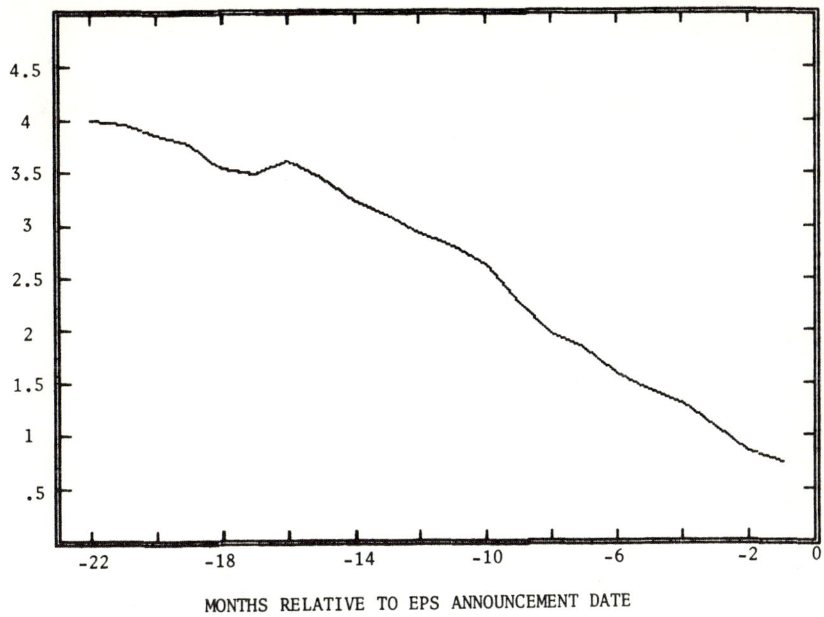

PANEL B: DECILES OF DISTRIBUTION

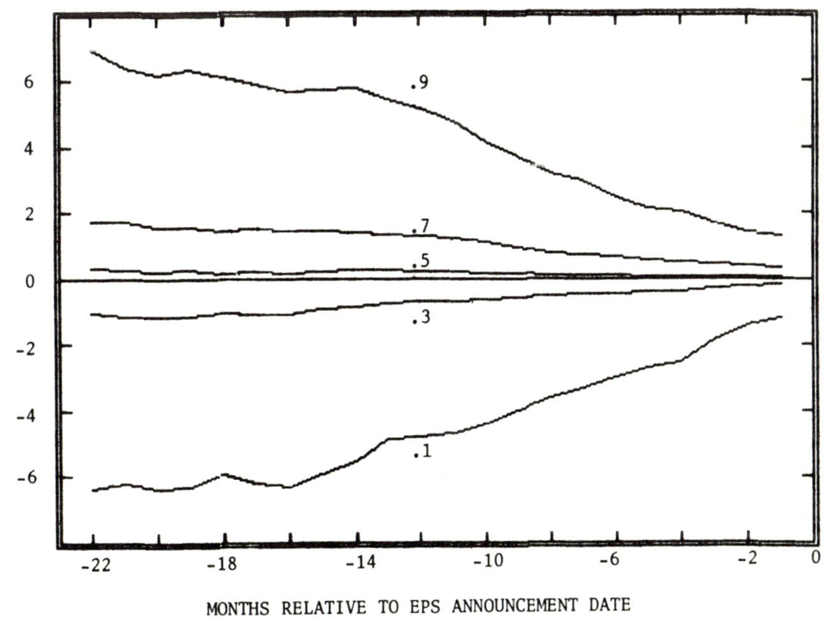

error measures that address forecast accuracy over time are the mean absolute error (M.AB.E.) and the mean square error (M.S.E.). Table 3.4 (columns 2 to 4) presents the median values of the distribution for the following M.AB.E. measures:

$$|\text{Actual EPS} - \text{Forecast EPS}| \tag{3.4}$$

$$\frac{|\text{Actual EPS} - \text{Forecast EPS}|}{\text{Average Absolute Change in Actual EPS (1976-1980)}} \tag{3.5}$$

$$\frac{|\text{Actual EPS} - \text{Forecast EPS}|}{\text{Security Price at End of Forecast Month}} \times 100 \tag{3.6}$$

where | ... | denotes that the absolute value of each observation is computed. Table 3.4 (columns 5 to 7) presents the median values of the distribution for the following equivalent M.S.E. measures:

$$[\text{Actual EPS} - \text{Forecast EPS}]^2 \tag{3.7}$$

$$\frac{[\text{Actual EPS} - \text{Forecast EPS}]^2}{\text{Average Absolute Change in Actual EPS (1976-1980)}} \tag{3.8}$$

$$\frac{[\text{Actual EPS} - \text{Forecast EPS}]^2}{\text{Security Price at End of Forecast Month}} \times 100 \tag{3.9}$$

All six error measures in Table 3.4 indicate that security analyst EPS forecasts become more accurate as the announcement month of the actual EPS is approached. One explanation for this increase in accuracy (and the reduction in dispersion) is the expansion of information available to analysts about the conditions that will prevail for the remainder of the fiscal period being forecast. For example, during the –8 to –1 month period, analysts are able to observe interim EPS figures that actually comprise a part of the annual EPS being forecast.

Tables 3.1 to 3.4 use the median as the proxy for consensus forecasts. Table 3.5 presents summary data for the use of the mean for consensus forecasts. The inferences drawn previously, about the dispersion and accuracy of consensus forecasts, also apply with the use of this alternative proxy.

Table 3.6 and Figure 3.4 present the distribution of the following statistic for each of the –22 to –1 event months:

$$\frac{\text{Absolute Change in EPS Forecast from Month T}-1\text{ to T}}{\text{Average Absolute Change in Actual EPS (1976-1980)}} \tag{3.10}$$

Our intuition was that (at least over the –11 to 0 month period), as the time to the actual EPS announcement decreases and thus there is less of the annual EPS to be predicted, consecutive revisions in forecast annual EPS would decline in absolute amount. This pattern is not a consistent one in Table 3.6 (or Figure 3.4). While there is some evidence of a decline in (3.10) from months –22 to –13, over the –12 to –2 month period there appears to be no discernible reduction in the magnitude of forecast revisions.

B. *Evidence on Bias*

A forecast is biased if the *expected* forecast error is not zero. We choose not to make

TABLE 3.4

Median Absolute and Squared Forecast Error Measures: Median is Used as a Proxy for the Consensus Forecast

EVENT MONTH	ABSOLUTE FORECAST ERROR			SQUARED FORECAST ERROR		
	(3.4)	(3.5)	(3.6)	(3.7)	(3.8)	(3.9)
-1	0.085	0.127	0.376	0.007	0.011	0.033
-2	0.100	0.151	0.422	0.010	0.015	0.043
-3	0.130	0.195	0.541	0.017	0.025	0.068
-4	0.150	0.242	0.653	0.023	0.037	0.098
-5	0.171	0.268	0.719	0.029	0.049	0.125
-6	0.200	0.310	0.820	0.040	0.065	0.163
-7	0.220	0.356	0.914	0.048	0.083	0.198
-8	0.240	0.392	1.000	0.058	0.093	0.241
-9	0.270	0.437	1.150	0.073	0.119	0.304
-10	0.290	0.477	1.333	0.084	0.147	0.371
-11	0.310	0.519	1.386	0.096	0.169	0.431
-12	0.339	0.569	1.471	0.115	0.196	0.498
-13	0.350	0.595	1.531	0.122	0.215	0.520
-14	0.350	0.623	1.600	0.123	0.229	0.549
-15	0.385	0.654	1.743	0.148	0.256	0.658
-16	0.405	0.674	1.814	0.164	0.286	0.725
-17	0.420	0.716	1.770	0.176	0.316	0.742
-18	0.435	0.732	1.804	0.189	0.331	0.777
-19	0.447	0.765	1.887	0.200	0.366	0.828
-20	0.446	0.793	1.929	0.199	0.375	0.883
-21	0.460	0.838	2.032	0.212	0.393	0.928
-22	0.473	0.887	2.035	0.224	0.422	1.041

MONTH 0 = MONTH IN WHICH ACTUAL EPS IS ANNOUNCED

TABLE 3.5

Forecast Error Measures: Mean Forecast is Used as a Proxy for the Consensus Forecast

PANEL A: MEDIAN OF THE DISTRIBUTION

EVENT	FORECAST ERROR			ABSOLUTE FORECAST ERROR			SQUARED FORECAST ERROR		
MONTH	(3.1)	(3.2)	(3.3)	(3.4)	(3.5)	(3.6)	(3.7)	(3.8)	(3.9)
-2	0.016	0.028	0.062	0.107	0.158	0.444	0.011	0.018	0.049
-4	0.015	0.028	0.058	0.155	0.247	0.677	0.024	0.039	0.102
-6	0.027	0.050	0.105	0.199	0.311	0.838	0.040	0.066	0.166
-8	0.038	0.072	0.141	0.244	0.397	1.026	0.060	0.100	0.253
-10	0.045	0.085	0.195	0.291	0.490	1.333	0.085	0.145	0.386
-12	0.057	0.116	0.242	0.340	0.559	1.471	0.116	0.195	0.503
-14	0.056	0.116	0.255	0.357	0.619	1.612	0.127	0.229	0.564
-16	0.051	0.103	0.203	0.403	0.668	1.759	0.162	0.284	0.675
-18	0.052	0.110	0.218	0.431	0.734	1.822	0.186	0.329	0.783
-20	0.057	0.116	0.238	0.447	0.800	1.929	0.200	0.380	0.869
-22	0.087	0.184	0.333	0.470	0.887	2.042	0.221	0.440	1.041

PANEL B: INTERQUARTILE RANGE

EVENT	FORECAST ERROR			ABSOLUTE FORECAST ERROR			SQUARED FORECAST ERROR		
MONTH	(3.1)	(3.2)	(3.3)	(3.4)	(3.5)	(3.6)	(3.7)	(3.8)	(3.9)
-2	0.213	0.318	0.874	0.224	0.286	1.025	0.068	0.086	0.284
-4	0.308	0.496	1.335	0.346	0.415	1.523	0.161	0.190	0.670
-6	0.395	0.623	1.659	0.438	0.521	1.845	0.257	0.303	1.016
-8	0.485	0.765	2.094	0.541	0.616	2.380	0.389	0.460	1.600
-10	0.584	0.949	2.619	0.652	0.745	3.007	0.566	0.642	2.346
-12	0.685	1.089	3.028	0.728	0.832	3.461	0.708	0.831	3.010
-14	0.731	1.209	3.162	0.785	0.891	3.694	0.842	0.950	3.664
-16	0.795	1.340	3.536	0.850	0.979	4.083	0.995	1.153	4.506
-18	0.865	1.468	3.518	0.933	1.030	4.087	1.188	1.329	4.778
-20	0.908	1.586	3.851	0.942	1.139	4.212	1.223	1.581	5.230
-22	0.929	1.736	3.984	1.066	1.285	4.708	1.529	1.868	5.951

MONTH 0 = MONTH IN WHICH ACTUAL EPS IS ANNOUNCED

TABLE 3.6

Distribution Statistics for Ratio of (i) Absolute Change in Median EPS Forecast from Month T–1 to Month T to (ii) Average Absolute Change in Annual EPS: Median as Proxy for Consensus Forecast

month	mean	deciles									inter-quartile range	N
		.1	.2	.3	.4	.5	.6	.7	.8	.9		
- 1	0.119	0.016	0.030	0.042	0.056	0.070	0.088	0.116	0.160	0.233	0.099	858
- 2	0.155	0.023	0.038	0.055	0.074	0.097	0.122	0.158	0.222	0.355	0.135	1303
- 3	0.165	0.024	0.040	0.056	0.073	0.098	0.128	0.172	0.238	0.350	0.146	1301
- 4	0.137	0.023	0.037	0.048	0.066	0.085	0.109	0.141	0.187	0.293	0.115	1131
- 5	0.150	0.025	0.041	0.058	0.074	0.094	0.121	0.161	0.230	0.320	0.139	1314
- 6	0.171	0.024	0.044	0.062	0.081	0.101	0.132	0.177	0.238	0.352	0.151	1287
- 7	0.154	0.023	0.038	0.054	0.071	0.089	0.115	0.150	0.217	0.322	0.132	1212
- 8	0.168	0.026	0.042	0.058	0.078	0.103	0.132	0.174	0.238	0.371	0.152	1266
- 9	0.176	0.025	0.044	0.064	0.082	0.108	0.137	0.174	0.246	0.367	0.150	1272
-10	0.167	0.025	0.043	0.059	0.077	0.100	0.134	0.174	0.238	0.367	0.154	1232
-11	0.171	0.028	0.047	0.061	0.082	0.105	0.132	0.176	0.251	0.379	0.156	1266
-12	0.158	0.026	0.040	0.054	0.069	0.091	0.112	0.147	0.210	0.337	0.132	1008
-13	0.160	0.025	0.040	0.054	0.072	0.092	0.124	0.155	0.207	0.339	0.132	915
-14	0.189	0.032	0.049	0.067	0.093	0.118	0.150	0.199	0.276	0.425	0.173	1081
-15	0.188	0.029	0.047	0.066	0.093	0.115	0.147	0.197	0.272	0.430	0.182	1078
-16	0.154	0.029	0.045	0.063	0.076	0.103	0.132	0.173	0.229	0.338	0.143	927
-17	0.191	0.032	0.051	0.071	0.097	0.123	0.155	0.205	0.270	0.402	0.172	1039
-18	0.215	0.033	0.054	0.072	0.099	0.131	0.166	0.225	0.316	0.475	0.203	1040
-19	0.228	0.035	0.056	0.078	0.107	0.141	0.179	0.235	0.304	0.471	0.202	950
-20	0.246	0.038	0.060	0.088	0.116	0.155	0.205	0.262	0.347	0.518	0.231	877
-21	0.283	0.042	0.066	0.097	0.135	0.173	0.219	0.292	0.387	0.595	0.256	676
-22	0.274	0.042	0.068	0.102	0.132	0.172	0.228	0.304	0.431	0.588	0.281	454

MONTH 0 = MONTH WHICH ACTUAL EPS IS ANNOUNCED

FIGURE 3.4

Distribution Statistics for Ratio of (i) Absolute Change in Median EPS Forecast From Month T–1 to Month T to (ii) Average Absolute Change in Annual EPS

PANEL A: INTERQUARTILE RANGE

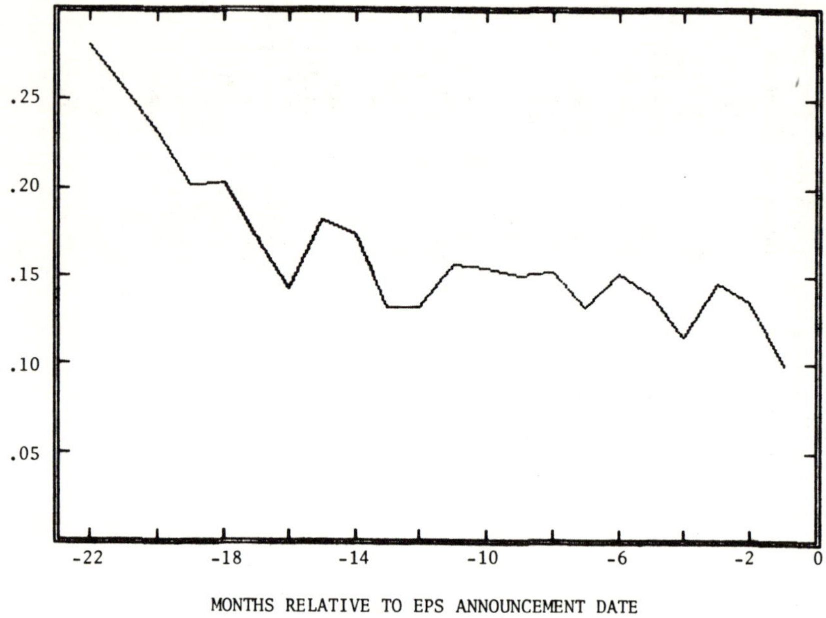

PANEL B: DECILES OF DISTRIBUTION

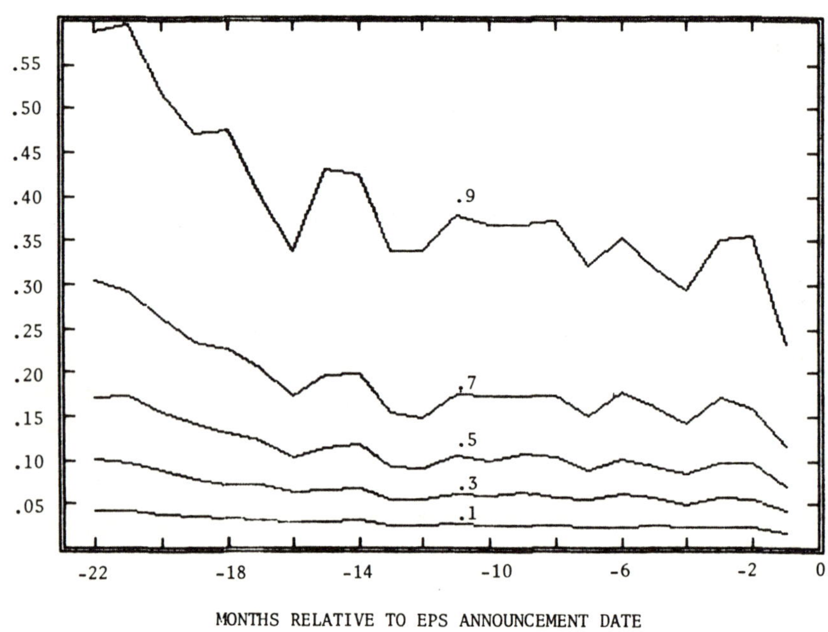

strong comments about bias due to the limited number of independent realizations available to make inferences about expectations. The comments we make are restricted to analysis of realizations in the 1976-1980 period. Focusing on the percent positive column in Tables 3.1 to 3.3, consensus forecasts are more likely to have underestimated the actual EPS reported by the company; the median forecast error is positive in each month of the –22 to –1 period. However, the mean of the forecast error distribution is more often negative over this –22 to –1 period. By inference, the magnitude of the average forecast overestimate exceeds the magnitude of the average forecast underestimate. The extreme observations for each error measure support this inference. Consider the five most extreme overestimates and underestimates for forecasts made in event month –12 for each of error measures (3.1) to (3.3):

(3.1)	(3.2)	(3.3)
–22.70	–5.06	–370.40
–20.02	–4.40	–318.60
–18.15	–4.32	–266.31
–17.83	–4.31	–237.04
–16.17	–4.27	–207.49
•		
•		
•		
5.28	2.86	31.30
5.88	2.87	32.44
6.81	2.97	34.35
8.33	3.15	40.21
9.41	3.89	46.76

The above results are for observations over the entire 1976 to 1980 period.

We also examined results on a year by year basis. Focusing on (3.3) for month –12, the following distribution statistics were obtained:

Fiscal Year-End	Mean (3.3)	Median (3.3)	Percent Positive
1976	–0.182	0.229	58.1
1977	–0.609	–0.095	47.3
1978	0.693	0.464	62.7
1979	0.795	0.715	67.0
1980	–2.217	0.000	50.5
1981	–1.105	–0.594	44.2

There is considerable year to year variation in the mean, median, and percent positive. A short time period, such as 1976 to 1980, may provide few reliable inferences about whether security analyst consensus forecasts are unbiased estimates of the actual EPS to be reported by companies.

C. Evidence on Divergence Within Consensus

The data in Tables 3.1 to 3.6 are based on the median or mean forecast for each company. No insight into the divergence across analysts for each company is provided in these tables. One statistic in the data base that relates to this topic is the standard deviation of analyst forecasts for each company. Table 3.7 and Figure 3.5 present distributional data for the standard deviation statistic.[4]

Prior evidence on the divergence (variation) across analysts is inconclusive. In a study of security analysts' forecasts for 46 firms over the 1967 to 1976 period, Crichfield-Dyckman-Lakonishok [1978] report that "while there is a tendency for the variation to decline, the decline [over the –13 to –1 month period] is uneven and often shows some increase in the middle months" (p. 665). Elton, Gruber and Gultekin [1982] report that "while there is some decline in the average dispersion as the estimates get closer to the end of the year, it is not uniform. Most of the decrease in dispersion across analysts occurs in the first four months of the year. From May on there is only a slight general decline and this decline does not occur in every month" (p. 18). Both these studies rely on the mean of the distribution when making the above inferences.

The results in Table 3.7 and Figure 3.5 are based on the fractiles of the distribution as well as the mean. The mean standard deviation of analysts' forecasts declines systematically over the –20 to –1 month event time period (especially in the –15 to –1 month period, where there is not one reversal in the pattern). Across all 9 deciles, there is also a systematic decline in the standard deviation of analysts' forecasts. The absolute magnitude of the decline is most marked for the .9 decile in Figure 3.5. However, there is a consistent relative decline across all nine deciles (again, especially in the –15 to –1 event month period). The overall conclusion is that as the time to the announcement of actual earnings is reduced, security analysts agree more on the EPS that each firm will announce.

Table 3.8 reports the correlation between the standard deviation of analysts' forecasts for each company in event month T and event month T + J. The correlations are based on the 1978 fiscal year observations. Similar patterns were observed in other years. The Spearman rank correlations range from a minimum of 0.77 to a maximum of 0.95. The overall pattern from Table 3.8 suggests that throughout the 20-month forecast horizon, security analysts disagree more on the same set of companies. (Note, however, that scaling differences between firms will also affect the correlations in Table 3.8.)

3.3 Interpretation Problems with Alternative Forecast Error Measures

Two interpretation problems cited in the literature reporting forecast errors relate to the effect of outliers and the effect of negative denominators. Due to our focus in Section 3.2 on the interquartile range and the deciles of the distribution, the presence of any outliers in our data base has limited effect on the inferences drawn in that section. In many prior studies, the mean of the distribution has been used to draw inferences about dispersion, forecast accuracy, or bias. To examine the effect of possible outliers on the mean, Table 3.9 presents the mean and truncated mean for a subset of the event

---

[4] Table 3.7 is based on the subsample for which six or more analysts make EPS forecasts for the month examined. This restriction was adopted so that the standard deviation was computed over a "sizeable" number of analysts. Distribution statistics are not reported for months with fewer than 200 observations.

TABLE 3.7

Distribution Statistics for Standard Deviation of Analysts' Forecasts

month	mean	deciles									inter-quartile range	N
		.1	.2	.3	.4	.5	.6	.7	.8	.9		
- 1	0.166	0.029	0.045	0.060	0.078	0.101	0.127	0.169	0.222	0.327	0.143	1570
- 2	0.184	0.036	0.052	0.070	0.087	0.113	0.146	0.197	0.254	0.387	0.164	1665
- 3	0.203	0.040	0.059	0.078	0.099	0.128	0.165	0.217	0.282	0.426	0.175	1670
- 4	0.208	0.044	0.063	0.082	0.105	0.131	0.170	0.217	0.280	0.439	0.174	1659
- 5	0.215	0.044	0.065	0.085	0.109	0.140	0.179	0.222	0.302	0.442	0.178	1648
- 6	0.227	0.046	0.068	0.090	0.115	0.146	0.185	0.240	0.315	0.471	0.192	1643
- 7	0.230	0.045	0.070	0.093	0.117	0.148	0.189	0.249	0.326	0.494	0.201	1633
- 8	0.238	0.047	0.070	0.096	0.122	0.153	0.195	0.253	0.339	0.497	0.204	1618
- 9	0.241	0.049	0.071	0.098	0.130	0.163	0.205	0.261	0.347	0.497	0.214	1594
-10	0.249	0.051	0.077	0.105	0.135	0.170	0.209	0.279	0.360	0.498	0.223	1570
-11	0.261	0.056	0.085	0.112	0.144	0.181	0.227	0.294	0.380	0.534	0.235	1567
-12	0.272	0.058	0.087	0.115	0.149	0.186	0.238	0.307	0.404	0.571	0.254	1546
-13	0.277	0.056	0.085	0.113	0.148	0.186	0.242	0.313	0.408	0.566	0.260	1499
-14	0.283	0.060	0.088	0.118	0.151	0.191	0.251	0.323	0.419	0.572	0.264	1332
-15	0.294	0.063	0.095	0.127	0.157	0.196	0.249	0.334	0.428	0.602	0.274	1230
-16	0.290	0.062	0.095	0.125	0.158	0.202	0.253	0.337	0.434	0.580	0.276	1154
-17	0.303	0.065	0.098	0.129	0.163	0.210	0.267	0.345	0.442	0.605	0.282	1069
-18	0.315	0.066	0.104	0.137	0.167	0.214	0.265	0.363	0.457	0.651	0.286	905
-19	0.310	0.066	0.102	0.132	0.160	0.209	0.267	0.342	0.458	0.646	0.267	690
-20	0.331	0.064	0.090	0.124	0.179	0.215	0.261	0.339	0.455	0.738	0.271	399

MONTH 0 = MONTH IN WHICH ACTUAL EPS IS ANNOUNCED

FIGURE 3.5

Distribution Statistics for Standard Deviation of Analysts' Forecasts

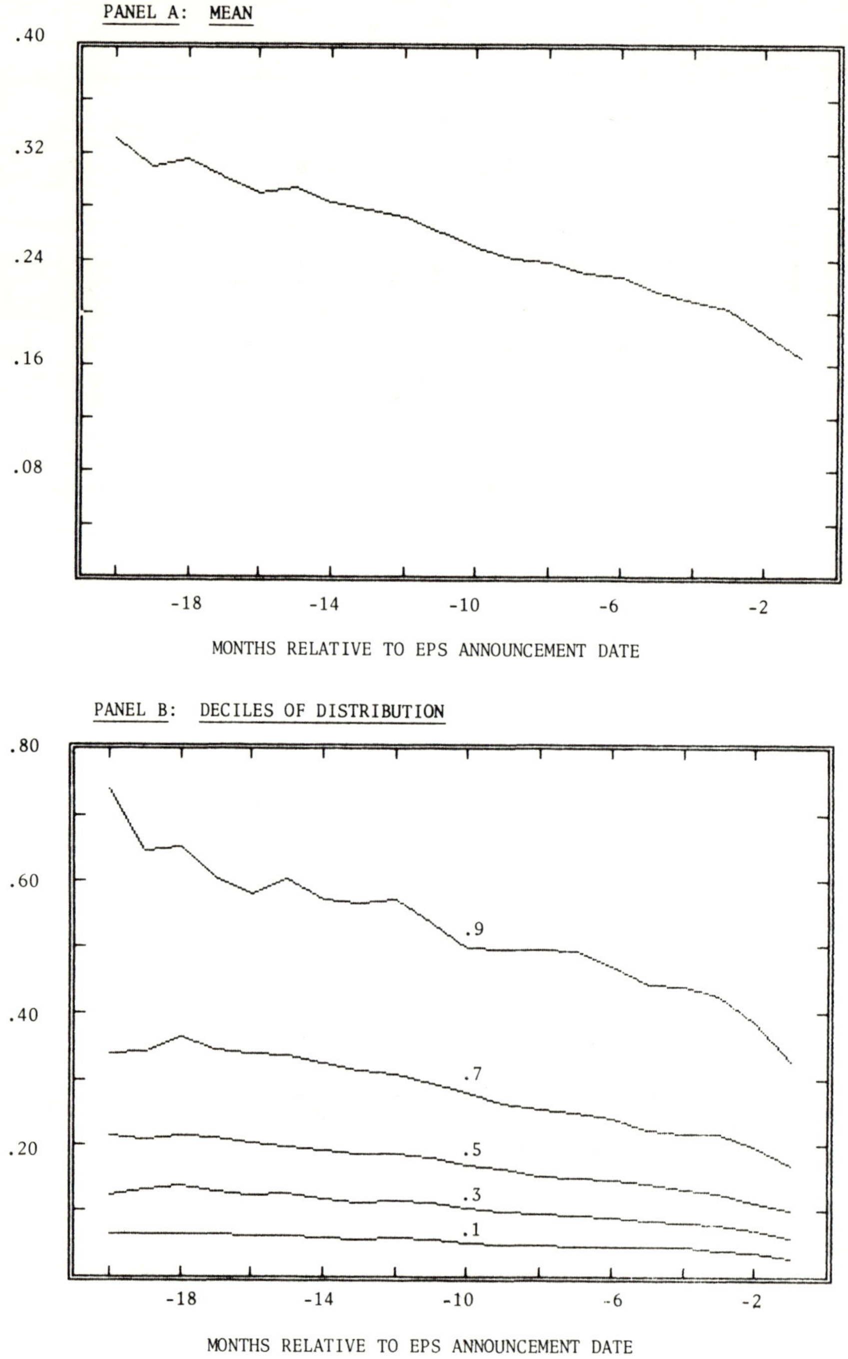

TABLE 3.8

Correlation Between Standard Deviation of Analysts' Forecasts in Event Month T and T + J for 1978 Fiscal Years' Earnings

EVENT MONTH	-2	-4	-6	-8	-10	-12	-14	-16	-18	-20
-2	-	0.91	0.88	0.71	0.73	0.63	0.70	0.71	0.69	0.85
-4	0.86	-	0.93	0.75	0.70	0.60	0.66	0.71	0.74	0.86
-6	0.86	0.94	-	0.86	0.76	0.68	0.75	0.81	0.83	0.88
-8	0.83	0.87	0.92	-	0.85	0.79	0.83	0.86	0.89	0.95
-10	0.82	0.83	0.88	0.90	-	0.93	0.82	0.84	0.84	0.79
-12	0.77	0.77	0.81	0.82	0.91	-	0.84	0.86	0.80	0.71
-14	0.85	0.85	0.85	0.86	0.86	0.83	-	0.95	0.88	0.78
-16	0.84	0.88	0.89	0.87	0.87	0.84	0.93	-	0.91	0.83
-18	0.82	0.87	0.89	0.90	0.87	0.84	0.91	0.95	-	0.94
-20	0.77	0.84	0.83	0.90	0.83	0.80	0.84	0.90	0.92	-

NOTES

1. Product Moment (Pearsonian) Correlations In Upper Right-hand Half of Matrix.

2. Spearman Rank Correlations in Lower Left-hand Half of Matrix.

3. Event Month 0 = Month in Which Actual EPS is Announced.

TABLE 3.9

Effect of Extreme Observations on Forecast Error Measures: Median Forecast as Proxy for the Consensus Forecast

PANEL A: FORECAST ERROR

EVENT	(3.1)		(3.2)		(3.3)		(3.11)	
MONTH	MEAN	TR.MEAN	MEAN	TR.MEAN	MEAN	TR.MEAN	MEAN	TR.MEAN
-2	-0.028	-0.004	-0.003	-0.003	-0.414	-0.163	-0.013	-0.008
-4	-0.053	-0.022	-0.023	-0.022	-0.683	-0.340	-0.069	-0.028
-6	-0.053	-0.021	-0.019	-0.017	-0.673	-0.353	-0.077	-0.031
-8	-0.062	-0.026	-0.025	-0.021	-0.677	-0.282	-0.080	-0.038
-10	-0.057	-0.014	-0.012	-0.008	-0.610	-0.156	-0.087	-0.042
-12	-0.041	0.011	-0.002	0.004	-0.363	0.050	-0.120	-0.051
-14	-0.051	0.011	-0.009	-0.004	-0.282	0.138	-0.158	-0.055
-16	-0.095	-0.026	-0.045	-0.038	-0.490	-0.047	-0.217	-0.082
-18	-0.081	-0.012	-0.042	-0.034	-0.212	0.118	-0.246	-0.090
-20	-0.083	-0.013	-0.051	-0.039	-0.019	0.251	-0.226	-0.083
-22	-0.094	0.007	-0.011	0.004	-0.039	0.393	-0.191	-0.060

PANEL B: ABSOLUTE FORECAST ERROR

EVENT	(3.4)		(3.5)		(3.6)		(3.12)	
MONTH	MEAN	TR.MEAN	MEAN	TR.MEAN	MEAN	TR.MEAN	MEAN	TR.MEAN
-2	0.255	0.220	0.274	0.259	1.559	1.184	0.102	0.076
-4	0.370	0.330	0.385	0.375	2.180	1.763	0.156	0.110
-6	0.461	0.415	0.472	0.462	2.575	2.103	0.183	0.133
-8	0.548	0.497	0.554	0.542	3.017	2.502	0.203	0.156
-10	0.650	0.591	0.655	0.644	3.531	2.956	0.231	0.183
-12	0.748	0.675	0.753	0.740	3.901	3.329	0.285	0.213
-14	0.812	0.728	0.829	0.815	4.346	3.690	0.329	0.223
-16	0.902	0.809	0.927	0.910	4.746	4.032	0.391	0.253
-18	0.937	0.844	0.990	0.972	4.439	3.879	0.428	0.269
-20	0.975	0.877	1.062	1.039	4.408	3.908	0.411	0.267
-22	1.080	0.939	1.140	1.111	4.692	3.968	0.390	0.256

PANEL C: SQUARED FORECAST ERROR

EVENT	(3.7)		(3.8)		(3.9)		(3.13)	
MONTH	MEAN	TR.MEAN	MEAN	TR.MEAN	MEAN	TR.MEAN	MEAN	TR.MEAN
-2	0.510	0.187	0.221	0.136	4.271	1.133	0.085	0.044
-4	0.803	0.353	0.324	0.246	6.042	2.121	0.149	0.085
-6	1.111	0.561	0.458	0.368	8.112	3.137	0.207	0.123
-8	1.478	0.812	0.614	0.513	10.061	4.316	0.254	0.164
-10	2.004	1.086	0.817	0.694	12.938	5.456	0.328	0.214
-12	2.740	1.380	1.080	0.896	15.698	6.844	0.488	0.300
-14	3.157	1.550	1.286	1.067	17.950	7.856	0.631	0.345
-16	3.721	1.863	1.564	1.311	20.568	9.050	0.881	0.462
-18	3.803	1.930	1.694	1.429	18.202	8.257	1.031	0.515
-20	4.060	2.018	1.892	1.575	17.897	8.158	1.029	0.521
-22	5.218	2.283	2.189	1.762	22.362	8.894	1.073	0.454

Note: Tr. Mean is the truncated mean which is computed by excluding the ten most extreme negative and the ten most extreme positive obervations.

MONTH 0 = MONTH IN WHICH ACTUAL EPS IS ANNOUNCED

months and forecast error measures examined previously. The truncated mean is computed by deleting the ten highest and ten lowest observations from each distribution. Note that this approach assumes that the most extreme values are outliers. To the extent that this assumption is not correct, the following examines only the effect on the mean of deleting extreme observations from the distribution.

Table 3.9 reports the mean and truncated mean for (3.1) to (3.3) and (3.4) to (3.6). In addition, the mean and truncated mean are reported for the following three forecast error measures frequently used in the literature:

$$\frac{\text{Actual EPS} - \text{Forecast EPS}}{\text{Actual EPS}} \qquad (3.11)$$

$$\frac{|\text{Actual EPS} - \text{Forecast EPS}|}{\text{Actual EPS}} \qquad (3.12)$$

$$\frac{[\text{Actual EPS} - \text{Forecast EPS}]^2}{\text{Actual EPS}} \qquad (3.13)$$

When Actual EPS is not positive, the observation is deleted from (3.11) to (3.13).

Use of the truncated mean in (3.1) to (3.3) systematically reduces the negative values reported using the mean; this pattern is predictable given the prior evidence that the magnitude of extreme overestimates exceeds the magnitude of extreme underestimates. Note, for instance, that using the truncated mean for (3.1), the average forecast error for months –12 to –2 ranges between only a 2.6 cents overestimate and a 1.1 cents underestimate. Use of the truncated mean in (3.4) to (3.6), while reducing the magnitude of the average absolute forecast error, does not change the previously drawn inference that as the actual EPS announcement month is approached the accuracy of consensus forecasts increases.

The use of the truncated mean in (3.11) also systematically reduces the negative values reported using the mean. Like (3.1) to (3.3), error measure (3.11) has a distribution where the magnitude of extreme overestimates exceeds the magnitude of extreme underestimates. Consider event month –12 for (3.11):

Most Extreme Overestimates	**Most Extreme Underestimates**
–25.25	1.63
–24.00	1.13
–24.00	1.01
–24.00	1.00
–13.42	1.00

Based on visual inspection of the extreme forecast errors for (3.1), (3.2), (3.3), and (3.11), it appears that (3.11) is most prone to giving large values due to the denominator approaching zero. For example, using (3.11) for event month –12, all of the ten largest overestimates had an actual EPS less than \$0.35. Prior studies using variants of (3.11) have adjusted for this small denominator effect in several ways. For instance, Beaver, Clarke and Wright [1979] omitted from the sample "percentage forecast error" observations where the denominator was less than \$0.20. Collins and Hopwood [1980] computed the absolute percentage forecast error with the restriction that any observation greater than 3 was assigned a value of 3. They noted that "the selection of the value of 3 as an indicator of an outlier was based on a visual analysis of the frequency distribution of the absolute percentage forecast error metric" (p. 395).

A second interpretation issue with (3.11) arises when the denominator is negative. For instance, when the numerator of (3.11) is negative, the forecast error measure can be reported as positive if the denominator is also negative. The relative frequency of such observations appears small. The observations underlying (3.11) can be classified into the following categories (excluding those with zero denominators):

Event Month	Numerator –, 0, or + / Denominator +	Numerator + or 0 / Denominator –	Numerator – / Denominator –
–2	98.08%	0.18%	1.64%
–4	97.93	0.09	1.98
–6	97.91	0.09	2.00
–8	97.90	0.09	2.01
–10	97.97	0.05	1.98
–12	98.15	0.00	1.85

The data for (3.11) in Table 3.9 exclude those observations with negative denominators. This is one of two frequently used heuristics for "handling" this problem; Elton, Gruber and Gultekin [1982] also adopt this approach. The other approach frequently observed in the literature is to use the absolute value of the denominator; Brown and Rozeff [1978] adopt this heuristic when comparing the relative accuracy of the forecasts of security analysts with the forecasts from time-series models.

CHAPTER 4

SECURITY ANALYST SINGLE YEAR EARNINGS FORECAST REVISIONS AND SECURITY PRICE CHANGES

4.1 Overview of Issues Examined and Results

This chapter examines three related issues, using the IBES data base:

1. The association between (i) one year ahead (FY1) earnings forecast errors and (ii) security returns in the period up to and including the month the actual FY1 earnings is announced. Significant associations between (i) and (ii) are found with both time-series and cross-sectional research designs.

2. The effects on portfolio returns of using more timely security analyst forecasts when classifying observations into negative or positive earnings forecast error portfolios. Contrary to some existing evidence in the literature, this chapter reports that the more timely the analyst forecast, the larger the portfolio return observed. This intuitive result is based on a more powerful design than that used in prior research.

3. The association between (i) security price movements in the period prior to the FY1 earnings forecast revision, and (ii) the sign or magnitude of the forecast revision. This test examines whether analysts act as if they are extracting information from security prices. With a design exploiting only the sign of the earnings forecast revision, there is a strong statistical association between (i) and (ii). However, using both time-series and cross-sectional designs, prior security price changes appear to explain no more than ten percent of the variance in earnings forecast revisions. The inference we draw is that either the structural form in which analysts extract information from security price changes is not as specified in this chapter or that prior security returns are a small component of the information sources security analysts use when revising their earnings forecasts. Econometric and economic modeling issues yet to be addressed in this area are discussed.

4.2 Association Between Analyst FY1 Forecast Errors and Security Price Changes: Company Earnings Announcement Date as Event Month 0

This section reexamines issues that have been well explored in the literature, e.g., McEnally [1971], Zacks [1979], Elton-Gruber-Gultekin [1981], and Fried and Givoly [1982]. There are several reasons why this section is included in the monograph. *First*, the results show that the data base is "well-behaved" relative to the results reported in prior studies. *Second*, in some sections we employ specific regressions not previously reported in the literature. These regressions play a central role in Chapter 5 where the issue of the incremental explanatory power of FY2 forecasts over FY1 forecasts is examined. Documenting in this chapter that FY1 has significant explanatory power in its own right makes the issue posed in Chapter 5 more interesting (and the hurdle for FY2 to "beat," higher). *Third*, in the process of reexamining prior findings, the sensitivity of the results to alternative definitions of consensus forecasts is examined. Finding that our results are robust to the use of either the median or the mean consensus forecast measure increases our confidence in the reliability of inferences drawn in this and subsequent sections of this monograph.

A. Portfolio Analysis Using Sign of Earnings Forecast Errors

The tests in this section require measures of both security price changes and earnings forecast errors. Appendix 4.A describes estimation of the average cumulative abnormal return (ACAR) measure; the market model is used to estimate the abnormal returns of each security. In this section, portfolios are formed based upon earnings forecast errors. The ACAR's of these portfolios are then computed. The earnings forecast error for month T is defined to be + (–) if the actual earnings by the company in month 0 exceeds (is less than) the earnings forecast for month T. Two definitions of consensus earnings forecasts are used: (1) the median earnings forecast and (2) the mean earnings forecast.

The research design is that employed in Ball and Brown [1968]. Appendix 4.B describes the non-parametric randomization type test used to estimate the statistical significance of the associations observed between the ACAR and the sign of the earnings forecast error. Briefly, the randomization test involves assigning earnings forecast errors to firms at random and recomputing the ACAR measures. This is done 100 times to develop an empirical distribution of the ACAR under the null hypothesis that abnormal returns and earnings forecast errors are statistically independent. Eleven overlapping time periods are examined: [–10,0], [–9,0], ..., [–1,0] and [0,0].[1]

Results are reported in Table 4.1. Consistent with prior studies, there is a significant association between the sign of the earnings forecast error and the sign and magnitude of the ACAR. For instance, the – earnings forecast portfolio (median forecast as consensus proxy) yields a –9.879% return over the [–10,0] period – see Panel A. This –9.879% return was exceeded in every one of 100 trials where firms were randomly assigned to the – and + earnings forecast error portfolios. The + earnings forecast portfolio has a 6.404% return over the same [–10,0] period. This 6.404% return was not exceeded on any of 100 trials where firms were randomly assigned to the – and + earnings forecast error portfolios. The strong association for both – and + earnings forecast error portfolios holds for all (overlapping) time periods examined in Table 4.1, and holds when either the median FY1 forecast or mean FY1 forecast is used as the proxy for the consensus forecast.

Some intuition for the relative importance of foreknowledge about the FY1 forecast error can be gained by comparing:

(i) the ACAR from foreknowledge of the sign of the earnings forecast error, with

(ii) the ACAR from foreknowledge of the sign of the cumulative abnormal return for each firm over the same time period.

[1] As the time periods overlap, the results for each time period are not independent. Due to small sample problems, results are not reported for those observations in which the actual EPS reported by the company equalled the consensus forecast in month T. This group ranged from 0.9% of all possible observations in month [–10] to 3.3% of all possible observations in month [0] (using the median forecast as the consensus forecast).

TABLE 4.1

Association Between FY1 Forecast Errors and Average Cumulative Abnormal Returns Portfolios Formed Using Sign of Earnings Forecast Error

PANEL A: AVERAGE CUMULATIVE ABNORMAL RETURNS (ACAR's)

FORECAST ERROR MODEL	PERIOD USED TO COMPUTE ACAR										
	-10,0	-9,0	-8,0	-7,0	-6,0	-5,0	-4,0	-3,0	-2,0	-1,0	0,0
MEDIAN FY1 USED TO COMPUTE FORECAST ERROR											
-	-9.879	-9.483	-9.419	-8.199	-6.937	-6.465	-5.494	-3.665	-2.706	-2.620	-1.433
+	6.404	5.664	4.994	4.354	3.625	2.969	3.250	2.825	1.676	1.755	1.529
MEAN FY1 USED TO COMPUTE FORECAST ERROR											
-	-9.973	-9.820	-9.234	-8.153	-6.833	-6.323	-5.238	-3.493	-2.591	-2.442	-1.361
+	6.562	5.702	4.679	4.168	3.374	2.823	3.050	2.694	1.425	1.499	1.369

PANEL B: RELATIVE FREQUENCY WITH WHICH OBSERVED ACAR WAS EXCEEDED IN 100 RANDOM TRIALS

FORECAST ERROR MODEL	PERIOD USED TO COMPUTE ACAR										
	-10,0	-9,0	-3,0	-7,0	-6,0	-5,0	-4,0	-3,0	-2,0	-1,0	0,0
MEDIAN FY1 USED TO COMPUTE FORECAST ERROR											
-	1.00	1.00	1.00	1.00	1.00	1.00	1.00	1.00	1.00	1.00	1.00
+	0.00	0.00	0.00	0.00	0.00	0.00	0.00	0.00	0.00	0.00	0.00
MEAN FY1 USED TO COMPUTE FORECAST ERROR											
-	1.00	1.00	1.00	1.00	1.00	1.00	1.00	1.00	1.00	1.00	1.00
+	0.00	0.00	0.00	0.00	0.00	0.00	0.00	0.00	0.00	0.00	0.00

MONTH 0 = MONTH IN WHICH ACTUAL EPS IS ANNOUNCED

For instance, for the – earnings forecast error group over the [–10,0] period, (i) is –9.879% while (ii) is –18.901%. (That is, if firms are sorted into the – and + portfolios based upon foreknowledge of the sign of the cumulative abnormal return, the average return for all firms with a negative cumulative abnormal return would have been –18.901%.) Thus, over this period, information that is impounded in the sign of the – earnings forecast error explains 52 percent (–9.879/–18.901) of the cumulative abnormal return (which is a proxy for all information that became available during this same period). The comparable percent figures for selected time periods are:

	Ratio of (i) to (ii) for – FY1 Earnings Forecast Error	**Ratio of (i) to (ii) for + FY1 Earnings Forecast Error**
[–10,0]	52%	38%
[–8,0]	54	34
[–6,0]	47	27
[–4,0]	46	29
[–2,0]	29	18
[0,0]	25	27

These percentages suggest that the FY1 forecast error variable has substantial explanatory power in its own right. Chapter 5 examines the incremental contribution of the FY2 forecast error variable in explaining security price revisions.

B. Cross-Section Regression Analysis Using Sign and Magnitude of Earnings Forecast Errors

This section adopts a cross-sectional approach to examining the association between FY1 security analyst forecast revisions and security price changes. The following regression format is employed:

$$ROR_i[t_0,t_1] = \gamma_0 + \gamma_1 \cdot X_{1i} + \gamma_2 \cdot X_{2i} + \epsilon_i \tag{4.1}$$

where $ROR_i[t_0,t_1]$ = return on security i between month t_0 and t_1.

X_{1i} = beta (relative risk) of security i; estimated using 60 months of data immediately prior to month t_0.

X_{2i} = FY1 analyst earnings forecast error for security i.

Several proxies for X_{2i} are examined:

$$\frac{\text{(Actual EPS for FY1 – Consensus EPS Forecast for FY1 at Month T)}}{\text{Consensus EPS Forecast for FY1 at Month T}} \tag{4.2}$$

$$\frac{\text{(Actual EPS for FY1 – Consensus EPS Forecast for FY1 at Month T)}}{\text{Security Price at Start of Month T}} \tag{4.3}$$

Results are reported using both the median and the mean as the measure of consensus EPS forecast.

The regression model in (4.1) assumes a linear relationship between $ROR_i[t_0,t_1]$ and X_{1i} and X_{2i}. Since the regression is cross-sectional, we assume (e.g., in our interpretation of t–statistics) that at any point in time all firms have the same coefficient for the relationship between $ROR_i[t_0,t_1]$ and FY1 forecast errors (and between

$ROR_i[t_0,t_1]$ and $Beta_i$).

Our motivation for including the beta coefficient in (4.1) is that the two-parameter asset pricing model has a strong theoretical foundation and is the most frequently used paradigm in empirical capital market research. Inclusion of beta as an independent variable in (4.1) is a more general approach than the alternative of relative risk-adjusting the ROR_i dependent variable; in (4.1) we do not assume that a specific structural relationship holds between ROR and relative risk in each period. All results reported for (4.1) are for X_{2i} first made orthogonal to X_{1i} by a linear regression of X_{2i} on X_{1i}; results were also run with no prior orthogonalization of X_{2i} with no change in the inferences drawn in this chapter.

Results for (4.1) are reported in Table 4.2 for both the [–10,0] and [–8,0] time periods for each year from 1977 to 1980; the [–10,0] and [–8,0] time periods are overlapping and hence the significance levels reported for the two regressions of each year are not independent. We will concentrate on the [–10,0] period when describing the results; the [–8,0] period was included due to its having a larger number of observations, especially in 1977 and 1978. The median FY1 forecast is used as the proxy for the consensus forecast; Panel A uses (4.2) as the FY1 measure while Panel B uses (4.3) as the FY1 measure.[2] In both Panels A and B, the coefficient on FY1 (γ_2) is statistically significant in each of the four years examined. This result is consistent with prior findings of a significant cross-sectional relationship between the sign and magnitude of earnings forecast errors and the sign and magnitude of security price revisions. The coefficient for the beta variable (γ_1) is not consistently significant.[3]

Specification Checks

1. The results in Table 4.2 are based on use of the median FY1 as a proxy for the consensus forecast. Table 4.3 reports a subset of the results when the mean FY1 is used as a proxy for the consensus forecast. The results in Table 4.2 are robust to the use of this alternative proxy. In particular, the coefficient on the FY1 variable is statistically significant across each of the four years examined.

2. The results in Tables 4.2 and 4.3 are based on use of either the (a) median FY1 forecast as the deflator or (b) security price as the deflator of the FY1 forecast error variable. Chapter 3 also reported forecast error metrics using the average absolute change in EPS over the 1976 to 1980 period as the deflator. Summary results when this deflator is used (for the [–10,0] time period with the median forecast used as the proxy for the consensus forecast) are:

---

[2] If the denominator of (4.2) is negative, the observation is excluded from the sample. At most, three percent of the observations in any of the regressions reported in Table 4.2 fall in this category. No such exclusions are necessary with (4.3), as the denominator is always positive.

[3] There are many explanations for this result. For example, (i) the two-parameter model is not descriptively valid, or (ii) there is significant measurement error in our estimates of beta. Note that this result for beta (β) is not affected by the orthogonalization procedure used to estimate X_{2i} in (4.1). The X_{1i} variable enters the regression without any prior orthogonalization. The theory underlying its inclusion specifies a linear relation between $ROR_i[t_0,t_1]$ and β_i.

TABLE 4.2

Cross-Section Regression of Security Return on Beta and Median FY1 Forecast Error

PANEL A: MEDIAN FY1 AS DEFLATOR OF FY1 FORECAST ERROR VARIABLE

	γ_0	$t(\gamma_0)$	γ_1 Beta	$t(\gamma_1)$	γ_2 FY1	$t(\gamma_2)$	NOB	ADJ.R^2
1977								
[-10,0]	0.109	2.577	-0.067	-1.446	0.269	3.558	132	.089
[- 8,0]	0.051	1.971	-0.019	-0.718	0.193	3.407	228	.043
1978								
[-10,0]	-0.075	-2.580	-0.005	-0.170	0.178	5.256	148	.149
[- 8,0]	-0.119	-5.368	0.053	2.371	0.105	4.573	263	.086
1979								
[-10,0]	0.060	2.101	0.037	1.291	0.062	3.422	234	.047
[- 8,0]	0.037	1.717	-0.019	-0.877	0.131	3.466	268	.039
1980								
[-10,0]	0.119	2.168	0.087	1.573	0.780	11.869	256	.357
[- 8,0]	0.052	1.071	0.115	2.385	0.474	8.787	292	.218

PANEL B: SECURITY PRICE AS DEFLATOR OF FY1 FORECAST ERROR VARIABLE

	γ_0	$t(\gamma_0)$	γ_1 Beta	$t(\gamma_1)$	γ_2 FY1	$t(\gamma_2)$	NOB	ADJ.R^2
1977								
[-10,0]	0.109	2.535	-0.066	-1.414	1.490	2.821	133	.057
[- 8,0]	0.056	2.042	-0.024	-0.873	1.097	2.706	233	.026
1978								
[-10,0]	-0.075	-2.524	-0.005	-0.166	1.080	4.484	148	.110
[- 8,0]	-0.119	-5.545	0.053	2.454	1.095	5.863	264	.127
1979								
[-10,0]	0.062	2.247	0.034	1.226	1.149	4.817	237	.088
[- 8,0]	.035	1.623	-0.016	-0.748	0.868	3.790	274	.045
1980								
[-10,0]	0.105	1.607	0.105	1.605	1.101	5.536	258	.108
[- 8,0]	0.060	1.132	0.104	1.985	0.666	4.609	294	.073

Notes

1. Regression is
   $ROR_i[t_0,t_1] = \gamma_0 + \gamma_1 X_{1i} + \gamma_2 X_{2i} + \varepsilon_{it}$
   where ROR_i = cumulative security return from t_0 to t_1
   X_{1i} = relative risk (beta) estimate
   X_{2i} = FY1 forecast error (orthogonalized relative to X_{1i}).

2. Month 0 = Month in Which Actual EPS is Announced.

TABLE 4.3

Cross-Section Regression of Security Return on Beta and FY1 Forecast Error: Comparison of Use of Median FY1 and Mean FY1 as Proxy for Consensus Forecast

	Median as Proxy for Consensus		Mean as Proxy for Consensus	
	t on FY1	Adj. R^2	t on FY1	Adj. R^2
1977				
[-10,0]	3.558	.089	3.200	.074
[-8,0]	3.407	.043	2.836	.028
1978				
[-10,0]	5.256	.149	5.563	.165
[-8,0]	4.573	.086	4.631	.087
1979				
[-10,0]	3.422	.047	2.145	.018
[-8,0]	3.466	.039	3.518	.040
1980				
[-10,0]	11.869	.357	12.052	.364
[-8,0]	8.787	.218	8.483	.206

Month 0 = Month in Which Actual EPS is Announced.

	t on FY1	Adjusted R^2
1977	3.941	.106
1978	7.116	.249
1979	6.061	.133
1980	9.898	.278

Again, the FY1 variable appears significant in each year.

3. As a final specification check, (4.1) was run excluding the X_{1i} variable and including the X_{2i} variable without any prior orthogonalization. Summary results for the [−10,0] time period (median forecast used as the proxy for the consensus forecast; average absolute change in EPS over the 1976 to 1980 period as the deflator) are:

	t on FY1	Adjusted R^2
1977	3.944	.099
1978	7.143	.254
1979	6.194	.137
1980	9.770	.269

Inclusion or exclusion of the beta (X_{1i}) variable from (4.1) makes very little difference to the coefficients on FY1 or their statistical significance.

4. Tables 4.2 and 4.3 and the above specification checks assume a linear relationship between security returns, beta, and the FY1 forecast error. The results reported in Table 4.1 (and in Tables 4.4 to 4.6 in the next section) do not assume a linear relationship between security returns and the FY1 forecast error. The consistency of the results across Tables 4.1 to 4.6 increases our confidence that they are not an artifact of one specific research design.

4.3 Effect on Association Measures of Updating Expectations Model

Many studies examining the association between earnings forecast errors and security price changes have used expectations models based on the past series of annual or interim earnings, e.g., Ball and Brown [1968], Brown and Kennelly [1972], and Foster [1977]. The time period used to cumulate security returns in these studies typically was the time period covered by the earnings series examined (i.e., twelve months when examining annual earnings and three months when examining interim earnings). This research design effectively precluded examination of the effect on the ACAR of updating the information set used to classify firms into earnings change portfolios. One potential advantage of the use of security analyst forecasts in association studies is the ability for frequent revision of the expectations model as the information set is expanded over time.

In a study of analysts' forecasts reported in *The Earnings Forecaster*, Fried and Givoly [1982] conclude that "timing... does not result in a significant improvement in the association of FAF [financial analyst forecasts] with stock price movements" (p.102). The data base used to support this conclusion was analyst forecasts issued in the January, February, March, and April months of the 1970 to 1979 period:

> We expect forecasts with a later release date to incorporate more (accounting and non-accounting) information and therefore to be superior to earlier forecasts. To

> examine whether this is so, we divided our sample into two groups of FAF: one, denoted as 'early' forecasts, consists of forecasts released in January and February, and the other, denoted as 'late' forecasts, consists of those released in March and early April. This particular grouping results in forecasts that were released on average, about six weeks apart. Only companies for which both early and late forecasts were available in a given year were considered... The average API over the 11 years is 12.78% and 13.15% for the early and late forecasts, respectively. The difference, although in the expected direction, when subjected to a t-test proved insignificant (p. 101).

The IBES data base used in this study makes possible a more extensive study of the timing issue than in Fried and Givoly [1982]; more firms are available, more analysts are represented and, most importantly, monthly revisions over a time period longer than four months are available.

The research design we use examines consensus analyst revisions in each of the 11 months up to and including the month the actual earnings are announced by the company. Results are reported in Table 4.4. Consider Panel A for the [–6,0] cumulation period. The relevant entries in the table are:

		Period Used to Compute ACAR
Month That		[–6,0]
Firm Placed	[–10]	–5.968
Into FY1	[–9]	–6.182
Negative	[–8]	–6.736
Earnings	[–7]	–6.852
Portfolio	[–6]	–6.937

The first row reports the ACAR over the [–6,0] period for observations classified into the FY1 – portfolio based on consensus forecasts available at the start of month –10 (i.e., the least timely month); ...the fifth row reports the ACAR over the [–6,0] period for observations classified into the FY1 – portfolio based on consensus forecasts available at the start of month –6 (i.e., the most timely month). The hypothesis that updating the expectations model increases the association measure predicts that the ACAR should be increasingly negative going down each column in Panel A (the FY1 – portfolio) and increasingly positive going down each column in Panel B (the FY1 + portfolio). There are very few observations in Table 4.4 for which this prediction does not hold. Note that the increase in the ACAR as the more timely expectations model is used is due to those observations where the revision in the consensus earnings forecast is sufficient to switch the sign of the earnings forecast error.

Appendix 4.B describes a non-parametric randomization procedure used to test the statistical significance of the results in Table 4.4. The test is based on the number of instances in which the predicted monotonicity pattern in Panels A and B is not observed. Panel A had fewer violations of the predicted monotonicity pattern than that observed on any of 100 random trials; the same result was observed for Panel B. Table 4.4 is computed using the median analyst FY1 forecast as a proxy for the consensus forecast in month T. Similar results (and the same significance levels) were obtained when the mean analyst FY1 forecast was used as a proxy for the consensus forecast in month T. The inference drawn is that the timeliness of the information set used to

TABLE 4.4

Effect on ACAR of Using More Timely Security Analyst Consensus (Median) Forecast When Classifying Observations into Negative or Positive Earnings Forecast Error Portfolios

PANEL A: ACAR's FOR FY1 NEGATIVE EARNINGS FORECAST ERROR PORTFOLIO

		Average Cumulative Abnormal Return For [-T,0] Months										
		-10,0	-9,0	-8,0	-7,0	-6,0	-5,0	-4,0	-3,0	-2,0	-1,0	0,0
	-10	-9.879	-9.147	-8.614	-7.371	-5.968	-5.339	-4.276	-2.648	-1.541	-1.073	-0.369
MONTH	- 9		-9.483	-8.981	-7.604	-6.182	-5.538	-4.392	-2.865	-1.666	-1.141	-0.449
THAT	- 8			-9.419	-8.071	-6.736	-5.857	-4.633	-2.980	-1.812	-1.272	-0.485
FIRM WAS	- 7				-8.199	-6.852	-6.105	-4.891	-3.263	-2.111	-1.470	-0.644
PLACED	- 6					-6.937	-6.226	-5.056	-3.266	-2.010	-1.517	-0.742
INTO	- 5						-6.456	-5.281	-3.473	-2.241	-1.776	-0.956
FY1	- 4							-5.494	-3.714	-2.544	-2.017	-1.099
NEGATIVE	- 3								-3.665	-2.526	-1.972	-1.057
EARNINGS	- 2									-2.706	-2.245	-1.188
PORTFOLIO	- 1										-2.620	-1.418
	- 0											-1.433

Frequency The Aggregated Kendall's Tau Statistic was Empirically Exceeded = 0 (in 100 trials)

PANEL B: ACAR's FOR FY1 POSITIVE EARNINGS FORECAST ERROR PORTFOLIO

		Average Cumulative Abnormal Return For [-T,0] Months										
		-10,0	-9,0	-8,0	-7,0	-6,0	-5,0	-4,0	-3,0	-2,0	-1,0	0,0
	-10	6.404	5.253	4.124	3.583	2.988	2.147	2.108	1.579	0.501	0.217	0.492
MONTH	- 9		5.664	4.642	3.890	3.230	2.359	2.269	1.723	0.564	0.278	0.519
THAT	- 8			4.994	4.289	3.600	2.615	2.464	1.835	0.679	0.442	0.578
FIRM WAS	- 7				4.354	3.594	2.766	2.636	2.084	0.910	0.600	0.682
PLACED	- 6					3.625	2.835	2.762	2.204	0.942	0.677	0.694
INTO	- 5						2.969	2.900	2.391	1.209	0.968	0.941
FY1	- 4							3.250	2.748	1.461	1.188	1.054
POSITIVE	- 3								2.825	1.557	1.250	1.057
EARNINGS	- 2									1.676	1.568	1.193
PORTFOLIO	- 1										1.755	1.381
	- 0											1.529

Frequency The Aggregated Kendall's Tau Statistic was Empirically Exceeded = 100 (in 100 trials)

NOTES:
1. Month 0 = Month in which actual EPS is announced.
2. See Appendix 4.B for an explanation of the Aggregated Kendall's Tau Statistic

compute earnings forecast errors is a significant determinant of the observed measure of association. (An interesting extension of the results in Table 4.4 would be to form portfolios using the magnitude as well as the sign of the earnings forecast error.)

The results in Table 4.4 are important in several areas of research. One area is studies that make inferences about the relative importance of information releases in explaining security price movements, e.g., a FIFO/LIFO change vis-a-vis an FY1 earnings forecast error. Where two (or more) information releases do not simultaneously appear in the "public domain," there is the potential to underestimate the relative importance of one by using a less timely expectations model; the results in Table 4.4 document that the earnings forecast error variable is subject to this underestimation problem. Another area where the results in Table 4.4 are important is research on the determinants of financial analyst forecast superiority over time-series models. Fried and Givoly [1982] use their non-significant timeliness result to infer that "it appears that the main factor behind the better performance of FAF is the broader information set used by them" (p.103). For the data underlying Table 4.4, it appears that this conclusion is worthy of reconsideration.

The results in Table 4.4 are consistent with those discussed in Chapter 3. In that chapter, it was reported that as the time to the actual FY1 earnings announcement decreases, security analyst consensus forecasts of FY1 become more accurate. Given this finding, it is not surprising that errors in the more timely (and more accurate) analyst FY1 forecasts better explain subsequent security price movements. The results in Table 4.4 also imply that while the IBES data base does have "reporting lags" (see Chapter 2), these lags are not so severe as to preclude the timeliness hypothesis being supported in a highly significant manner.[4]

4.4 Association Between Analyst FY1 Forecast Revisions and Security Price Changes: IBES Revision Month as Event Month 0

The tests in Section 4.2 and 4.3 defined month 0 to be the actual earnings announcement month. The tests in this section define month 0 to be the IBES forecast revision month.[5]

A. Portfolio Analysis Using Sign of Forecast Revisions

Consensus earnings forecasts of FY1 for each month are classified into one of four categories:

- FY1 Consensus Revised Down = –
- FY1 Consensus Not Changed = 0
- FY1 Consensus Revised Up = +
- Data Not Available on IBES Summary Tape = *

[4] We are assuming that the "reporting lags" are not the same for each analyst for each month for all securities examined; i.e., they add "noise" into the classification of observations across columns in Table 4.4 and not just a mislabeling of the actual release date of each column.

[5] These two foci are not independent. Indeed, one could view the focus on the actual announcement month as a subset of the focus on the IBES revision month, with that revision being a forecast with zero error.

For the median and mean proxies for consensus forecasts, the current and the prior month's forecasts are required when classifying firms into the above categories. The third proxy used in this research compares the number of analysts revising FY1 up with the number of analysts revising FY1 down; firms fall in the –, 0, or + categories depending on whether (#↑) < (#↓), (#↑) = (#↓) or (#↑) > (#↓), respectively. The relative percentage of observations falling into the first three categories are:

	Median as Proxy	**Mean as Proxy**	**(#↑)–(#↓) as Proxy**
–	26.3%	39.4%	33.2%
0	42.4	13.2	26.1
+	31.3	47.4	40.7

The number of observations in each category is 19,582 for the median and mean proxies and 22,264 for the (#↑)–(#↓) proxy.[6]

Table 4.5 reports the ACAR for the –, 0, and + categories for the following event time periods: [–12 to –2], [–1], [0], [–1,0] and [+1 to +12]. Two significance tests are presented in Table 4.5. The first is a conventional parametric t-test. The second is a non-parametric randomization test. Appendix 4.B contains a description of this latter test.

Focusing on the [–12 to –2] period, there is a statistically significant association between security price changes and the *subsequent* earnings forecast revision. For instance, using the median forecast proxy, –(+) forecast revisions in month [0] had on average a security return of –7.91% (5.37%) in the [–12 to –2] month period. Figure 4.1 plots the ACAR for the median consensus proxy over the [–12 to +12] period. The most striking pattern in Figure 4.1 is the increasing divergence in security returns of the – and + portfolios in the period prior to the earnings forecast revision month. This result is supported by both the parametric t-test and the non-parametric randomization test and is found for all three proxies for consensus forecasts. These results are consistent with security analysts extracting information from security price movements when developing their earnings forecast revisions. An alternative explanation is that security analysts use information for their own trading purposes prior to encoding that information in publicly released earnings forecasts.

Interpretation of the results for [–1] and [0] turns, in part, on how systematic are either (i) the prior distribution of forecasts by individual analysts to their own clients, or (ii) the reporting lags between the date of a forecast revision by an individual analyst and its inclusion in the IBES file made available to IBES subscribers. If both (i) and (ii) are minimal, [0] could be interpreted as the announcement month and [–1] as being in the pre-announcement period. If the combined effect of (i) and (ii) for individual firms is a lag of up to one month, month [–1] could include both pre-announcement and announcement effects. The results in Table 4.5 indicate that while month [–1] has a

---

[6] The data base examined in this section is a subset of that described in Chapter 2. Observations were required to have (i) security return data available, and (ii) both FY1 and FY2 forecasts available in the month examined. Restriction (ii) was imposed to make the results comparable with those reported in Chapter 5. A subset of tests were run without restriction (ii) with no change in the inferences drawn.

TABLE 4.5

Consensus Forecast Revisions and Security Price Revisions

	Months -12 to -2			Month -1			Month 0			Months -1 to 0			Months +1 to +12		
	ACAR	t	FREQ	AAR	t	FREQ	AAR	t	FREQ	ACAR	t	FREQ	ACAR	t	FREQ
A. MEDIAN AS PROXY FOR CONSENSUS															
-	-7.91	-25.80	1.00	-1.41	-14.18	1.00	-0.77	-7.61	1.00	-2.18	-15.59	1.00	-3.69	-10.53	1.00
0	-1.17	- 5.00	1.00	-0.12	- 1.67	0.86	-0.24	-3.14	1.00	-0.36	- 3.43	1.00	-1.22	- 4.68	0.99
+	5.37	19.14	0.00	1.02	11.24	0.00	0.55	6.34	0.00	1.56	12.70	0.00	0.87	2.87	0.00
B. MEAN AS PROXY FOR CONSENSUS															
-	-7.48	-31.42	1.00	-1.16	-14.94	1.00	-0.75	-9.37	1.00	-1.91	-17.39	1.00	-3.80	-13.84	1.00
0	1.50	3.12	0.00	0.08	0.53	0.15	-0.04	-0.24	0.49	0.04	0.20	0.30	1.94	3.72	0.00
+	3.91	17.71	0.00	0.72	10.13	0.00	0.35	5.14	0.00	1.07	10.94	0.00	0.04	0.17	0.24
C. (#+) - (#+) AS PROXY FOR CONSENSUS															
-	-8.57	-35.37	1.00	-1.48	-18.71	1.00	-0.85	-10.35	1.00	-2.33	-20.84	1.00	-3.89	-13.81	1.00
0	1.08	3.54	0.00	0.10	1.08	0.01	0.03	0.28	0.23	0.13	0.96	0.04	0.55	1.68	0.01
+	4.39	19.46	0.00	0.91	12.60	0.00	0.44	6.19	0.00	1.35	13.60	0.00	0.13	0.53	0.17

NOTES

1. Month 0 = Forecast Revision Month in IBES Data Base
2. ACAR = Average Cumulative Abnormal Return
3. AAR = Average Abnormal Return

FIGURE 4.1

Average Cumulative Abnormal Returns Surrounding IBES Earnings Forecast Revision Month for FY1 Portfolios: Median Forecast as Proxy for Consensus Forecast

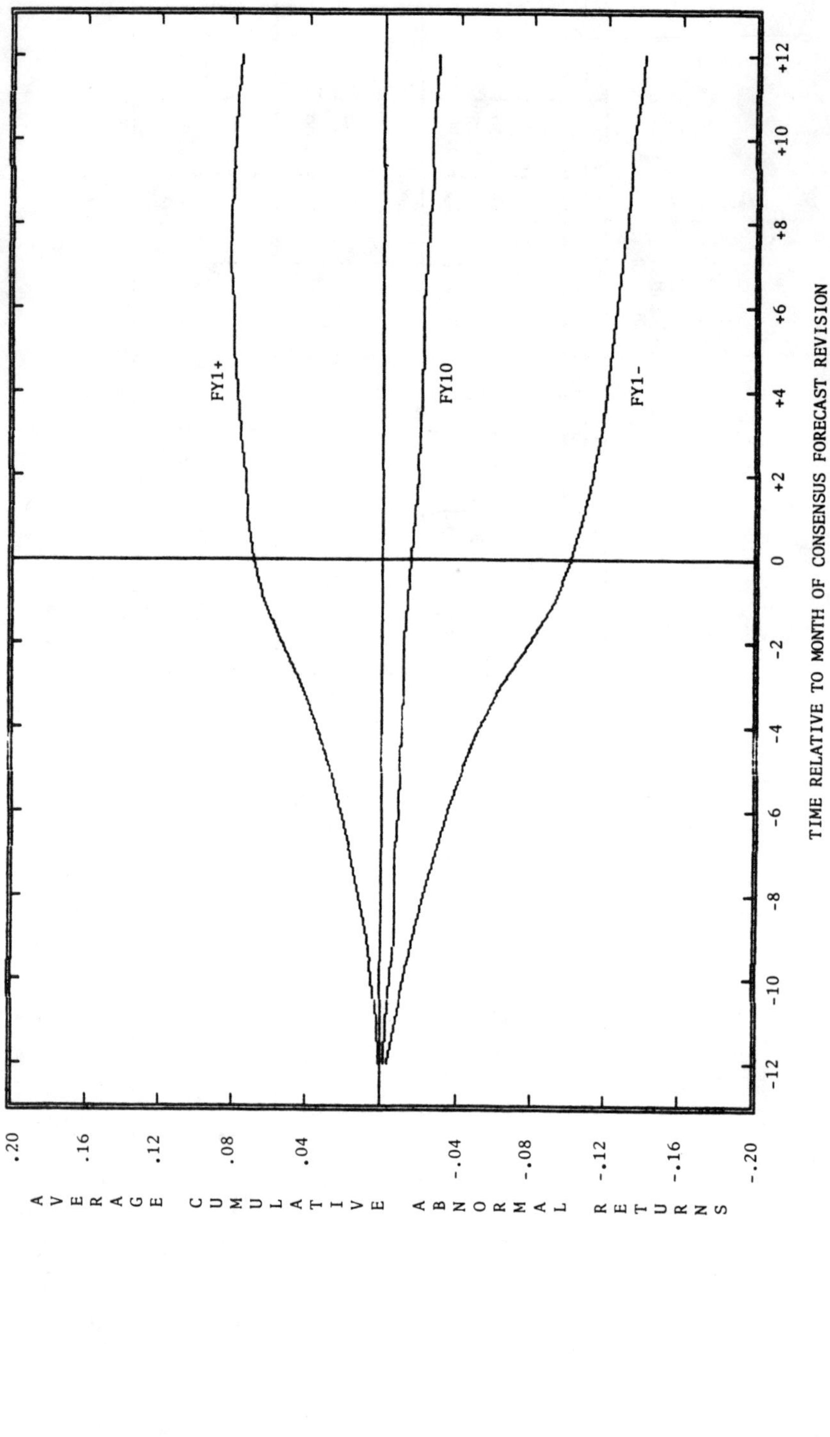

stronger association between security returns and earnings forecast revisions in month 0 than does month [0], both months [–1] and [0] have highly significant associations in a statistical sense.

The focus of the research in this monograph is not on post-announcement drifts in security returns. This topic raises difficult issues relating to market efficiency tests that are worthy of a separate study – see Ball [1978] and Foster [1984]. However, ACAR results covering the [+1 to +12] month period can be obtained at minimal cost. Table 4.5 reports ACAR's for each of the three proxies for consensus forecasts. Only for the – earnings forecast revision group do all three proxies report a statistically significant post-announcement drift in the same direction: –3.69% for the median, –3.80% for the mean and –3.89% for the (# ↑)–(# ↓) proxy. Prior studies on post-announcement drifts have reported conflicting findings. Zacks [1979] reported finding "no relation between forecast EPS growth and actual price movements ...This finding is consistent with efficient market concepts" (p. 54). Elton-Gruber-Gultekin [1981] report "no discernible pattern in the cumulative [post- announcement] excess returns... This is what one would expect if expectations are incorporated into security price" (pp. 983, 984). In contrast, Givoly and Lakonishok [1979] conclude that "the market does not respond instantaneously to financial analyst forecast revisions; significant abnormal returns are observed during the two months following the month of the revision" (pp. 183-184). Hawkins-Chamberlin-Daniel [1983] likewise conclude that "revisions in consensus earnings estimates can be used to predict subsequent stock price performance and that the market is not efficient in processing such information" (p.20).

Subsample Analysis

Chapter 2 reported statistics on the serial correlation over time of consensus forecasts and on the unconditional and conditional frequency distributions of forecast revisions. One limitation of the research design underlying Table 4.5 is that a firm's membership in a given forecast revision portfolio is not independent over time – see Table 2.6. At a minimum, this suggests that the degrees of freedom in our significance tests are overstated; it also raises the possibility that the effects observed are proxying for some omitted variable other than the sign of the forecast revision – see Ball [1978]. To address this issue, we replicated Table 4.5 for 13 mutually-exclusive subsamples of the data. Forecast revisions 13 months apart were chosen to minimize the month by month persistences documented in Chapter 2. (Subsample 1 includes forecast revisions in January 1976, February 1977, March 1978; Subsample 2 includes forecast revisions in February 1976, March 1977, April 1978, ..., etc.) Every 13th month was also chosen to avoid the same month of each year appearing in any subsample.

Table 4.6 presents the ACAR's for the –, 0, and + earnings forecast revision categories over the [–12 to –2] period. In each of the 13 mutually exclusive subsamples, the ACAR ranking is – < 0 < + and in each subsample the –(+) group has a negative (positive) ACAR. These results reinforce the inferences previously drawn from Table 4.5.

B. Price-Extraction Tests: Cross-Section Analysis

The results in Table 4.5 are consistent with security analysts using information in security price-movements (what we term "extraction of information from price") when

TABLE 4.6

Consensus Forecast Revisions and Security Price Revisions: ACAR for [–12 to –2] Period Using Median as Consensus Proxy for Thirteen Mutually Exclusive Subsamples and for Total Sample

SUB-SAMPLES	- GROUP for [-12,-2]	0 GROUP for [-12,-2]	+ GROUP for [-12,-2]
1	-7.37	-0.76	6.37
2	-8.91	-2.55	6.76
3	-8.21	-1.54	4.79
4	-8.27	-3.03	5.70
5	-7.51	-3.10	3.67
6	-7.63	-1.18	4.39
7	-8.35	-0.61	4.03
8	-8.41	-1.27	5.65
9	-8.18	-0.79	4.98
10	-8.29	0.70	5.53
11	-6.77	-0.12	5.46
12	-5.67	-2.00	7.05
13	-9.22	0.53	9.20
TOTAL SAMPLE	-7.91	-1.17	5.37

Month 0 = Forecast Revision Month in IBES Data Base.

revising their earnings forecasts. This and the next section further examine this finding using cross-sectional and time-series tests. As a first pass, the following cross-sectional regression is run centered on each forecast revision month:

$$\Delta F\hat{Y}1_i = \gamma_o + \gamma_1 \cdot R\hat{O}R_i[-T,-1] + \epsilon_i \qquad (4.4)$$

where $\Delta F\hat{Y}1_i$ = change in the median consensus earnings forecast for ith firm.

$R\hat{O}R_i[-T,-1]$ = security rate of return of ith firm in the [–T,–1] period.

Given the results in Table 4.5, month [–1] was included in the pre-forecast revision period when computing $R\hat{O}R_{it}$. To the extent that [–1] is the revision month itself, this will bias upward our estimates of the amount of extraction of information from price. $R\hat{O}R_i$ was estimated over 12 overlapping time periods – [–1,–1], [–2,–1], ..., [–11,–1], [–12,–1]. Clearly, significance levels across these time periods are not independent. Regression (4.4) was run for each month from February 1976 to December 1980, yielding 59 estimates of the Pearsonian correlation between $\Delta F\hat{Y}1_i$ and $R\hat{O}R_i$.

Table 4.7 (Panel A) reports distribution statistics for the 59 cross-sectional correlations in (4.4) for $R\hat{O}R_i$, measured both as ("raw") security returns and as abnormal returns (see Appendix 4.A). The median at [–1,–1] is a correlation of .09. It increases to .20 at [–4,–1] for both measures of $R\hat{O}R_i$. The incremental effect of extending backwards the prior security returns period beyond month [–4] appears minimal. These results are consistent with a positive linear relation between FY1 forecast revisions and prior security returns. However, the largest median correlation is .22 which means that in the structural form in (4.4), prior security returns explain less than five percent of the variance in FY1 forecast revisions across firms. Table 4.7 (Panel B) reports results from the use of $\Delta F\hat{Y}2_i$ as the dependent variable in (4.4). The highest median correlation is .16, which means that less than three percent of the variance in FY2 forecast revisions across firms can be explained by prior security return movements.

There are several explanations for the results in Table 4.7. One explanation is that prior security returns are indeed a small component of the information sources security analysts use when revising their earnings forecasts. Another explanation is that (4.4) is misspecified; for instance, it assumes that all analysts use the same prior time period for each and every security to extract information from security price movements and that all firms have the same coefficient for the relationship between $\Delta F\hat{Y}1_i$ ($\Delta F\hat{Y}2_i$) and $R\hat{O}R_i$.

C. Price-Extraction Tests: Time-Series Analysis

This section relaxes the assumption that all firms have the same coefficient for the relationship between $\Delta F\hat{Y}1$ ($\Delta F\hat{Y}2$) and $R\hat{O}R$ by adopting a time-series analysis. Results from the following regressions are reported in Table 4.8 (Panel A):

$$\Delta F\hat{Y}1_t = \gamma_0 + \gamma_1 \cdot \Delta F\hat{Y}1_{Mt} + \epsilon_t \qquad (4.5)$$

$$\Delta F\hat{Y}1_t = \gamma_0 + \gamma_1 \cdot \Delta R\hat{O}R_t[-T,-1] + \epsilon_t \qquad (4.6)$$

$$\Delta F\hat{Y}1_t = \gamma_0 + \gamma_1 \cdot \Delta F\hat{Y}1_{Mt} + \gamma_2 \cdot R\hat{O}R_t[-T,-1] + \epsilon_t \qquad (4.7)$$

where $\Delta F\hat{Y}1_{Mt}$ = change in the median consensus forecast for the "market" in

TABLE 4.7

Distribution Statistics for Cross-Sectional (Pearsonian) Correlation Between FY1 and FY2 Median Forecast Revisions and Prior Security Returns

PANEL A: FY1 MEDIAN FORECAST REVISION AS DEPENDENT VARIABLE

TIME PERIOD FOR ROR CUMULATION	SECURITY RETURNS		ABNORMAL RETURNS	
	MEAN	MEDIAN	MEAN	MEDIAN
-1, -1	.10	.09	.10	.09
-2. -1	.14	.13	.15	.14
-3, -1	.17	.16	.17	.17
-4, -1	.19	.20	.19	.20
-5, -1	.20	.19	.20	.21
-6, -1	.21	.19	.22	.21
-7, -1	.21	.20	.22	.21
-8, -1	.21	.21	.22	.21
-9, -1	.21	.21	.22	.22
-10, -1	.21	.21	.21	.21
-11, -1	.20	.20	.21	.21
-12, -1	.19	.20	.20	.19

PANEL B: FY2 MEDIAN FORECAST REVISION AS DEPENDENT VARIABLE

TIME PERIOD FOR ROR CUMULATION	SECURITY RETURNS		ABNORMAL RETURNS	
	MEAN	MEDIAN	MEAN	MEDIAN
-1,-1	.07	.04	.07	.05
-2,-1	.10	.09	.11	.09
-3,-1	.12	.10	.12	.10
-4,-1	.13	.13	.13	.13
-5,-1	.15	.13	.15	.13
-6,-1	.16	.14	.16	.14
-7,-1	.15	.15	.15	.14
-8,-1	.15	.15	.16	.16
-9,-1	.13	.15	.15	.14
-10,-1	.13	.15	.15	.15
-11,-1	.13	.14	.14	.15
-12,-1	.13	.15	.14	.15

Notes

1. Month 0 = Forecast Revision Month in IBES Data Base.

2. Correlation Reported is from the following Regressions:

PANEL A: $\Delta FY1_i = \hat{\gamma}_0 + \hat{\gamma}_1 \cdot ROR_i\,[-T,-1] + \varepsilon_i$

PANEL B: $\Delta FY2_i = \hat{\gamma}_0 \quad \hat{\gamma}_1 \cdot \hat{ROR}_i\,[-T,-1] + \varepsilon_i$

TABLE 4.8

Distribution Statistics of R^2 for Time-Series Regression of FY1 (FY2) Median Forecast Revision Against Market FY1 (FY2) Forecast Revision and Prior Security Returns

PANEL A: FY1 MEDIAN FORECAST ERROR AS DEPENDENT VARIABLE

TIME PERIOD FOR ROR CUMULATION	R^2 OF (4.5)		R^2 OF (4.6) SECURITY RETURNS		R^2 OF (4.6) ABNORMAL RETURNS		R^2 OF (4.7) SECURITY RETURNS		R^2 OF (4.7) ABNORMAL RETURNS	
	MEAN	MEDIAN	MEAN	MEDIAN	MEAN	MEDIAN	MEAN	MEDIAN	MEAN	MEDIAN
	.13	.08	-	-	-	-	-	-	-	-
-1,-1	-	-	.03	.01	.04	.02	.16	.12	.16	.12
-2,-1	-	-	.05	.02	.06	.03	.17	.13	.18	.13
-3,-1	-	-	.05	.02	.06	.03	.17	.14	.18	.15
-4,-1	-	-	.05	.02	.06	.03	.18	.14	.19	.17
-5,-1	-	-	.05	.02	.06	.03	.18	.15	.20	.17
-6,-1	-	-	.05	.02	.06	.03	.18	.15	.19	.16
-7,-1	-	-	.05	.02	.06	.03	.19	.16	.20	.17
-8,-1	-	-	.05	.02	.06	.03	.19	.16	.20	.18
-9,-1	-	-	.05	.02	.06	.03	.19	.17	.20	.18
-10,-1	-	-	.05	.02	.06	.03	.19	.16	.20	.17
-11,-1	-	-	.05	.02	.06	.03	.19	.16	.20	.17
-12,-1	-	-	.05	.02	.06	.03	.18	.15	.19	.16

PANEL B: FY2 MEDIAN FORECAST ERROR AS DEPENDENT VARIABLE

TIME PERIOD FOR ROR CUMULATION	R^2 OF (4.5)		R^2 OF (4.6) SECURITY RETURNS		R^2 OF (4.6) ABNORMAL RETURNS		R^2 OF (4.7) SECURITY RETURNS		R^2 OF (4.7) ABNORMAL RETURNS	
	MEAN	MEDIAN	MEAN	MEDIAN	MEAN	MEDIAN	MEAN	MEDIAN	MEAN	MEDIAN
	.16	.13	-	-	-	-	-	-	-	-
-1,-1	-	-	.04	.02	.04	.02	.20	.16	.20	.16
-2,-1	-	-	.05	.02	.06	.02	.20	.17	.21	.18
-3,-1	-	-	.05	.02	.06	.02	.20	.17	.21	.19
-4,-1	-	-	.05	.02	.06	.02	.20	.17	.21	.18
-5,-1	-	-	.05	.02	.06	.02	.20	.17	.21	.18
-6,-1	-	-	.05	.02	.06	.02	.20	.17	.21	.19
-7,-1	-	-	.05	.02	.06	.02	.21	.17	.21	.18
-8,-1	-	-	.05	.02	.06	.02	.21	.18	.21	.18
-9,-1	-	-	.05	.02	.06	.02	.21	.18	.21	.18
-10,-1	-	-	.05	.02	.06	.02	.20	.18	.21	.18
-11,-1	-	-	.05	.02	.06	.02	.20	.18	.21	.19
-12,-1	-	-	.05	.02	.06	.02	.20	.18	.21	.18

Notes

1. Month 0 = Forecast Revision Month in IBES Data Base.

2. In Panel A Regression (4.5) is $\Delta \hat{FY1}_t = \gamma_0 + \gamma_1 \cdot \Delta \hat{FY1}_{Mt} + \epsilon_t$

(4.6) is $\Delta \hat{FY1}_t = \gamma_0 + \gamma_1 \cdot ROR_t[-T,-1] + \epsilon_t$

(4.7) is $\Delta \hat{FY1}_t = \gamma_0 + \gamma_1 \cdot \Delta \hat{FY1}_{Mt} + \gamma_2 \cdot ROR_t[-T,-1] + \epsilon_t$

In Panel B dependent variable of (4.5) to (4.7) is $\Delta \hat{FY2}_t$; independent variables as above.

month t ("market" defined as arithmetic average of $\Delta F\hat{Y}1_t$ for all December 31 fiscal year firms).[7]

$\Delta FY1$ and $\hat{ROR}$ are as defined for (4.4). A separate time-series regression is run for each firm using the February 1976 to December 1980 time period. Table 4.8 (Panel A) reports the mean and median for the R^2 statistic from (4.5), (4.6), and (4.7) across the 347 December 31 fiscal year firms in the sample. Results are reported for (4.6) and (4.7) using both "raw" security returns and risk-adjusted security returns.

Using this time-series approach, the explanatory power of the $\hat{ROR}$ variable again appears relatively small. The highest mean R^2 is .05 (.06) when raw security returns (risk-adjusted security returns) are used to estimate $\hat{ROR}$. The market consensus forecast revision variable, on average, explains 13 percent of the variance in individual firm earnings forecast revisions. In combination, the two independent variables explain at most 20 percent of the variance in individual firm earnings forecast revisions.

Panel B of Table 4.8 reports results from the use of $\Delta F\hat{Y}2_t$ as the dependent variable in (4.5), (4.6), and (4.7). They are similar to the results for $\Delta F\hat{Y}1_t$. Note that one explanation for the relatively low explanatory power of the $\hat{ROR}_t$ variable in (4.6) could be that, over time for a firm, the same fixed period is not always used to extract information from security price changes.

Both the cross-sectional and time-series models reported in Tables 4.7 and 4.8 provide evidence consistent with analysts extracting forecast revision information from security price changes, albeit both models appear to have low explanatory power. From an econometric perspective, we regard the inferences drawn from the [–1,–1] time period as most reliable. Individual regressions for time periods [–2,–1], ..., [–11,–1, [–12,–1] are affected by overlapping data observations. These overlapping observations can induce positive serial correlation into the residuals of the regressions.

From an economic modeling perspective it is likely that the process is considerably more complex than that assumed by the linear models underlying Tables 4.7 and 4.8; e.g., for specific securities, an individual analyst may be a "market leader" in which case not all individuals would simultaneously revise their earnings forecasts as is assumed implicitly in both linear models. (To probe this explanation, the researcher would need access to the individual forecasts underlying the consensus measures available on the IBES Summary Data Base.) In addition, it is likely that neither linear model fully captures all the information cues used by analysts when revising earnings forecasts. For example, the announcement in month 0 (say) of a new product or R&D development may not be reflected in security returns in the [–12,–1] period, but may prompt analysts to make a sizeable revision in their forecast of FY1 earnings in month 0.

---

[7] When computing (4.5) and (4.7), a "Dimson" estimation approach is used – see Dimson [1979]. Operationally, $\Delta F\hat{Y}1_{M,t-1}$, $\Delta F\hat{Y}1_{M,t}$ and $\Delta F\hat{Y}1_{M,t+1}$ were included as independent variables in each firm's regression for (4.5) and (4.7). The motivation for using this estimation approach was to take into account reporting lags between individual analysts revising their forecasts and the inclusion of those revisions in the consensus forecast measures in the IBES data base.

Appendix 4.A

Estimating Abnormal Security Returns

The abnormal returns reported in Chapters 4 and 5 are based on the following returns-generating model:

$$r_{jt} - r_{ft} = \alpha_j + \beta_j (r_{mt} - r_{ft}) + \epsilon_{jt} \qquad (4.A.1)$$

where

r_{jt} = the discrete return on the common stock of firm j in month t,

r_{ft} = the return on 30-day Treasury Bills in month t (the time-series was acquired from Salomon Brothers),

r_{mt} = the equally weighted average return of all firms in the IBES and Wells Fargo data bases in month t,

α_j, β_j = firm-specific parameters, and

ϵ_{jt} = error term for firm j in month t.

The parameters α_j and β_j were estimated by regressing $r_{jt} - r_{ft}$ on $r_{mt} - r_{ft}$ using up to 60 months of returns. Suppose we are interested in estimating the abnormal return for firm j in month T. Then α_j and β_j would be estimated by using all available returns between months T-60 and T-1 (providing there are at least two returns available). Since the parameters α_j and β_j will differ for each period T, we subscript the estimates by T (i.e., $\hat{\alpha}_{jT}, \hat{\beta}_{jT}$).

The abnormal return in period T for firm j we define as

$$e_{jT} = (r_{jT} - r_{fT}) - \hat{\beta}_{jT}(r_{mT} - r_{fT}) \qquad (4.A.2)$$

Note that the parameter $\hat{\alpha}_{jT}$ does not appear in the expression defining the abnormal return. We omit $\hat{\alpha}_{jT}$ from the definition of the abnormal return for a number of reasons. First, Ross [1976] demonstrates that under plausible conditions, the returns-generating model (4.A.1) is consistent with the absence of arbitrage opportunities only if $\alpha_j = 0$. Thus, there are theoretical grounds to suspect that α_j is zero and any difference between $\hat{\alpha}_{jT}$ and zero is simply estimation error. Second, the abnormal return defined by (4.A.2) can actually be realized by forming portfolios ex-ante, whereas any abnormal return measure that incorporates $\hat{\alpha}_{jT}$ cannot actually be realized.[8]

In short, the abnormal returns in this study were computed by subtracting from the return on a security: 1) the return on 30-day Treasury Bills and 2) $\hat{\beta}_{jT}$ times the difference between the average return for the samples and the 30-day Treasury Bill rate. The parameter $\hat{\beta}_{jT}$ was determined from an ordinary least-squares regression of $r_{jT} - r_{fT}$ on $r_{mt} - r_{ft}$ using all available data in the immediately preceding 60 months.

---

[8] The abnormal return e_{jT} can be realized (ignoring transactions costs and restrictions on short-selling) by investing in firm j, r_f and r_m in the proportions 1, $\hat{\beta}_{jT-1}$, and $-\hat{\beta}_{jT}$. Note that this would require no net investment and hence any abnormal return that is realized would be (approximately) an arbitrage profit – providing, of course, that the variance of e_{jT} is sufficiently small.

Each month in the IBES data base corresponds to the IBES reporting cycle, which ends on the third Thursday of each calendar month; r_{jt} and r_{mt} are computed from the third Thursday of month t–1 to the third Thursday of month t. (A daily series for 30-day Treasury Bill rates was not available; r_{ft} is defined over calendar months.)

We typically perform tests on cumulative abnormal returns between two months. If t_0 is the initial month and t_1 is the final month in the cumulation period, the cumulative abnormal return, $CAR_j(t_0, t_1)$, is defined to be

$$CAR_j(t_0, t_1) = \sum_{t=t_0}^{t_1} e_{jt} \cdot \sigma(e_{jt}) \qquad (4.A.3)$$

$$\text{where } \sigma(e_{jt}) = \begin{cases} 1 \text{ if } e_{jt} \text{ is not missing} \\ 0 \text{ if } e_{jt} \text{ is missing} \end{cases}$$

The abnormal return, e_{jt}, is missing if r_{jt} is missing or if there were insufficient data in the previous 60 months (i.e., less than two months) to estimate the parameter $\hat{\beta}_{jT}$.

The average cumulated abnormal return, ACAR (t_0, t_t), is defined to be

$$ACAR\,(t_0, t_1) = \frac{\sum_{j=1}^{N} CAR_j\,(t_0,t_1) \cdot \sigma(e_{jt*})}{\sum_{j=1}^{N} \sigma(e_{jt*})} \qquad (4.A.4)$$

where N is the number of firms in the portfolio and t* is either t_0 or t_1, depending upon the focus of a test. In Tables 4.1 and 4.4 (and 5.1, 5.2, and 5.3), the focus is on the incremental benefit of earlier portfolio formation and the focus of the test is on the initial month in the cumulation period. Hence, t* is t_0 in Tables 4.1 and 4.4. In Tables 4.5 and 4.6 (and 5.11, 5.12, and 5.13), the focus is on the final month in the cumulation period, so t* is t_1.

This treatment of missing data is a compromise. At one extreme, we could have deleted all firms with any data missing during the cumulation period. At the other extreme, we could have included all firms – regardless of how many data were missing. We chose instead to delete only those firms with data missing for the month that is the focus of the test. An implication is that our average cumulative abnormal return measure excludes some firms with well-defined abnormal returns in at least some of the cumulation period. It may also include some firms with missing data during the cumulation period. In fact, all of the firms in the sample have a continuous returns history. In other words, once a firm is added to the sample, it stays in the sample and there are no missing data. This implies that when t* is t_0, there are no missing data for any firm included in the ACAR measure. When t* is t_1, some firms may be missing some data during the cumulation period.

Appendix 4.B

Nonparametric Tests of Statistical Significance

We perform nonparametric tests, similar in spirit to a randomization test, on the average cumulative abnormal returns.[9] These tests, in contrast to parametric tests such as the t-test, are distribution-free and, if properly designed, can overcome problems due to statistical dependence. Randomization-type tests, on the other hand, typically require far more computation than comparable parametric tests. With the rapid decline in the costs of computing, randomization-type tests are becoming more attractive.[10]

Testing the Abnormal Returns from Forming Portfolios on the Basis of Forecast Errors

In the terminology that is usually employed to describe such tests, the firms are the subjects and the treatment consists of assigning a subset of the firms to mutually exclusive portofolios (e.g., – or + portfolios based upon the sign of an earnings forecast error). The statistic that we focus on is the average cumulative abnormal return (ACAR) for a portfolio.

The null hypothesis is that the statistic ACAR is independent of the assignment of firms (subjects) to the portfolios (treatments). The distribution of the statistic ACAR under the null hypothesis can be determined exactly by permuting the data. For example, suppose there are N firms, and based on an earnings forecast error, n firms are assigned to one portfolio and N-n are assigned to another portfolio. There are N!/n!(N-n)! different possible combinations of n firms in one portfolio and N-n in another. For each of these possible combinations, the statistic ACAR can be computed. If the probability of rejecting the null, when it is in fact true, is set at α, then the null should be rejected if the ACAR for the actual portfolio assignment exceeds $(1 - \alpha) \times 100$ percent of the ACARs generated by creating all possible combinations of portfolios of size n and N-n.

The only distributional assumption that is made is that each possible combination of portfolios is equally likely. The abnormal returns themselves can have any distributional properties, including cross-sectional dependence, and the test is still valid.

The disadvantage of the test is that it requires computation of N!/n!(N-n)! different ACARs. With N on the order of 300-400 firms in most of our tests, the number of computations required would be economically infeasible with the computer equipment available to us. Nevertheless, the exact distribution of the statistic ACAR under the null hypothesis can be approximated by random sampling. This is accomplished by repeatedly sampling at random from the set of possible combinations of portfolios of size n and N-n and then computing the statistic ACAR for each random combination of

---

[9] See Siegel [1956, pp. 88-92] and Cox and Hinkley [1974, pp. 196-198] for examples of randomization tests. L. Marais of the University of Chicago is currently conducting research on accounting applications in this area.

[10] Examples of recent empirical work employing randomization or bootstrapping tests include Bowen, Lacey and Noreen [1981], Noreen and Sepe [1981], Foster, Olsen and Shevlin [1984], and Marais [1984].

portfolios. Mechanically, this can be done by randomly shuffling the order of the N firms, assigning the first n to portfolio one and the last N-n to portfolio two, computing the ACAR, and then starting all over again.[11] The resulting sample distribution of ACAR will approach the exact distribution of ACAR as the number of drawings from the distribution of ACAR increases. Due to the cost of this procedure, we limited the sample size to 100 draws from the distribution of ACAR under the null. Stated another way, we shuffled the order of the firms and computed the resulting ACARs 100 times.

For example, in Table 4.1, the ACAR for the "–" portfolio when the median FY1 is used to compute forecast error is –9.879 between months –10 and 0. The ACAR for the "+" portfolio is 6.404. In order to assess the statistical significance of these ACARs, we randomly drew 100 observations from the ACAR distributions under the null hypothesis. This was accomplished by randomly assigning firms to the "–" and to the "+" portfolios. Equivalently, since the only relevant attribute of the firms at this point was their cumulative abnormal returns, these cumulative abnormal returns were randomly assigned to the "–" and to the "+" portfolios. In one hundred such trials, no ACAR was greater than 6.404 and none was less than –9.879.

Relative to the conventional t-test, the randomization-type test described above requires more computation. However, unlike the conventional t-test, the validity of the randomization-type test is not threatened by possible statistical properties of abnormal returns such as non-normality, cross-sectional temporal dependence, and differing variance.

Test of the Effect on ACAR of Using More Timely Security Analyst Forecasts

Panels A and B of Table 4.4 were constructed in order to test the null hypothesis that ACARs are independent of the timeliness of security analyst forecasts. The alternative hypothesis is that more timely forecasts (i.e., those that are closer to the announcement date) can be used to generate larger ACARs than less timely forecasts. In other words, at time T relative to the announcement month 0, a larger ACAR will result if earnings forecasts as of time T are used in forming portfolios than if less timely earnings forecasts are used. In terms of the layout in Table 4.4, this implies that the absolute value of the ACARs should be monotonically increasing down the columns.

To test this hypothesis, the following procedure was employed. Kendall's tau (a rank correlation between the actual ordering and the hypothesized ordering of the ACARs) was computed for each column independently. For example, Kendall's tau for the column headed [–9, 0] in Panel B of Table 4.5 is +1, since the second entry exceeds the first, as predicted. Kendall's tau for the column headed [–8, 0] in Panel B is +3 since entry two exceeds entry one, entry three exceeds entry one, and entry three exceeds entry two. The test statistic was defined to be the sum of these Kendall's taus across columns. A large positive number would indicate that the entries do indeed monotonically increase down the column.

To calibrate the significance of this aggregated Kendall's tau, a randomization-type test was employed. The null hypothesis is that the pattern of the ACARs by column is

---

[11] We ran a subset of our tests forming portfolios by sampling both with and without replacement from the set of firms. The results were indistinguishable between the two methods. The results reported in Chapters 4 and 5 are for sampling with replacement.

independent of the timeliness of the earnings forecast (or in the terms employed in Table 4.4, of the month a firm was placed into a portfolio). The distribution of the test statistic under the null could be determined exactly by permuting the rows of the full 11 x 11 matrix of ACARs. For each of the 11! possible permutations of rows, the aggregated Kendall's tau test statistic could be computed and then the value of the test statistic for the actual ordering of the rows could be assessed relative to the exact distribution. To economize on computation costs, we sampled from the exact distribution by shuffling the order of the rows 100 times and after each shuffle, the aggregated Kendall's tau test statistic was computed. This procedure automatically takes into account the fact that the ACARs across a row are not independent. A formal test of the hypothesis hardly seems necessary since there are so few entries in Panels A and B that are out of predicted order. It should not be surprising that the actual value of the test statistic was not exceeded on any of the 100 trials.

CHAPTER 5

SECURITY ANALYST MULTI-YEAR EARNINGS FORECAST REVISIONS AND SECURITY PRICE CHANGES

5.1 Overview of Issues Examined and Results

This chapter examines four related issues using the IBES (issues 1, 2, and 3) and Wells Fargo data bases (issue 4):

1. The association between (i) two year ahead (FY2) earnings forecast errors or revisions, and (ii) security returns in the period up to and including the month the actual FY1 earnings is announced. The results of two tests are consistent with a significant relationship existing between (i) and (ii) for firms in the IBES data base.

2. The association between (i) two year ahead (FY2) earnings forecast revisions, and (ii) security returns in the period up to and including the month the forecast revision is reported. The results of two tests are consistent with a significant relationship existing between (i) and (ii) for firms in the IBES data base.

3. The incremental explanatory power of (i) FY2 relative to FY1, and (ii) FY1 relative to FY2. The research designs adopted in this chapter reflect the fact that FY1 and FY2 earnings forecast errors (and FY1 and FY2 earnings forecast revisions) are positively correlated. Using a cross-sectional regression approach, the incremental explanatory power of FY2 relative to FY1 is examined. When the correlation between FY1 and FY2 is attributed to FY1, both FY1 and FY2 have significant coefficients in a multiple regression. This result suggests that prior studies focusing exclusively on FY1 have underestimated the power of future earnings revisions as an explainer of security price revisions. When the correlation between FY1 and FY2 is attributed to FY2, only FY2 has a consistently significant coefficient in a multiple regression. There are several possible explanations for this result. One explanation is that FY1 has a higher "transitory" earnings component than does FY2. An alternative (but related) explanation is that security analysts consciously tailor their FY1 forecast to the GAAP-based number to be reported by the company but that they use the FY2 forecast to convey their expectations about "permanent" earnings.

4. The association between (i) individual security analyst earnings per share forecast revisions for each year of a five year ahead horizon, and (ii) security returns in the eleven-month period up to and including the end of the FY1 fiscal year. Using a regression approach, forecast revisions of years beyond FY1 have statistically significant explanatory power for firms in the Wells Fargo data base. In particular, forecast revisions of FY2 and FY3 are significant explanatory variables. This result is consistent with (i) the capital market having a multi-year earnings horizon, and (ii) the forecast for FY1 not capturing fully the signal embodied in revisions to the earnings sequence over that multi-year horizon.

5.2 Association Between Analyst FY2 Forecast Errors and Security Price Changes: Company Earnings Announcement Date as Event Month 0

This section extends the tests on FY1 reported in Section 4.2 to incorporate information about the sign or magnitude of the FY2 forecast error. The IBES data base is used in this and the next section.

A. Portfolio Analysis Using Sign of FY1 and FY2 Earnings Forecast Errors

Section 4.2A reported ACAR results, based on a Ball and Brown [1968] design for two portfolios formed using the sign of the FY1 earnings forecast error: FY1– and FY1 +. This section reports results for four portfolios formed using the signs of both the FY1 and FY2 forecast errors:

- FY1– and FY2– = – –
- FY1– and FY2 + = – +
- FY1 + and FY2– = + –
- FY1 + and FY2 + = + +

Two approaches to measuring the FY2 forecast error are reported in this section:

(i) EPS Forecast for FY2 in Month 0 – EPS Forecast for FY2 at the start of Month T.

(ii) Actual EPS for FY2 – EPS Forecast for FY2 at the start of Month T.

Month 0 is the month the company reports its FY1 earnings. The advantage of measure (i) is that information available in month 0 of the association period is used to determine the sign of both the FY1 and FY2 forecast errors. Measure (ii) utilizes information not released until (typically) twelve months beyond the period used to compute the ACAR association metric. We prefer (i) for this reason. However, (i) has the disadvantage that if analysts rely exclusively on security price changes in the [–T,0] period when revising their FY2 earnings forecast, then its use will guarantee a significant ACAR association, by construction.[1] Inclusion of (ii) provides a check on the sensitivity of inferences drawn from (i).[2] Recall that while Chapter 4 presented evidence consistent with extraction of information from prior security returns by security analysts, no more than ten percent of the variance in security analyst forecast revisions could be explained by prior security returns. Moreover, it would be difficult to explain the continued employment of security analysts to forecast earnings and the development of data bases like IBES if the pure "extraction of information from price" description of analyst behavior was appropriate.

Table 5.1 (5.2) reports ACAR results for the FY1 and FY1/FY2 based portfolios when the median (mean) forecast is used as the proxy for consensus forecasts.[3] The results in Tables 5.1 and 5.2 are consistent with FY2 having incremental explanatory power over and above FY1. For instance, the ACARs for [–10,0] for FY2 measured using (i) are:

---

[1] This is a common problem in research examining associations between analyst forecasts and security prices (or returns). Malkiel and Cragg [1970] face a similar problem when regressing PE (price to earnings) ratios against security analyst earnings growth forecasts; if analysts rely exclusively on PE ratios to forecast earnings growth, the regression exercise in Malkiel and Cragg [1970] will be circular.

[2] One limitation of the use of (ii) is that the EPS forecast for FY2 made at the start of month T may be for a different entity than exists when the FY2 results are announced (e.g., due to acquisitions, divestitures, or spinoffs). This problem exists with (i), but to a lesser degree than with (ii).

[3] Table 5.1 (and 5.2) excludes observations where there is no forecast error for FY1 or FY2.

TABLE 5.1

Association Between FY1/FY2 Forecast Errors and Average Cumulative Abnormal Returns: Portfolios Formed Using Signs of FY1/FY2 Earnings Forecast Error with Median Forecast Used as Proxy for Consensus Forecast

PANEL A: AVERAGE CUMULATIVE ABNORMAL RETURNS

	-10,0	-9,0	-8,0	-7,0	-6,0	-5,0	-4,0	-3,0	-2,0	-1,0	0,0
SINGLE YEAR: FY1 ONLY											
−	-9.879	-9.483	-9.419	-8.199	-6.937	-6.465	-5.494	-3.665	-2.706	-2.620	-1.433
+	6.404	5.664	4.994	4.354	3.625	2.969	3.250	2.825	1.676	1.755	1.529
MULTI-YEAR: FY1, FY2[2]											
− −	-11.200	-11.625	-10.842	-9.725	-8.422	-7.524	-6.471	-4.403	-3.162	-3.309	-1.508
− +	-7.982	-6.624	-6.108	-3.781	-1.498	-1.645	-0.513	-0.799	-1.192	-0.944	-1.330
+ −	0.126	-0.936	0.033	-0.364	-0.117	0.099	0.335	-0.221	-0.552	0.261	0.179
+ +	8.028	8.201	6.986	6.749	5.610	4.694	5.013	4.789	3.849	3.507	2.620
MULTI-YEAR: FY1, FY2[3]											
− −	-12.114	-12.091	-11.330	-10.485	-8.919	-8.332	-7.061	-5.082	-4.008	-3.863	-2.063
− +	-7.771	-6.597	-6.153	-3.756	-2.560	-1.912	-1.744	-0.230	0.014	-0.343	-0.409
+ −	-3.369	-3.783	-3.089	-1.916	-1.927	-1.067	-0.282	-0.286	-0.596	0.367	0.509
+ +	8.433	8.167	7.541	6.600	5.683	4.547	4.596	4.110	2.709	2.361	1.994

PANEL B: RELATIVE FREQUENCY WITH WHICH OBSERVED ACAR WAS EXCEEDED IN 100 RANDOM TRIALS

	-10,0	-9,0	-8,0	-7,0	-6,0	-5,0	-4,0	-3,0	-2,0	-1,0	0,0
SINGLE YEAR: FY1 ONLY											
−	1.00	1.00	1.00	1.00	1.00	1.00	1.00	1.00	1.00	1.00	1.00
+	0.00	0.00	0.00	0.00	0.00	0.00	0.00	0.00	0.00	0.00	0.00
MULTI-YEAR: FY1, FY2[2]											
− −	1.00	1.00	1.00	1.00	1.00	1.00	1.00	1.00	1.00	1.00	1.00
− +	1.00	1.00	1.00	0.99	0.83	0.80	0.58	0.72	0.86	0.85	0.95
+ −	0.51	0.81	0.55	0.72	0.61	0.35	0.34	0.81	0.86	0.38	0.41
+ +	0.00	0.00	0.00	0.00	0.00	0.00	0.00	0.00	0.00	0.00	0.00
MULTI-YEAR: FY1, FY2[3]											
− −	1.00	1.00	1.00	1.00	1.00	1.00	1.00	1.00	1.00	1.00	1.00
− +	1.00	1.00	1.00	1.00	0.99	0.96	0.95	0.54	0.38	0.67	0.80
+ −	0.95	0.99	0.99	0.92	0.95	0.77	0.61	0.70	0.85	0.31	0.20
+ +	0.00	0.00	0.00	0.00	0.00	0.00	0.00	0.00	0.00	0.00	0.00

Notes

1. Month 0 = Month in Which Actual EPS is Announced.
2. Multi-Year: Forecast FY2 refers to portfolios formed using the sign of FY1 and FY2 forecast errors. FY2 forecast error is (EPS Forecast for FY2 in Month 0 - EPS Forecast for FY2 at the Start of Month T).
3. Multi-Year: Actual FY2 refers to portfolios formed using the sign of FY1 and FY2 forecast errors. FY2 forecast error is (Actual EPS for FY2 - EPS Forecast for FY2 at the Start of Month T).

TABLE 5.2

Association Between FY1/FY2 Forecast Errors and Average Cumulative Abnormal Returns: Portfolios Formed Using Signs of FY1/FY2 Earnings Forecast Error with Mean Forecast Used as Proxy for Consensus Forecast

PANEL A: AVERAGE CUMULATIVE ABNORMAL RETURNS

	-10,0	-9,0	-8,0	-7,0	-6,0	-5,0	-4,0	-3,0	-2,0	-1,0	0,0
SINGLE YEAR: FY1 ONLY											
−	- 9.973	- 9.820	- 9.234	- 8.153	- 6.833	- 6.323	- 5.238	- 3.493	- 2.591	- 2.442	- 1.361
+	6.562	5.702	4.679	4.168	3.374	2.823	3.050	2.694	1.425	1.499	1.369
MULTI-YEAR: FY1, FY2[2]											
− −	-10.896	-11.723	-10.779	- 9.742	- 8.040	- 7.373	- 6.243	- 4.278	- 3.147	- 3.297	- 1.647
− +	- 8.588	- 7.631	- 5.826	- 3.904	- 2.034	- 1.823	- 0.050	- 0.371	- 0.657	- 0.639	- 0.977
+ −	- 0.407	- 0.489	- 0.785	- 0.728	- 0.975	0.236	- 0.425	- 0.009	- 0.795	- 0.186	- 0.251
+ +	8.410	7.823	6.895	6.404	5.351	4.208	4.473	4.375	2.813	2.583	1.959
MULTI-YEAR: FY1, FY2[3]											
− −	-11.912	-12.310	-11.280	-10.269	- 8.823	- 8.167	- 6.907	- 4.804	- 3.833	- 3.567	- 1.853
− +	- 8.139	- 7.086	- 5.926	- 3.953	- 2.361	- 1.728	- 1.138	- 0.398	- 0.017	- 0.260	- 0.521
+ −	- 3.807	- 3.435	- 3.332	- 2.480	- 2.591	- 1.518	- 0.995	- 0.684	- 1.080	0.259	0.009
+ +	8.751	8.053	7.274	6.535	5.584	4.474	4.625	4.099	2.546	2.076	1.943

PANEL B: RELATIVE FREQUENCY WITH WHICH OBSERVED ACAR WAS EXCEEDED IN 100 RANDOM TRIALS

	-10,0	-9,0	-8,0	-7,0	-6,0	-5,0	-4,0	-3,0	-2,0	-1,0	0,0
SINGLE YEAR: FY1 ONLY											
−	1.00	1.00	1.00	1.00	1.00	1.00	1.00	1.00	1.00	1.00	1.00
+	0.00	0.00	0.00	0.00	0.00	0.00	0.00	0.00	0.00	0.00	0.00
MULTI-YEAR: FY1, FY2[2]											
− −	1.00	1.00	1.00	1.00	1.00	1.00	1.00	1.00	1.00	1.00	1.00
− +	1.00	1.00	1.00	1.00	0.89	0.86	0.44	0.65	0.73	0.78	0.98
+ −	0.67	0.66	0.76	0.78	0.84	0.42	0.42	0.66	0.98	0.81	0.68
+ +	0.00	0.00	0.00	0.00	0.00	0.00	0.00	0.00	0.00	0.00	0.00
MULTI-YEAR: FY1, FY2[3]											
− −	1.00	1.00	1.00	1.00	1.00	1.00	1.00	1.00	1.00	1.00	1.00
− +	1.00	1.00	1.00	1.00	0.98	0.93	0.79	0.57	0.46	0.69	0.86
+ −	0.99	1.00	1.00	1.00	1.00	0.92	0.82	0.87	0.94	0.45	0.61
+ +	0.00	0.00	0.00	0.00	0.00	0.00	0.00	0.00	0.00	0.00	0.00

Notes

1. Month 0 = Month in Which Actual EPS is Announced.
2. Multi-Year: Forecast FY2 refers to portfolios formed using the sign of FY1 and FY2 forecast errors. FY2 forecast error is (EPS Forecast for FY2 in Month 0 - EPS Forecast for FY2 at the Start of Month T).
3. Multi-Year: Actual FY2 refers to portfolios formed using the sign of FY1 and FY2 forecast errors. FY2 forecast error is (Actual EPS for FY2 - EPS Forecast for FY2 at the Start of Month T).

FY1– = –9.879

- FY1–;FY2– = –11.200
- FY1–;FY2+ = –7.982

FY1+ = 6.404

- FY1+;FY2– = 0.126
- FY1+;FY2+ = 8.028

The same general pattern emerges from Tables 5.1 and 5.2 whether the FY2 forecast error is measured using (i) the FY2 forecast at month 0, or (ii) the actual FY2 reported by the company approximately twelve months after month 0. Similarly, the findings are robust to whether the median or mean is used as the proxy for consensus forecasts.

Inferences drawn about the incremental information content of FY2, from the research design in Tables 5.1 and 5.2, are most reliable when the sign of the FY1 and FY2 forecast errors are independent – see Foster [1975] and Brown, Finn and Hancock [1977]. We have already noted (Chapter 4) an association between the magnitudes of the FY1 variable and security price revisions. If the sign of the FY2 forecast error is conditional on the magnitude of the FY1 forecast error, the apparent significance of FY2 could be due to the FY1/FY2 categories being proxies for the magnitude of the FY1 variable.

To examine this possibility, the FY1 forecast error was scaled by the security price at the start of month –T. If the FY1/FY2 categories proxy for the magnitude of the FY1 forecast error, then this scaled FY1 forecast error should differ in a predictable manner between the FY1/FY2 categories. Table 5.3 reports the median scaled FY1 forecast error for each FY1/FY2 category. The conclusion from this table is that the research design in Figure 5.1 (and 5.2) does confound the magnitude of the FY1 forecast error effect with the (potential) incremental information content of the FY2 forecast error.

The next section reports results from a test that controls for the magnitude of the FY1 forecast error when examining the FY2 forecast error variable.

B. Cross-Section Regression Analysis Using Sign and Magnitude of FY1 and FY2 Earnings Forecast Errors

This section extends the cross-sectional regression approach outlined in Section 4.2B. The following regression format is employed initially:[4]

$$ROR_i[t_0,t_1] = \gamma_0 + \gamma_1 . X_{1i} + \gamma_2 . X_{2i} + \epsilon_i \qquad (5.1)$$

where $ROR_i[t_0,t_1]$ = return on security i between month t_0 and t_1.

[4] Unless stated otherwise, in all regressions reported in this Chapter (as in Chapter 4), the X_{2i} variable is orthogonalized relative to the X_{1i} variable (and X_{3i} orthogonalized relative to X_{1i} and X_{2i}). Orthogonalization was accomplished via a linear regression of X_{2i} on X_{1i} (X_{3i} on X_{2i} and X_{1i}). This approach facilitates computing the weights on individual variables reported in Table 5.7.

TABLE 5.3

Magnitude of FY1 Forecast Error (Deflated By Security Price) for Categories Based on the Signs of the FY1 and FY1/FY2 Forecast Errors Using Median Forecast as Proxy for Consensus Forecast

	SCALED FY1 FORECAST ERROR AT START OF MONTH T										
	-10	-9	-8	-7	-6	-5	-4	-3	-2	-1	0
FY1 CATEGORIZATION											
-	-.013	-.013	-.012	-.012	-.011	-.010	-.008	-.008	-.006	-.004	-.004
+	.013	.010	.009	.008	.008	.007	.007	.006	.005	.004	.004
FY1/FY2 CATEGORIZATIONS											
--	-.015	-.015	-.014	-.013	-.013	-.013	-.010	-.010	-.007	-.006	-.005
-+	-.011	-.007	-.005	-.006	-.005	-.005	-.006	-.005	-.005	-.004	-.005
+-	.008	.006	.006	.005	.005	.004	.004	.004	.004	.003	.003
++	.015	.012	.011	.010	.009	.008	.008	.007	.006	.005	.004

NOTE:

MONTH 0 = MONTH IN WHICH ACTUAL EPS IS ANNOUNCED

X_{1i} = beta (relative risk) of security i; estimated using 60 months of data immediately prior to month t_0.

X_{2i} = FY2 analyst earnings forecast error for security i.

In this section the FY2 forecast error is measured as (EPS forecast for FY2 in Month 0 – EPS forecast for FY2 at the start of month T). The robustness of the results to the use of the alternative FY2 forecast error measure is examined in a subsequent subsection.

Table 5.4 reports the results from (5.1). These results are presented to document that the FY2 forecast error has significant explanatory power in its own right. The following data, drawn from Tables 4.2 and 5.4 (Panel B for [–10,0]), compare FY1 and FY2 to illustrate this point:

	t on FY1 from (4.1)	**Adj. R^2 from (4.1)**	**t on FY2 from (5.1)**	**Adj. R^2 from (5.1)**
1977	2.821	.057	5.079	.165
1978	4.484	.110	6.493	.215
1979	4.817	.088	7.394	.187
1980	5.536	.108	9.140	.248

The next section examines the incremental explanatory power of FY2.

FY2 Incremental to FY1

This section reports results from the following regression:

$$ROR_i[t_0,t_1] = \gamma_0 + \gamma_1 . X_{1i} + \gamma_2 . X_{2i} + \gamma_3 . X_{3i} + \epsilon_i \qquad (5.2)$$

where X_{1i} = beta (relative risk as in (4.1)) of security i,

X_{2i} = FY1 analyst earnings forecast error for security i (component orthogonal to X_{1i}), and

X_{3i} = FY2 analyst earnings forecast error for security i (component orthogonal to X_{1i} and X_{2i}).

The historical evolution of research has been to examine FY1, with limited analysis of FY2. Given this evolution, (5.2) examines whether the prior focus on FY1 has underestimated the explanatory power of the vector of future earnings forecast errors.

Results using regression model (5.2) are reported in Table 5.5. The median FY1(FY2) forecast is used as the deflator of the FY1(FY2) forecast error in Panel A and the security price at the start of period T as the deflator in Panel B. These cross-sectional results provide strong support for both FY1 and FY2 variables having significant explanatory power. For instance, the t– statistics from Panel B (for [–10, 0]) are:

	FY1	**FY2**
1977	2.987	4.096
1978	4.759	4.395
1979	5.094	5.362
1980	6.390	9.263

TABLE 5.4

Cross-Section Regression of Security Return on Beta and Median FY2 Forecast Error

PANEL A: MEDIAN FY2 FORECAST AS DEFLATOR OF FY2 FORECAST ERROR VARIABLE

	γ_0	$t(\gamma_0)$	γ_1 Beta	$t(\gamma_1)$	γ_2 FY2	$t(\gamma_2)$	NOB	ADJ.R^2
1977								
[-10,0]	0.109	2.602	-0.067	-1.460	0.208	3.926	132	.106
[- 8,0]	0.051	1.979	-0.019	-0.720	0.151	3.662	228	.050
1978								
[-10,0]	-0.075	-2.823	-0.005	-0.186	0.470	7.850	148	.289
[- 8,0]	-0.119	-5.338	0.053	2.357	0.143	4.216	263	.075
1979								
[-10,0]	0.060	2.161	0.037	1.328	0.165	5.081	234	.099
[- 8,0]	0.037	1.785	-0.019	-0.911	0.265	5.870	268	.111
1980								
[-10,0]	0.119	2.570	0.087	1.865	1.165	17.333	256	.542
[- 8,0]	0.052	1.289	0.115	2.870	1.006	15.538	292	.460

PANEL B: SECURITY PRICE AT START OF MONTH -T AS DEFLATOR OF FY2 FORECAST ERROR VARIABLE

	γ_0	$t(\gamma_0)$	γ_1 Beta	$t(\gamma_1)$	γ_2 FY2	$t(\gamma_2)$	NOB	ADJ.R^2
1977								
[-10,0]	0.109	2.694	-0.066	-1.502	2.803	5.079	133	.165
[- 8,0]	0.056	2.043	-0.024	-0.873	1.209	2.759	233	.027
1978								
[-10,0]	-0.075	-2.687	-0.005	-0.177	2.140	6.493	148	.215
[- 8,0]	-0.119	-5.607	0.053	2.482	1.635	6.408	264	.147
1979								
[-10,0]	0.062	2.381	0.034	1.299	2.420	7.394	237	.187
[- 8,0]	0.035	1.674	-0.016	-0.772	1.382	5.727	274	.103
1980								
[-10,0]	0.105	1.750	0.105	1.748	2.338	9.140	258	.248
[- 8,0]	0.060	1.231	0.104	2.158	2.310	8.838	294	.216

Notes

1. Month 0 = Month in Which Actual EPS is Announced
2. Median Forecast Used as Proxy for Consensus Forecast
3. Regression is

$$ROR_i\ [t_0, t_1] = \gamma_0 + \gamma_1 . X_{1i} + \gamma_2 . X_{2i} + \varepsilon_i$$

TABLE 5.5

Cross-Section Regression of Security Return on Beta, FY1 Forecast Error and FY2 Forecast Error: FY1 Orthogonal to Beta; FY2 Orthogonal to Beta and FY1

PANEL A: MEDIAN FY1 (FY2) FORECAST AS DEFLATOR OF FY1 (FY2) FORECAST ERROR VARIABLE

	γ_0	$t(\gamma_0)$	γ_1 Beta	$t(\gamma_1)$	γ_2 FY1	$t(\gamma_2)$	γ_3 FY2	$t(\gamma_3)$	NOB	ADJ.R^2
1977										
[-10,0]	0.109	2.627	-0.067	-1.474	0.269	3.627	0.150	2.467	132	.123
[- 8,0]	0.051	1.996	-0.019	-0.727	0.193	3.450	0.115	3.450	228	.067
1978										
[-10,0]	-0.075	-2.823	-0.005	-0.186	0.178	5.749	0.422	5.431	148	.288
[- 8,0]	-0.119	-5.366	0.053	2.370	0.105	4.572	0.054	0.936	263	.085
1979										
[-10,0]	0.060	2.176	0.037	1.337	0.062	3.545	0.290	4.224	234	.111
[- 8,0]	0.037	1.781	-0.019	-0.910	0.131	3.597	0.265	4.625	268	.107
1980										
[-10,0]	0.119	2.595	0.087	1.883	0.780	14.202	1.001	10.500	256	.551
[- 8,0]	0.052	1.288	0.115	2.868	0.474	10.565	1.051	11.393	292	.459

PANEL B: SECURITY PRICE AT START OF MONTH -T AS DEFLATOR OF FY1 AND FY2 FORECAST ERROR VARIABLES

	γ_0	$t(\gamma_0)$	γ_1 Beta	$t(\gamma_1)$	γ_2 FY1	$t(\gamma_2)$	γ_3 FY2	$t(\gamma_3)$	NOB	ADJ.R^2
1977										
[-10,0]	0.109	2.685	-0.066	-1.497	1.490	2.987	2.933	4.096	133	.159
[- 8,0]	0.056	2.048	-0.024	-0.875	1.097	2.714	0.798	1.525	233	.031
1978										
[-10,0]	-0.075	-2.678	-0.005	-0.176	1.080	4.759	2.051	4.395	148	.210
[- 8,0]	-0.119	-5.625	0.053	2.490	1.095	5.948	1.150	2.932	264	.152
1979										
[-10,0]	0.062	2.377	0.034	1.297	1.149	5.094	2.583	5.362	237	.184
[- 8,0]	0.035	1.672	-0.016	-0.771	0.868	3.904	1.315	4.191	274	.100
1980										
[-10,0]	0.105	1.856	0.105	1.853	1.101	6.390	5.317	9.263	258	.331
[- 8,0]	0.060	1.254	0.104	2.198	0.666	5.103	3.469	8.164	294	.244

Notes

1. Month 0 = Month in Which Actual EPS is Announced.
2. Median Forecast Used as Proxy for Consensus Forecast.
3. Regression is

$$ROR_i\ [t_0, t_1] = \gamma_0 + \gamma_1 . X_{1i} + \gamma_2 . X_{2i} + \gamma_3 . X_{3i} + \varepsilon_i$$

Given that FY2 is orthogonalized relative to FY1, the ability of the FY2 variable to explain security price movements in the [–10,0] period is especially impressive.

FY1 Incremental to FY2

This section reports results from the following regression:

$$ROR_i[t_0,t_1] = \gamma_0 + \gamma_1 . X_{1i} + \gamma_2 . X_{2i} + \gamma_3 . X_{3i} + \epsilon_i \tag{5.3}$$

where X_{1i} = beta (relative risk as in (4.1)) of security i,

X_{2i} = FY2 analyst earnings forecast error for security i (component orthogonal to X_{1i}), and

X_{3i} = FY1 analyst earnings forecast error for security i (component orthogonal to X_{1i} and X_{2i}).

Table 5.6 reports results for (5.3). A consistent result in Table 5.6 is the significance of the FY2 variable. For instance, the t statistics from Panel B (for [–10,0]) are:

	FY2	FY1
1977	5.061	–0.287
1978	6.472	0.270
1979	7.382	–0.463
1980	9.692	–5.719

Whereas the coefficient on FY2 is highly significant in each year examined, the coefficient on FY1 is not and does not have the same sign in all four years.[5]

---

[5] As part of our specification checks, we studied the distributions of the residuals from the regressions reported in Tables 5.5 and 5.6, Panel B. While there was some evidence of skewness and kurtosis, as often occurs in rate of return data, the correlation between the absolute value of the regression residual and the predicted rate of return ranged between a minimum of –0.057 and a maximum of 0.136.

One explanation for skewness and kurtosis is undetected "errors" remaining in the data base. A useful heuristic is to re-run (5.2) and (5.3) excluding a subset of observations generating the largest absolute residuals; the assumption being that "data errors" are more likely to be associated with large values of the residuals. We re-ran (5.2) and (5.3) using 98% and 90% of the data (excluding, respectively, the two percent and ten percent of observations with the largest absolute residuals). Inferences drawn about the significance of FY2 in both (5.2) and (5.3) are unchanged. For instance, results for Panel B of (5.2) – see Table 5.5 – for [–10,0] are:

	t–statistic for FY2 in (5.2)		
	All Observations	98% of Observations	90% of Observations
1977	4.096	4.342	4.692
1978	4.395	4.563	5.299
1979	5.362	5.716	6.666
1980	9.263	9.650	8.905

The only change in the inferences drawn about FY1 was that the significant negative coefficient in 1980 for (5.3) became positive in the smaller samples. Results for Panel B of (5.3) – see Table 5.6 – for [–10,0] are:

(Footnote continued on page 96)

TABLE 5.6

Cross-Section Regression of Security Return on Beta, FY2 Forecast Error and FY1 Forecast Error: FY2 Orthogonal to Beta; FY1 Orthogonal to Beta and FY2

PANEL A: MEDIAN FY2 (FY1) FORECAST AS DEFLATOR OF FY2 (FY1) FORECAST ERROR VARIABLE

	γ_0	$t(\gamma_0)$	γ_1 Beta	$t(\gamma_1)$	γ_2 FY2	$t(\gamma_2)$	γ_3 FY1	$t(\gamma_3)$	NOB	ADJ.R^2
1977										
[-10,0]	0.109	2.627	-0.067	-1.474	0.208	3.964	0.161	1.879	132	.123
[- 8,0]	0.051	1.996	-0.019	-0.727	0.151	3.694	0.135	2.236	228	.067
1978										
[-10,0]	-0.075	-2.823	-0.005	-0.186	0.470	7.849	0.039	0.971	148	.288
[- 8,0]	-0.119	-5.366	0.053	2.370	0.143	4.239	0.076	1.952	263	.085
1979										
[-10,0]	0.060	2.176	0.037	1.337	0.165	5.116	-0.076	-2.056	234	.111
[- 8,0]	0.037	1.781	-0.109	-0.910	0.265	5.859	0.000	0.003	268	.107
1980										
[-10,0]	0.119	2.595	0.087	1.883	1.165	17.497	0.189	2.409	256	.551
[- 8,0]	0.052	1.288	0.115	2.868	1.006	15.523	-0.043	-0.675	292	.459

PANEL B: SECURITY PRICE AT START OF MONTH -T AS DEFLATOR OF FY1 AND FY2 FORECAST ERROR VARIABLES

	γ_0	$t(\gamma_0)$	γ_1 Beta	$t(\gamma_1)$	γ_2 FY2	$t(\gamma_2)$	γ_3 FY1	$t(\gamma_3)$	NOB	ADJ.R^2
1977										
[-10,0]	0.109	2.685	-0.066	-1.497	2.803	5.061	-0.185	-0.287	133	.159
[- 8,0]	0.056	2.048	-0.024	-0.875	1.209	2.765	0.692	1.431	233	.031
1978										
[-10,0]	-0.075	-2.678	-0.005	-0.176	2.140	6.472	0.086	0.270	148	.210
[- 8,0]	-0.119	-5.625	0.053	2.490	1.635	6.428	0.462	1.627	264	.152
1979										
[-10,0]	0.062	2.377	0.034	1.297	2.420	7.382	-0.153	-0.463	237	.184
[- 8,0]	0.035	1.672	-0.016	-0.771	1.382	5.718	0.098	0.339	274	.100
1980										
[-10,0]	0.105	1.856	0.105	1.853	2.338	9.692	-2.344	-5.719	258	.331
[- 8,0]	0.060	1.254	0.104	2.198	2.310	8.999	-0.739	-3.422	294	.244

Notes

1. Month 0 = Month in Which Actual EPS is Announced
2. Median Forecast Used as Proxy for Consensus Forecast
3. Regression is

$$ROR_i\,[t_0,t_1] = \gamma_0 + \gamma_1 . X_{1i} + \gamma_2 . X_{2i} + \gamma_3 . X_{3i} + \epsilon_i$$

Relative Importance of the FY1 and FY2 Variables

The X_{2i} and X_{3i} variables in (5.2) and (5.3) are orthogonalized prior to being included in the regression. This procedure facilitates computing the percentage of the variance in the rate of return that is associated with the addition of each independent variable. Table 5.7 presents summary data for these percentages for FY2 incremental to FY1 (Panel A) and FY1 incremental to FY2 (Panel B). Consider in Panel A, the second to the last column – 1979 results for when security price is used as the deflator. The beta (relative risk) variable explains 0.6% of the variance in ROR_{it} over the [–10,0] period; FY1 explains 9.0%; FY2 (orthogonalized) explains 9.9%. The sum of these percentages is 19.5%, which translates to an unadjusted R^2 of .195. The most striking pattern in Table 5.7 is in Panel B for the FY1 variable. Once FY2 enters the regression, the explanatory power of FY1 appears relatively small. This is a systematic result across all four years, across both deflators and across both the [–10,0] and [–8,0] time periods examined. The same pattern is not observed in Panel A; FY1 does not systematically dominate FY2 in explanatory power when FY1 enters the regression first. For instance, when security price is used as the deflator in Panel A, FY2 has more explanatory power than does FY1 in two of the four years examined (1979 and 1980).

Several (related) explanations for the results in Tables 5.5 to 5.7 are based on a dichotomy of reported earnings per share (E_i^R) into a permanent earnings (E_i^P) component and a transitory earnings (E_i^T) component.[6] Assume a valuation model of the following kind:

$$P_i = M_i \cdot E_i^P \tag{5.4}$$

where P_i is the price of one equity share in firm i and M_i is the multiple applied to the permanent earnings to determine P_i (M_i in the Miller-Modigliani [1966] risk-class version of (5.4) is the reciprocal of the firm's cost of capital). A permanent component of E_i^R is one for which $M_i \neq 0$. A transitory component of E_i^R is one for which

[5] *(Continued)*

	t–statistic for FY1 in (5.3)		
	All Observations	**98% of Observations**	**90% of Observations**
1977	–0.287	–0.391	0.136
1978	0.270	0.626	0.241
1979	–0.463	–0.228	0.108
1980	–5.719	1.955	1.742

Plots of the regression residuals for the smaller samples exhibited less evidence of skewness and kurtosis.

The reliability of the t-statistics was also checked by a randomization procedure, analogous to that described in Appendix 4B. The results (based on 1000 trials) were closely consistent with the inferences that may be drawn from the t-statistics reported in Tables 5.5 and 5.6.

[6] The "permanent earnings" term does not imply that the future vector of permanent earnings always can be represented by a scalar. For some statistical time-series processes (e.g., integrated moving average), this representation is possible. However, for other statistical time-series processes (e.g., autoregressive), no single number is a sufficient statistic for the future sequence of permanent earnings.

TABLE 5.7

Cross-Section Regression of Security Return on Beta, FY1 Forecast Error and FY2 Forecast Error: Relative Importance of Independent Variables

PANEL A: SEQUENCE IS FY1 FIRST THEN ORTHOGONALIZED FY2

	Median FY1(FY2) as Deflator of FY1(FY2) Forecast Error				Security Price as Deflator of FY1(FY2) Forecast Error			
	1977	1978	1979	1980	1977	1978	1979	1980
[-10,0]								
Unadjusted R^2	.143	.303	.123	.556	.178	.226	.195	.339
Weighting (%)								
Beta	1.5	0.0	0.7	0.6	1.4	0.0	0.6	0.9
FY1	8.8	16.0	4.8	35.5	5.7	12.2	9.0	10.6
FY2	4.1	14.3	6.8	19.4	10.7	10.4	9.9	22.3
[-8, 0]								
Unadjusted R^2	.079	.096	.118	.464	.044	.162	.110	.252
Weighting (%)								
Beta	0.2	2.0	0.3	1.5	0.3	2.0	0.2	1.2
FY1	4.9	7.3	4.3	20.8	3.1	11.4	5.0	6.7
FY2	2.8	0.3	7.1	24.1	1.0	2.8	5.8	17.2

PANEL B: SEQUENCE IS FY2 FIRST THEN ORTHOGONALIZED FY1

	Median FY1(FY2) as Deflator of FY1(FY2) Forecast Error				Security Price as Deflator of FY1(FY2) Forecast Error			
	1977	1978	1979	1980	1977	1978	1979	1980
[-10,0]								
Unadjusted R^2	.143	.303	.123	.556	.178	.226	.195	.339
Weighting (%)								
Beta	1.5	0.0	0.7	0.6	1.4	0.0	0.6	0.9
FY2	10.5	29.8	10.0	53.9	16.3	22.5	18.8	24.5
FY1	2.4	0.5	1.6	1.0	0.1	0.0	0.1	8.5
[-8, 0]								
Unadjusted R^2	.079	.096	.118	.464	.044	.162	.110	.252
Weighting (%)								
Beta	0.2	2.0	0.3	1.5	0.3	2.0	0.2	1.2
FY2	5.6	6.3	11.5	44.8	3.2	13.3	10.8	20.9
FY1	2.1	1.3	0.0	0.1	0.9	0.9	0.0	3.0

Notes

1. Month 0 = Month in Which Actual EPS is Announced.

2. Weighting refers to the percentage of the variance in the rate of return that is associated with each independent variable. The orthogonalization procedure is aimed at computing these weights. The weights may not sum to 100 x R-square because of minor rounding errors.

$M_i = 0$.[7] Although the accounting profession distinguishes between "extraordinary" and "ordinary" income, there need not be a one for one correspondence between the guidelines used in generally accepted accounting principles (GAAP) and the earnings concept (E_i^P) implicit in the capital market's pricing of equity securities. For instance, reported earnings per share (E_i^R) may include the effect of a major labor stoppage or strike; however, the capital market may adjust E_i^R due to its placing a low probability on another major stoppage occurring in (say) the next three years.

The results in Tables 5.5 to 5.7 of this monograph are consistent with the transitory component of the FY1 earnings forecast error being large relative to the transitory component of the FY2 earnings forecast error. This explanation assumes that analysts, when forecasting both FY1 and FY2, attempt to forecast the GAAP-based number the company will report. A related explanation for the results in Tables 5.5 to 5.7 is that analysts consciously tailor their FY1 forecasts to the GAAP-based number the company will report, but that they use their FY2 forecast to convey their expectations about permanent earnings. This latter explanation assumes that as the time to the announcement of actual earnings is reduced (say, over the –22 month to 0 month horizon), analysts switch the earnings concept they are forecasting.

Specification Checks

This subsection reports five specification checks on the results presented in Tables 5.5 to 5.7.

1. Table 5.8 presents results comparing the use of the median and mean proxies for consensus earnings forecasts. Consistent with the results reported in Tables 4.3 and 5.2, both proxies yield similar cross-sectional regression results; there is no change in the inference drawn previously that the FY2 forecast error variable is statistically significant in its own right and also when it is made orthogonal to the FY1 forecast error variable.

2. The second specification check reports results for [–T,–1] as the period used to compute the ROR_i dependent variable. Recall that the numerator of the FY2 forecast error in Tables 5.5 to 5.7 is measured as (EPS Forecast for FY2 in Month 0 – EPS Forecast for FY2 in Month T), where month 0 is the month the company reports the actual FY1 EPS figure. If (i) there are no reporting lags by analysts, and (ii) analysts use the actual FY1 to revise their FY2 forecast instantaneously, the possibility exists that the ACAR for [–T,0] will incorporate as an FY2 effect the market reaction to the actual FY1 in its announcement month.[8] Table 5.9 reports results for regressions (5.2) and (5.3) using the [–10,–1] and [–8,–1] event time periods; this excludes the FY1 announcement month effect from the dependent variable. This variation of the research design does not change the inferences drawn previously from Tables 5.5 to 5.7.

3. The third specification check involves altering the numerator of the FY2 forecast

---

[7] A transitory component has $M_i = 0$ *by definition*. We are not implying that empirically any single line item in the income statement literally will have a zero multiple. Indeed, there may be a spectrum of values associated with different components of the reported earnings series. Bowen [1981] reports evidence consistent with the capital market placing different (non-zero) multiples on components of the reported earnings series of electric utility companies.

[8] This possibility was raised at several seminars at which an earlier version of this research was presented.

TABLE 5.8

Cross-Sectional Regression of Security Return on Beta, FY1 Forecast Error and FY2 Forecast Error: Comparison of Use of Median Forecast and Mean Forecast as Proxies for Consensus When Estimating FY1 and FY2 Forecast Errors

PANEL A: SEQUENCE IS FY1 FIRST THEN ORTHOGONALIZED FY2

	Median as Proxy for Consensus			Mean as Proxy for Consensus		
	t on FY1	t on FY2	Adj. R^2	t on FY1	t on FY2	Adj. R^2
1977						
[-10,0]	3.627	2.467	.123	3.255	2.335	.104
[-8,0]	3.450	3.450	.067	2.883	2.904	.059
1978						
[-10,0]	5.749	5.431	.288	6.056	5.276	.295
[-8,0]	4.572	0.936	.085	4.632	1.060	.088
1979						
[-10,0]	3.545	4.224	.111	2.300	5.958	.145
[-8,0]	3.597	4.625	.107	3.666	4.882	.116
1980						
[-10,0]	14.202	10.500	.551	14.131	9.788	.537
[-8,0]	10.565	11.393	.459	10.047	10.838	.434

PANEL B: SEQUENCE IS FY2 FIRST THEN ORTHOGONALIZED FY1

	Median as Proxy for Consensus			Mean as Proxy for Consensus		
	t on FY2	t on FY1	Adj. R^2	t on FY2	t on FY1	Adj. R^2
1977						
[-10,0]	3.964	1.879	.123	3.986	-0.401	.104
[-8.0]	3.694	2.236	.067	3.965	1.011	.059
1978						
[-10,0]	7.849	0.971	.288	7.959	1.079	.295
[-8,0]	4.239	1.952	.085	4.367	1.871	.088
1979						
[-10,0]	5.116	-2.056	.111	4.977	-4.001	.145
[-8,0]	5.859	0.003	.107	6.105	-0.036	.116
1980						
[-10,0]	17.497	2.409	.551	17.000	2.542	.537
[-8,0]	15.523	-0.675	.459	14.750	-0.928	.434

Note

1. Month 0 = Month in Which Actual EPS is Announced.

TABLE 5.9
Cross-Sectional Regression of Security Return on Beta, FY1 Forecast Error and FY2 Forecast Error: Effect of Using [–10,–1] and [–8,–1] as Cumulation Period

PANEL A: SEQUENCE IS FY1 FIRST THEN ORTHOGONALIZED FY2

	Median FY1(FY2) as Deflator of FY1(FY2) Forecast Error			Security Price as Deflator of FY1(FY2) Forecast Error		
	t on FY1	t on FY2	Adj. R^2	t on FY1	t on FY2	Adj. R^2
1977						
[-10,-1]	4.917	2.158	.170	5.262	2.607	.199
[-8,-1]	4.730	1.240	.085	4.292	1.626	.075
1978						
[-10,-1]	6.452	3.356	.259	5.272	2.205	.173
[-8,-1]	3.630	2.155	.058	5.799	2.524	.128
1979						
[-10,-1]	3.391	5.417	.174	4.656	6.811	.245
[-8,-1]	3.944	4.297	.110	3.375	5.554	.132
1980						
[-10,-1]	13.134	8.360	.493	5.624	7.712	.270
[-8,-1]	10.190	6.450	.348	3.985	7.835	.223

PANEL B: SEQUENCE IS FY2 FIRST THEN ORTHOGONALIZED FY1

	Median FY1(FY2) as Deflator of FY1(FY2) Forecast Error			Security Price as Deflator of FY1(FY2) Forecast Error		
	t on FY2	t on FY1	Adj. R^2	t on FY2	t on FY1	Adj. R^2
1977						
[-10,-1]	4.479	2.961	.170	5.690	1.453	.199
[-8,-1]	3.062	3.812	.085	4.238	1.760	.075
1978						
[-10,-1]	6.984	2.029	.259	5.275	2.199	.173
[-8,-1]	4.192	-0.496	.058	6.264	0.868	.128
1979						
[-10,-1]	5.419	-3.387	.174	7.921	-2.309	.245
[-8,-1]	5.822	0.359	.110	6.444	-0.842	.132
1980						
[-10,-1]	15.395	2.317	.493	7.996	-5.212	.270
[-8,-1]	12.023	0.940	.348	6.988	-5.332	.223

Note

1. Month 0 = Month in Which Actual EPS is Announced.

error variable to (Actual EPS for FY2 – EPS Forecast for FY2 in Month T). This numerator uses a forecast available at the start of the [–T,0] ROR_i event time period and an actual FY2 figure that is released (typically) twelve months after the end of the event period. Even if analysts do extract information from security price changes in the [–T,0] period when revising forecasts made subsequent to –T, these forecast revisions will not be reflected in the Actual EPS component of the numerator of the FY2 forecast error variable. Thus, this numerator helps circumvent any observed association between security price changes and analyst forecast revisions being significant by construction of the FY2 error measure. Table 5.10 reports results for both (5.2) and (5.3). Again the inferences drawn previously appear robust to this specification check.

4. The results in Tables 5.4 to 5.10 are based on use of either (i) the actual FY1 (FY2) forecast, or (ii) security price as the deflator of the FY1 (FY2) forecast error. Chapter 3 also reported forecast error measures using a third deflator – the average absolute change in actual EPS over the 1976-1980 period. Summary results for (5.2) and (5.3) with the use of this deflator (for the [–10,0] period using the median forecast as the proxy for the consensus forecast) are:

	(5.2)		**(5.3)**	
	t on FY1	**t on FY2**	**t on FY2**	**t on FY1**
1977	4.051	2.890	4.914	0.783
1978	7.164	1.713	6.465	3.529
1979	6.252	4.005	7.138	2.045
1980	11.167	8.401	13.608	3.177

These results reinforce the prior findings for FY2. The results for FY1 in (5.3) are the most significant found in the alternative specifications examined in this research.

5. As a final specification check, (5.2) and (5.3) were run with the beta variable excluded from the regression and excluded from any orthogonalization procedure. Results using the average absolute change in actual EPS over the 1976-1980 period as the deflator of the FY1 and FY2 forecast errors (for the [–10,0] period using the median forecast as the proxy for the consensus forecast) are:

	(5.2) excluding X_{1i}		**(5.3) excluding X_{1i}**	
	t on FY1	**t on FY2**	**t on FY2**	**t on FY1**
1977	4.038	2.876	4.891	0.779
1978	7.188	1.719	6.487	3.541
1979	6.243	3.999	7.127	2.042
1980	11.101	8.352	13.528	3.158

These results are similar to those reported above in 4. for when the beta variable is included in (5.2) and (5.3).

Summary

Based on the analysis in Section 5.2, three findings are robust across all the specifications examined:

TABLE 5.10

Cross-Section Regression of Security Return on Beta, FY1 Forecast Error and FY2 Forecast Error: Effect of Using Actual FY2 in Numerator of FY2 Forecast Error Measure

PANEL A: SEQUENCE IS FY1 FIRST THEN ORTHOGONALIZED FY2

	Actual FY1(FY2) as Deflator of FY1(FY2) Forecast Error			Security Price As Deflator of FY1(FY2) Forecast Error		
	t on FY1	t on FY2	Adj. R^2	t on FY1	t on FY2	Adj. R^2
1977						
[-10,0]	3.644	2.703	.131	2.917	3.162	.118
[-8,0]	3.546	4.443	.116	2.792	3.974	.084
1978						
[-10,0]	5.561	4.283	.240	4.558	2.415	.139
[-8,0]	4.593	1.808	.094	5.912	2.316	.142
1979						
[-10,0]	3.417	0.501	.043	4.905	3.104	.120
[-8,0]	3.744	6.715	.176	3.921	4.488	.108
1980						
[-10,0]	13.777	9.426	.522	5.601	2.644	.129
[-8,0]	9.946	9.069	.389	4.639	2.191	.085

PANEL B: SEQUENCE IS FY2 FIRST THEN ORTHOGONALIZED FY1

	Actual FY1(FY2) as Deflator of FY1(FY2) Forecast Error			Security Price As Deflator of FY1(FY2) Forecast Error		
	t on FY2	t on FY1	Adj. R^2	t on FY2	t on FY1	Adj. R^2
1977						
[-10,0]	4.316	1.398	.131	4.010	1.558	.118
[-8,0]	5.643	0.681	.116	4.769	0.916	.084
1978						
[-10,0]	6.397	2.889	.240	4.649	2.235	.139
[-8.0]	4.439	2.158	.094	5.494	3.183	.142
1979						
[-10,0]	3.324	0.936	.043	5.391	2.152	.120
[-8,0]	7.574	1.317	.176	5.878	0.985	.108
1980						
[-10,0]	15.348	6.564	.522	6.192	-0.126	.129
[-8,0]	12.495	5.004	.389	5.128	0.175	.085

Note

1. Month 0 = Month in Which Actual EPS is Announced.

(1) the FY1 forecast error variable is significant when it enters the regression prior to the FY2 forecast error variable,

(2) the FY2 forecast error variable is significant when it enters the regression prior to the FY1 forecast error variable, and

(3) the FY2 forecast error variable is significant when it enters the regression after having been made orthogonal to the FY1 forecast error variable.

Inferences about the significance of the FY1 forecast error variable when it enters the regression after having been made orthogonal to the FY2 forecast error variable are contingent on the regression specification examined. The specification showing the strongest level of significance is when the average absolute change in EPS (1976-1980) is used as the deflator; the coefficients on FY1 are positive in all four years and statistically significant (at the .01 level) in three of those four years. Other specifications show at least one year with a negative coefficient for FY1 and typically lower levels of statistical significance across all four years.

5.3 Association Between Analyst FY2 Forecast Revisions and Security Price Changes: IBES Revision Month as Event Month 0

The tests in Section 5.2 defined month 0 to be the actual earnings announcement. The tests in this section define month 0 to be the IBES revision month. This section extends the FY1 analysis in Section 4.4 to incorporate information about the sign and magnitude of the FY2 forecast revision.

A. Portfolio Analysis Using Sign of FY1 and FY2 Forecast Revisions

For firms with data available for the sign of the consensus forecast revision in month 0 for both FY1 (–, 0, or +) and FY2 (–, 0, or +), observations are classified into one of nine categories. The percentages of observations falling into these nine categories for each of the three proxies for consensus earnings forecasts are:

			Median as Proxy	Mean as Proxy	(# ↑)–(# ↓) as Proxy
FY1– and FY2–	=	– –	14.0%	25.3%	15.6%
FY1– and FY20	=	– 0	8.0	4.9	14.9
FY1– and FY2+	=	– +	4.3	9.2	2.7
FY10 and FY2–	=	0 –	9.8	2.3	2.5
FY10 and FY20	=	0 0	23.0	8.7	20.7
FY10 and FY2+	=	0 +	9.6	2.2	2.9
FY1+ and FY2–	=	+ –	5.8	11.8	3.2
FY1+ and FY20	=	+ 0	8.9	5.4	17.8
FY1+ and FY2+	=	+ +	16.6	30.2	19.7

The number of observations is 19,582 for both the median and the mean proxy and 22,264 for the (# ↑)–(# ↓) proxy.

Tables 5.11, 5.12, and 5.13 present the ACAR for the above nine FY1/FY2 portfolios (and for the three FY1 portfolios) using the median, mean, and [(# ↑)–(# ↓)] proxies for consensus earnings forecasts, respectively. Figure 5.1 presents the behavior of the ACAR over the [–12, +12] event month period for the

TABLE 5.11

FY1/FY2 Consensus Forecast Revisions and Security Price Revisions: Median Forecast as Proxy for Consensus Forecast; IBES Reporting Month as Month 0

	MONTHS -12 TO -2			MONTH -1			MONTH 0			MONTHS -1 TO 0			MONTHS 1 TO 12		
	ACAR	t	FFEQ	AAR	t	FFEQ	AAR	t	FREQ	ACAR	t	FREQ	ACAR	t	FREQ
A. SINGLE YEAR: FY1															
-	-7.91	-25.80	1.00	-1.41	-14.18	1.00	-0.77	-7.61	1.00	-2.18	-15.59	1.00	-3.69	-10.53	1.00
0	-1.17	- 5.00	1.00	-0.12	- 1.67	1.00	-0.24	-3.14	1.00	-0.36	- 3.43	1.00	-1.22	- 4.68	0.99
+	5.37	19.14	0.00	1.02	11.24	0.00	0.55	6.34	0.00	1.56	12.70	0.00	0.87	2.87	0.00
B. MULTI-YEAR: FY1, FY2															
--	-10.03	-24.47	1.00	-2.00	-15.17	1.00	-1.27	-9.24	1.00	-3.27	-17.56	1.00	-4.22	-8.79	1.00
-0	- 6.88	-12.38	1.00	-0.95	- 5.16	1.00	-0.36	-1.96	0.98	-1.31	- 5.21	1.00	-3.66	-5.70	1.00
-+	- 3.00	- 3.81	1.00	-0.36	- 1.41	0.91	0.07	0.26	0.34	-0.29	- 0.79	0.68	-2.04	-2.40	0.97
0-	- 4.56	-10.69	1.00	-0.54	- 3.86	1.00	-0.55	-3.59	0.99	-1.09	- 5.30	1.00	-3.72	-7.27	1.00
00	- 0.53	- 1.61	0.76	-0.13	- 1.25	0.81	-0.19	-1.79	0.96	-0.32	- 2.17	0.96	-0.11	-0.29	0.36
0+	0.76	1.59	0.04	0.31	2.01	0.01	-0.04	-0.25	0.47	0.28	1.28	0.05	-1.35	-2.56	0.88
+-	1.49	2.36	0.00	0.33	1.57	0.05	-0.09	-0.48	0.58	0.23	0.83	0.21	-0.45	-0.65	0.64
+0	3.55	6.94	0.00	0.60	3.79	0.00	0.29	1.83	0.04	0.89	4.11	0.00	0.18	0.32	0.29
++	7.72	19.74	0.00	1.48	11.55	0.00	0.91	7.53	0.00	2.39	13.72	0.00	1.70	4.02	0.00

NOTES

1. ACAR = Average Cumulative Abnormal Return; AAR = Average Abnormal Return

2. FREQ = Frequency with which the ACAR or AAR was exceeded in 100 trials in which assignment of firms to FY1 and FY1/FY2 categories were random

TABLE 5.12

FY1/FY2 Consensus Forecast Revisions and Security Price Revisions: Mean Forecast as Proxy for Consensus Forecast; IBES Reporting Month as Month 0

	MONTHS [-12 TO -2]			MONTH [-1]			MONTH [0]			MONTHS [-1 TO 0]			MONTHS [+1 TO +12]		
	ACAR	t	FREQ	AAR	t	FREQ	AAR	t	FREQ	ACAR	t	FREQ	ACAR	t	FREQ
A. SINGLE YEAR: FY1															
-	-7.48	-31.42	1.00	-1.16	-14.94	1.00	-0.75	-9.37	1.00	-1.91	-17.39	1.00	-3.80	-13.84	1.00
0	1.50	3.12	0.00	0.08	0.53	0.15	-0.04	-0.24	0.49	0.04	0.20	0.30	1.94	3.72	0.00
+	3.91	17.71	0.00	0.72	10.13	0.00	0.35	5.14	0.00	1.07	10.94	0.00	0.04	0.17	0.24
B. MULTI-YEAR: FY1, FY2															
--	-9.04	-31.34	1.00	-1.56	-16.54	1.00	-1.05	-10.65	1.00	-2.60	-19.58	1.00	-4.57	-13.31	1.00
-0	-5.72	-7.78	1.00	-1.20	-5.13	1.00	-0.37	-1.51	0.94	-1.57	-4.70	1.00	-2.35	-2.97	0.99
-+	-4.15	-8.36	1.00	-0.07	-0.43	0.61	-0.13	-0.82	0.73	-0.20	-0.88	0.77	-2.46	-4.41	1.00
0-	-2.06	-2.13	0.91	-0.29	-0.92	0.78	-0.39	-1.30	0.90	-0.68	-1.59	0.92	-2.16	-1.98	0.95
00	2.84	4.49	0.00	0.05	0.23	0.25	0.10	0.51	0.26	0.15	0.54	0.25	3.25	4.80	0.00
0+	-0.03	-0.03	0.36	0.59	1.80	0.07	-0.22	-0.69	0.70	0.37	0.81	0.18	1.06	0.93	0.14
+-	0.53	1.27	0.06	-0.09	-0.69	0.64	-0.35	-2.68	0.99	-0.44	-2.42	0.97	-1.97	-4.16	1.00
+0	2.77	3.97	0.00	0.57	2.61	0.00	0.31	1.49	0.05	0.88	2.89	0.00	1.32	1.73	0.03
++	5.43	19.60	0.00	1.07	11.75	0.00	0.64	7.29	0.00	1.70	13.65	0.00	0.60	1.99	0.02

NOTES

1. ACAR = Average Cumulative Abnormal Return; AAR = Average Abnormal Return

2. FREQ = Frequency with which the ACAR or AAR was exceeded in 100 trials in which assignment of firms to FY1 and FY1/FY2 categories were random.

TABLE 5.13

FY1/FY2 Consensus Forecast Revisions and Security Price Revisions: (# ↑)–(# ↓) as Proxy for Consensus Forecast; IBES Reporting Month as Month 0

	MONTHS [-12 TO -2]			MONTH [-1]			MONTH [0]			MONTHS [-1 TO 0]			MONTHS [+1 TO +12]		
	ACAR	t	FREQ	AAR	t	FREQ	AAR	t	FREQ	ACAR	t	FREQ	ACAR	t	FREQ
A. SINGLE YEAR: FY1															
-	-8.57	-35.37	1.00	-1.48	-18.71	1.00	-0.85	-10.35	1.00	-2.33	-20.84	1.00	-3.89	-13.81	1.00
0	1.08	3.54	0.00	0.10	1.08	0.01	0.03	0.28	0.23	0.13	0.96	0.04	0.55	1.68	0.01
+	4.39	19.46	0.00	0.91	12.60	0.00	0.41	6.19	0.00	1.35	13.60	0.00	0.13	0.53	0.17
B. MULTI-YEAR: FY1, FY2															
--	-10.87	-31.43	1.00	-2.18	-19.44	1.00	-1.24	-10.49	1.00	-3.41	-21.51	1.00	-4.68	-11.12	1.00
-0	-7.26	-19.75	1.00	-1.00	-8.39	1.00	-0.57	-4.52	1.00	-1.57	-9.31	1.00	-3.44	-8.40	1.00
-+	-2.62	-3.26	0.99	-0.08	-0.28	0.60	-0.20	-0.76	0.68	-0.28	-0.72	0.69	-1.78	-1.86	0.88
0-	-2.00	-2.32	0.90	-0.73	-2.80	1.00	-0.62	-2.05	0.96	-1.41	-3.51	1.00	-4.78	-4.65	1.00
00	1.20	3.44	0.00	0.07	0.69	0.08	0.10	0.88	0.08	0.17	1.11	0.04	1.38	3.65	0.00
0+	3.01	3.26	0.00	1.10	3.96	0.00	0.10	0.38	0.27	1.20	3.03	0.00	-0.67	-0.77	0.63
+-	-2.17	-3.07	0.97	-0.54	-2.28	0.96	-0.54	-2.41	0.95	-1.08	-3.40	0.99	-3.49	-4.06	0.99
+0	2.96	8.83	0.00	0.77	6.65	0.00	0.39	3.60	0.00	1.10	7.37	0.00	0.24	0.66	0.20
++	6.74	20.43	0.00	1.33	12.42	0.00	0.64	6.28	0.00	1.97	13.62	0.00	0.62	1.73	0.13

NOTES

1. ACAR = Average Cumulative Abnormal Return; AAR = Average Abnormal Return
2. FREQ = Frequency with which the ACAR or AAR was exceeded in 100 trials in which assignment of firms to FY1 and FY1/FY2 categories were random.

FIGURE 5.1

Average Cumulative Abnormal Returns Surrounding IBES Earnings Forecast Revision Month for FY1/FY2 Portfolios: Median Forecast as Proxy for Consensus Forecast

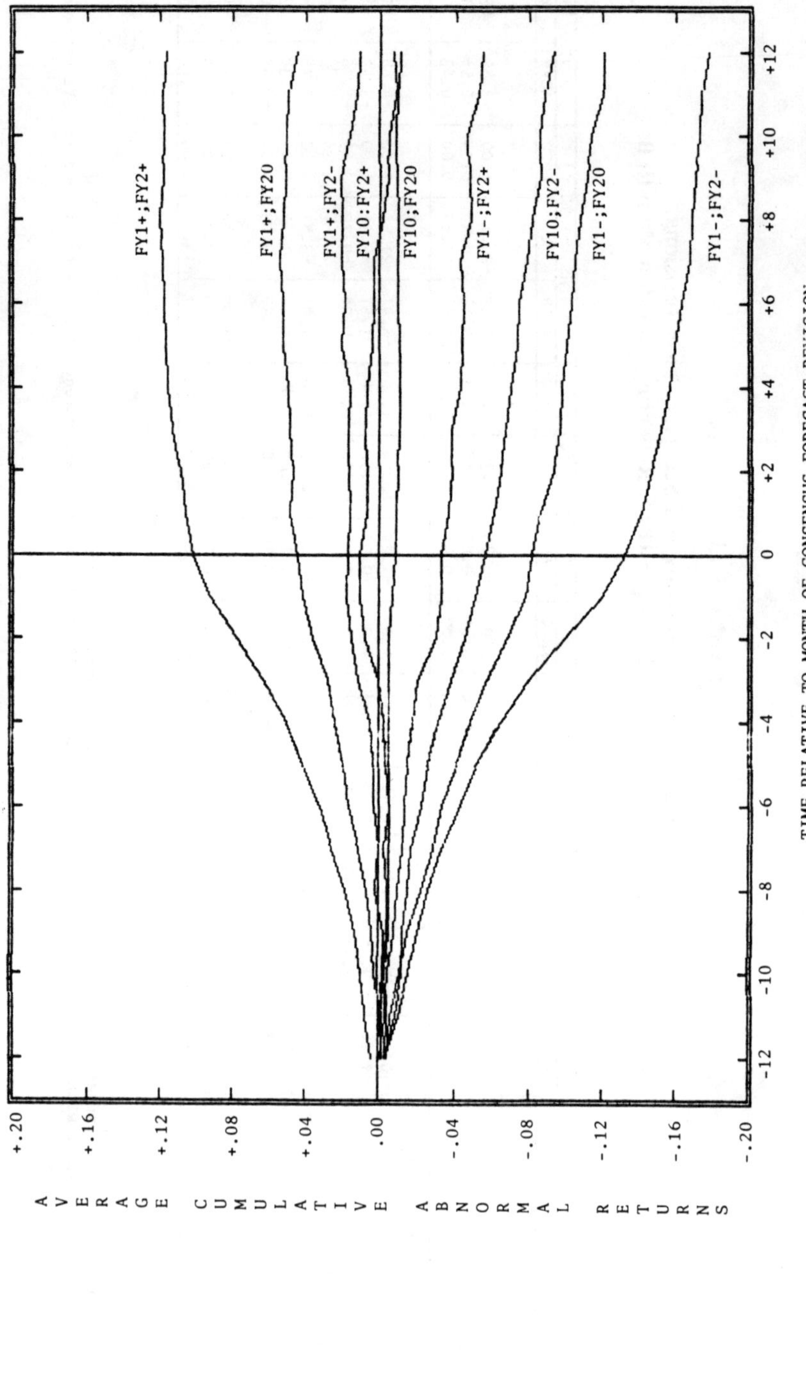

Table 5.11 data. Focusing on the [–12,0] event time, the predicted multi-year triples for each single year forecast revision category, if the capital market distinguishes between alternative combinations of FY1 and FY2 earnings forecast revisions, are:

(i) $ACAR^{--} < ACAR^{-0} < ACAR^{-+}$

(ii) $ACAR^{0-} < ACAR^{00} < ACAR^{0+}$

(iii) $ACAR^{+-} < ACAR^{+0} < ACAR^{++}$

The only violations of the above predictions are in category (ii) (FY1 = 0); violations are observed for months [–12,–2] and month [0] for the mean proxy and month [0] for the [(# ↑)–(# ↓)] proxy. The above predictions hold for categories (i) and (iii) across all three proxies and for category (ii) using the median proxy in each of the [–12 to –2], [–1], [0], and [–1,0] time periods.

Although the results in Tables 5.11 to 5.13 are consistent with FY2 conveying additional information over and above that in FY1, the research design does not control for the magnitude of FY1 forecast revisions – see Section 5.2A for further discussion. To examine this possible confounding variable, the magnitude of the FY1 forecast revision for all observations in the nine FY1/FY2 (and the three FY1) portfolios was calculated and the deciles of the distribution for each portfolio calculated. Table 5.14 presents these results. At best, the magnitude of the FY1 revision only partially explains the CAR results. Consider the median FY1 forecast error and ACAR of each FY1/FY2 category:

	Magnitude of Scaled FY1 Forecast Revision	**ACAR for [–12,–2]**	**ACAR for [–1,0]**
– –	–.118	–10.03	–3.27
– 0	–.080	–6.88	–1.31
– +	–.081	–3.00	–0.29
+ –	.079	1.49	0.23
+ 0	.075	3.55	0.89
+ +	.101	7.72	2.39

While the magnitude of the FY1 effect may partially explain the –– (vis-a-vis the –0 and – +) and the + + (vis-a-vis the + – and + 0) ACAR results, it does not explain the ACAR results of –0 (–6.88%) vis-a-vis – + (–3.00%) or the ACAR results of + 0 (3.55%) vis-a-vis + – (1.49%).

B. Portfolio Analysis Using Sign and Magnitude of FY2 Revisions When FY1 Revision = 0

One subset of the data examined in Tables 5.11 to 5.13 contains a built-in control for the magnitude of the FY1 forecast revision when examining the FY2 forecast revision, i.e., the subset for which FY1 = 0 but FY2 ≠ 0. This section examines this subset for when the median is used as the proxy for consensus forecasts. The median proxy has

TABLE 5.14

Magnitude of FY1 Forecast Revision (Deflated by Average Absolute Change in Actual EPS) for Portfolios Formed Using the Signs of the FY1 and FY1/FY2 Forecast Errors: Deciles for Each Portfolio Using Median Forecast as Proxy for Consensus Forecast

	DECILES OF DISTRIBUTION								
	.1	.2	.3	.4	.5	.6	.7	.8	.9
FY1 BASED PORTFOLIOS									
-	-.387	-.240	-.172	-.131	-.100	-.075	-.057	-.041	-.024
0	.000	.000	.000	.000	.000	.000	.000	.000	.000
+	.023	.039	.054	.070	.088	.111	.144	.193	.296
FY1/FY2 BASED PORTFOLIOS									
--	-.455	-.291	-.204	-.153	-.118	-.093	-.069	-.050	-.029
-0	-.313	-.196	-.143	-.111	-.080	-.061	-.048	-.035	-.020
-+	-.291	-.182	-.136	-.100	-.081	-.062	-.046	-.033	-.021
0-	.000	.000	.000	.000	.000	.000	.000	.000	.000
00	.000	.000	.000	.000	.000	.000	.000	.000	.000
0+	.000	.000	.000	.000	.000	.000	.000	.000	.000
+-	.020	.032	.046	.062	.079	.096	.127	.067	.244
+0	.020	.034	.046	.060	.075	.093	.116	.161	.236
++	.028	.044	.062	.081	.101	.130	.167	.231	.344

the largest number of observations in the 0– and 0+ portfolios.[9] A t–test was performed on the mean difference between the ACAR of the two portfolios with the following significant results:[10]

	Holding Periods		
	[−12, −2]	**[−1, 0]**	**[+1, +12]**
ACAR for 0+ less ACAR for 0–	5.32%	1.37%	2.37%
t–test for difference	8.30	5.17	3.10

To further probe the FY1 = 0; FY2 ≠ 0 categories, the observations in each of the 0– and 0+ portfolios were ranked using the magnitude of the FY2 revision and formed into five sub-portfolios. Table 5.15 reports the ACAR results for these sub-portfolios. For both the [–12,–2] and [–1,0] periods, there is a significant correlation between the sign and rank of the FY2 forecast revision and the sign and rank of the ACAR. This result confirms the finding of prior sections that the FY2 variable is a significant variable in explaining security price changes.

5.4 Extensions to Wells Fargo Individual Analyst Multi-Year Earnings Forecast Data Base

One attractive feature of the Wells Fargo data base described in Chapter 2 is that it contains earnings forecasts for each year of a five-year horizon. This section extends the Section 5.2B cross-sectional regression analysis to incorporate forecast revisions for this horizon. The unavailability (as of 1983) of actual results covering the full five-year horizon precluded computation of forecast error measures over this horizon. The following regression was estimated for 1977, 1978, and 1979:

$$ROR_{it} = \gamma_0 + \gamma_1 . X_{1i} + \gamma_2 . X_{2i} + \gamma_3 . X_{3i} + \gamma_4 . X_{4i} + \gamma_5 . X_{5i} + \gamma_6 . X_{6i} + \epsilon_i \qquad (5.4)$$

where ROR_{it} = security rate of return (February to December of year t),

X_{1i} = beta of security i, and

X_{2i} to X_{6i} = relative change in EPS forecasts from January 31 to December 31 of year t for each year of the five-year horizon.

As with the other regressions reported in this chapter, X_{2i} is made orthogonal to X_{1i}; X_{3i} is made orthogonal to X_{1i} and X_{2i}; ...; X_{6i} is made orthogonal to X_{1i}, X_{2i}, X_{3i}, X_{4i}, and X_{5i}. This procedure facilitates computing the weighting statistics reported in Table

[9] Clearly each proxy measures the consensus forecast construct with error. What we interpret as FY1 = 0 is probably better described as FY1 ≈ 0. This is accentuated if analysts choose not to report to IBES updates of their forecasts if they only contain minor revisions of their prior forecasts.

[10] The non-parametric randomization test, described in Appendix 4.B, was also employed. In none of the 100 trials was the observed mean difference for (0 +)–(0–) exceeded in any of the three time periods examined.

TABLE 5.15
ACAR's of Portfolios Using Magnitude of FY2 for Subset of Observations with FY1 = 0: Event Month 0 is Forecast Revision Month as Reported by IBES

MAGNITUDE OF FY2	CUMULATION PERIOD [-12, -2]	[-1, 0]	[+1, +12]
N5 (20% most negative FY2)	-5.52	-1.37	-5.41
N4	-5.69	-1.33	-5.98
N3	-3.55	-0.69	-2.78
N2	-4.47	-0.53	-2.35
N1 (20% least negative FY2)	-3.69	-1.30	-1.85
P1 (20% least positive FY2)	0.34	0.40	1.54
P2	1.10	-0.46	-0.63
P3	0.26	0.28	-2.85
P4	0.32	0.63	-2.75
P5 (20% most positive FY2)	1.47	0.49	-3.55
Spearman Rank Correlation Between Magnitude of FY2 and ACAR	.885	.915	.285

5.7 for the IBES data base. In order to facilitate comparison with the prior work in this chapter, the forecast years were entered into the orthogonalization sequence in two ways:

(i) FY1 first, then FY2, FY3, FY4, FY5

(ii) FY5 first, then FY4, FY3, FY2, FY1.

Summary results are presented in Table 5.16.

Consider Panel A of Table 5.16 which reports the FY1, FY2, ..., FY5 orthogonalization sequence. The most striking feature is the relative significance of the forecast years beyond FY1, in particular FY2. This finding is consistent with that reported using the IBES data base.

Panel B of Table 5.16 reports the FY5, FY4, ..., FY1 orthogonalization sequence. One feature of the Wells Fargo data base noted in Chapter 2 was the increasingly high correlation in successive adjacent forecast years across the forecast horizon; the median correlation for FY5 and FY4 forecast revisions across the sample of firms exceeds .95 – see Table 2.9. Given this finding, the results in Panel B of Table 5.16 are not surprising. Once FY5 is included in the regression, adding FY4 has minimal incremental explanatory power. In terms of relative explanatory power, the FY5 variable is the most important one in all three years examined.

The above results provide evidence consistent with (i) the capital market having an earnings forecast horizon longer than one year, and (ii) FY1 not fully capturing the signal embodied in revisions to the earnings sequence over the multi-year horizon. These findings reinforce those found with the IBES consensus forecast data base.

TABLE 5.16

Cross-Sectional Regression of Security Returns[1] on Beta and Wells Fargo Analyst Earnings Forecast Revisions for Five-Year Horizon Period

PANEL A: VARIABLE ORTHOGONALIZATION SEQUENCE IS FY1, FY2, FY3, FY4, FY5

Statistic	1977	1978	1979
R^2 (unadj.)	.425	.529	.367
t-statistics:			
--constant	-3.41	-2.15	7.05
--beta	-0.17	5.10	-1.66
--FY1	11.59	9.11	5.67
--FY2	5.11	8.41	6.63
--FY3	1.11	8.42	3.47
--FY4	-0.42	1.08	6.63
--FY5	0.19	3.26	0.66
Weighting (%):[2]			
--beta	0.0	5.9	0.7
--FY1	35.3	16.7	8.7
--FY2	6.8	14.2	12.0
--FY3	0.3	14.2	3.3
--FY4	0.0	0.2	11.9
--FY5	0.0	2.1	0.1
NOB	226	242	240

PANEL B: VARIABLE ORTHOGONALIZATION SEQUENCE IS FY5, FY4, FY3, FY2, FY1

Statistic	1977	1978	1979
R^2 (unadj.)	.425	.529	.367
t-statistics:			
--constant	-3.41	-2.15	7.05
--beta	-0.17	5.10	-1.66
--FY5	10.92	14.98	10.96
--FY4	2.05	0.93	1.29
--FY3	4.61	2.09	-1.10
--FY2	3.96	1.55	3.25
--FY1	1.19	2.12	0.68
Weighting[2]:			
--beta	0.0	5.9	0.7
--FY5	31.3	45.0	32.6
--FY4	1.1	0.2	0.5
--FY3	5.6	0.9	0.3
--FY2	4.1	0.5	2.9
--FY1	0.4	0.9	0.1
NOB	226	242	240

Notes

1. Security returns are measured over the eleven month period up to and including the end of the FY1 fiscal year.

2. "Weight" refers to the percentage of the variance in the rate of return that is associated with each independent variable. The orthogonalization procedure is aimed at computing these weights. The weights may not sum to 100 x R-square because of minor rounding errors.

CHAPTER 6

OVERVIEW OF FINDINGS AND THEIR RESEARCH IMPLICATIONS

6.1 Introduction

This chapter discusses the major findings in the monograph, possible extensions of the research, and how our findings may affect inferences drawn from the existing literature. The following discussion does not provide a detailed statement of the importance of our results (see Chapter 1 – Introduction and Summary). Nor does this chapter provide a detailed linking of our results with the results of the many prior studies in the earnings forecast literature (see Appendix – Research on Earnings Forecasts: A Literature Review and Classified Bibliography).

6.2 The Association Between Security Analysts' Multi-Year Earnings Forecasts and Security Returns

The most important result in this monograph is that earnings forecast errors or forecast revisions for fiscal years beyond the current one are important when explaining security returns in the period up to and including the month the current year's earnings are announced. This result is found in several time series and cross-sectional tests using the IBES data base and in cross-sectional tests using the Wells Fargo data base. Results for each year of the 1977 to 1980 period using the IBES data base and each year of the 1977 to 1979 period using the Wells Fargo data base are presented. The consistency of the findings across data bases, tests, and years examined greatly increases our confidence in the inference that the capital market has a multi-year earnings horizon and is not fixated on the current year's GAAP-based earnings.

The finding that horizon years beyond FY1 have important explanatory power gives added interest to benchmark studies comparing the forecasts of security analysts, management, and mechanical models using a multi-year horizon period in their analysis. The existing literature has concentrated on comparisons using forecasts of interim or annual earnings in the FY1 period. (See Section 6 of the Appendix.)

Our finding that years beyond FY1 have important explanatory power also has implications for studies on the capital market reaction to accounting changes or accounting policy decisions. One popular research design is to conduct a cross-sectional regression with the dependent variable being security returns and the independent variables including an FY1 earnings forecast error term and a term coding the accounting change or regulatory intervention. Our results imply that such a regression has an omitted variable – i.e., earnings forecast revisions for years beyond FY1 are omitted. (Whether this omitted variable affects inferences drawn from the regression will depend on the correlation between the omitted variable and the variable coding the accounting change or regulatory intervention.)

One explanation for the Chapter 5 result that FY2 has incremental explanatory power to FY1, but not vice versa, is that the reported earnings figure for FY1 has a substantial transitory earnings component. An extension of our research would be to operationalize the transitory earnings component. Such research could examine (i) whether there are items below the earnings before extraordinary items figure in the FY1 income statement that the capital market views as permanent (i.e., assigns a positive multiple (say M) in price determination), and (ii) whether there are items above the earnings before extraordinary items figure that the capital market views as transitory (i.e., assigns a zero multiple in price determination). The permanent-transitory dichotomy of reported earnings is used for analytical purposes. It is likely that empirical research will find that valuation at 0 (transitory) or M (permanent) represents end points of a spectrum with line items in the income statement having differing multiples between 0 and M. Such a finding would be inconsistent with the single earnings series (with a single multiple) equity valuation models found in many finance textbooks.

6.3 The Effect of Information Timeliness on Capital Market Association Measures

Chapter 4 presents evidence that use of a more timely expectations model enables a researcher to better approximate the capital market's classification of firms into "bad news" (actual earnings released in month 0 is less than forecasted earnings in month –T) or "good news" (actual earnings released in month 0 exceeds earnings forecasted in month –T) categories. This finding has implications for the many announcement effect studies in the accounting and finance literatures. By using less timely expectations models, researchers may underestimate the revaluation implications of a given signal.

One area where the choice of a timely expectations model is important is research on the information content of management forecasts. Early research (e.g., Patell [1976]) raised the issue of whether the *act* of management voluntarily releasing an earnings forecast conveys "good news" information. One approach to addressing this issue is to use the most recent security analyst forecast as the expectations model when classifying management forecasts into "bad news" and "good news" categories. Security analysts can update their expectations in a more timely way than can expectations models based on the past series of reported annual or interim earnings.

The research in Chapter 4 on timeliness can be extended in several ways. One direction is to exploit the magnitude as well as the sign of the earnings forecast error. A second direction is to use sequences of forecasts from individual security analysts rather than the consensus forecasts used in Chapter 4. The advantage of the consensus forecast data base is that a sequence of monthly updates can be accessed for a large number of firms. The disadvantage is that consensus forecasts typically are aggregates of individual forecasts of varying degrees of timeliness. By focusing specifically on individual analyst forecasts, the researcher can control better for timing differences. (However, it is likely that forecast revisions of many individual analysts are made at less regular intervals than one month, and non-uniform periods exist between those revisions.)

Another research direction associated with timeliness issues is to explore the effect of using alternative samples when computing consensus forecasts for each month. Two alternative samples are:

1. Use the forecasts of all analysts, irrespective of whether a revision is reported to IBES in that month. The mean and median consensus measures used in this research are computed by IBES using this sample.
2. Use the forecasts of only those analysts who report a revision to IBES in that month. This approach implicitly assumes that a no-revision observation is due to an analyst not reconsidering the prior forecast, rather than no update being reported to

IBES due to the analyst still believing the prior forecast to be appropriate. The ((#↑)–(#↓)) consensus measure used in this research is computed using this sample.

The results reported in Table 4.5 and Tables 5.11 to 5.13 are consistent with both samples yielding similar inferences for the specific issue examined in those tables. An interesting extension would be to examine (in a variety of research contexts) those cases where the different samples give different predictions as to the sign and direction of consensus forecast changes.

6.4 The Properties of Security Analysts' Multi-Year Earnings Forecasts

Chapters 4 and 5 report that the sign and magnitude of security returns in the twelve-month period *preceding* a revision in consensus security analyst earnings forecasts are positively associated with the sign of the single year and multi-year forecast revisions. Alternative explanations for this finding include:

- security prices impound information to which analysts do not yet have access (insider trading by management is one mechanism by which information internal to the firm can be impounded into security prices),
- security analysts are less efficient processors of publicly available information than is the aggregate capital market,
- security analysts deliberately delay releasing an earnings forecast revision until they have used it to trade on their personal account,
- severe time lags exist between individual analyst revisions being made public and their inclusion in consensus forecast data bases (or the methods used to compute consensus forecasts in those data bases overly weight non-timely forecasts), and
- security analysts use price changes as a cue to revise earnings forecasts.

An important future research area is discriminating between the above (and other) explanations. For example, one direction would be to examine security returns preceding forecast revisions by *individual* analysts. Such research would avoid the explanation that severe time lags exist with consensus forecast data bases. This research direction would also contribute to the issue of whether security analysts are rational (in the sense of fully exploiting available information) in their forecast revisions – see Givoly and Lakonishok [1983a] for further discussion.

Chapter 4 presented preliminary evidence on the relative contribution of prior security returns in explaining security analyst forecast revisions. The conclusion is that the explanatory power, at the individual security level, is not large (no more than ten percent). Future work in this area could explore econometric and economic modeling issues not addressed in our preliminary analysis. One econometric issue arises from overlapping time periods in a subset of the regressions reported in Section 4.4. This problem could be reduced by sampling every nth revision rather than including revisions for every month when examining security return periods longer than [–1,–1]; e.g., when examining security returns in the [–11,–1] period, the researcher could sample monthly forecast revisions twelve months apart. Economic modeling issues include (a) the choice of the time period that analysts "use" in their forecast revision analysis (this may differ over time or across different securities) and (b) the possible role that key individuals may play as ''lead'' analysts in an industry. The data base required to examine (b) would include information on the timing and amount of individual security analysts' forecasts.

The most reliable evidence we present that security returns precede (lead) analyst consensus earnings forecast revisions is in Figures 4.1 and 5.1. The remaining analysis is little more than tentative explorations of an issue whose importance is matched by its complexity.

APPENDIX

RESEARCH ON EARNINGS FORECASTS: A LITERATURE REVIEW AND CLASSIFIED BIBLIOGRAPHY

A.1 Introduction

The purpose of this Appendix is to provide a detailed review of prior research on earnings forecasts, with particular attention paid to where the findings in this monograph extend that research. In Table A.1 we classify the topics covered in the earnings forecast literature into five categories:

I. Properties of Earnings Forecasts by Security Analysts

II. Capital Markets and Security Analyst Earnings Forecasts

III. Properties of Earnings Forecasts by Management

IV. Capital Markets and Management Earnings Forecasts

V. Benchmark Comparisons of Security Analyst, Management, and Mechanical Model Earnings Forecasts.

Sections A.2 to A.6 of this chapter provide a review of research in these five areas. Included in each section is a classified bibliography of research in that area. The subsections in Sections A.2 to A.6 correspond to the subsections outlined in Table A.1.[1] Results from individual studies cited in that bibliography will be used to illustrate research trends in the literature or to highlight unresolved issues.[2]

A.2 Properties of Earnings Forecasts by Security Analysts

Researchers can access security analyst earnings forecasts via primary sources (the reports of individual analysts) or secondary sources (the reports of services that collect and distribute earnings forecasts made by analysts at several institutions).

Primary sources of earnings forecasts can be classified as follows:

(i) Security analyst forecasts not typically given external circulation. For example, Cragg and Malkiel [1968] used forecasts from five (unnamed) institutions, two of which were "large New York City banks heavily involved in trust management" (p. 68). One issue that arises in such a study is whether firms that permit researchers access to internal data are a random sample or whether they are (say) those that, ex post, had superior forecasting experience.

(ii) Security analyst forecasts circulated to external clients but not in a pre-

---

[1] As with any classified bibliography, arbitrary decisions as to both (i) inclusion/exclusion, and (ii) classification to specific categories are made. Where a single study contains research related to several topic areas, it is listed in each of those topic areas. Work-in-progress (e.g., drafts of dissertation research and working papers) is cited in Tables A.2 to A.6 but is not discussed in any detail in the text of this Appendix.

[2] The writing of this Appendix was facilitated by the following review articles: Abdel-khalik and Thompson[1977-1978], Richards and Fraser [1978], Abdel-khalik [1980], Hitschler [1980], Armstrong [1983], Givoly and Lakonishok [1983a] and Westwick [1983].

TABLE A.1

CATEGORIZATION OF RESEARCH ON EARNINGS FORECASTS

I. Properties of Earnings Forecasts by Security Analysts

A. Security Analyst Forecast Errors: Statistics on Forecast Error Distributions and Their Determinants

B. Security Analyst Forecast Revisions: Statistics on Frequency of Forecast Revisions and Their Determinants

C. Security Analyst Consensus Forecasts: Properties of and Issues in Aggregating Individual Analyst Forecasts

D. Divergence of Security Analyst Forecasts

E. Security Analyst Earnings Forecast Process: Experimental and Survey Research

II. Capital Markets and Security Analyst Earnings Forecasts

A. Announcement Effect of Security Analyst Forecasts

B. Association Between Security Analyst Earnings Forecast Errors or Forecast Revisions and Security Returns

C. Association Between Security Analyst Earnings Forecast-Based Variables and Capital Market Risk or Return

D. Cross-Sectional Valuation: Role of Security Analyst Forecasts in Explaining Price, PE Ratios, or in Active Equity Valuation Analysis

III. Properties of Earnings Forecasts by Management

A. Management Earnings Forecast Errors: Statistics on Forecast Error Distributions and Their Determinants

B. Management Earnings Forecast Process and Disclosure Decisions: Experimental and Survey Research

C. Characteristics of Firms with Voluntarily Disclosed Management Forecasts

IV. Capital Markets and Management Earnings Forecasts

A. Announcement Effect of Management Forecasts

B. Association Between Management Earnings Forecasts and Security Returns

V. Benchmark Comparisons of Security Analyst, Management, and Mechanical Model Earnings Forecasts

A. Forecasts of Security Analysts vs. Forecasts of Mechanical Models

B. Forecasts of Security Analysts vs. Forecasts of Management

C. Forecasts of Management vs. Forecasts of Mechanical Models

D. Composite Forecast Analysis

announced reporting date sequence for a pre-announced population. Researchers using this source typically have sought permission of the institution to facilitate collection of data; e.g., Elton and Gruber [1972] used forecasts provided by "a large pension fund, a well-known investment advisory service, and a large brokerage house" (p. B.418). They explicitly noted that "these three institutions were not selected at random....The investment advisory service was selected after analysts in a number of financial institutions indicated that this was the service in whose projections they placed the greatest faith. Furthermore, the other two institutions were the only ones among those contacted who were willing to expose their forecasts to rigorous testing" (p. B.418). One issue that faces a researcher here is ensuring access to all the forecasts made at the chosen institution(s); files for subsets may be (inadvertently or deliberately) missing.

(iii) Security analyst forecasts of one institution that are circulated to external clients in a pre-announced reporting date sequence for a pre-announced population, e.g., the Value Line Investment Survey. This source contains earnings forecasts for one to five quarters ahead for 1600 firms. Studies using the Value Line forecasts include Abdel-khalik and Espejo [1978], Brown and Rozeff [1978, 1979, 1980], Jaggi [1978], and Collins and Hopwood [1980].

Secondary sources of earnings forecasts include:[3]

(i) Standard and Poor's, *The Earnings Forecaster*. Started in the late 1960's, this service reports the earnings forecasts made at a cross-section of brokerage and investment institutions. Studies using this source include Niederhoffer and Regan [1972], Barefield and Comiskey [1975], Gonedes, Dopuch and Penman [1976], Fraser and Richards [1978, 1978a], and Fried and Givoly [1982].

(ii) Lynch, Jones and Ryan's *Institutional Brokers Estimate System* (IBES). Started in the early 1970's, this service covers (in 1983) over 2500 stocks with forecasts contributed by more than 70 brokerage firms. Chapter 2 of this monograph describes the data base and subsequent chapters examine properties of IBES consensus forecast data. Other studies using the IBES data base include Zacks [1979], Elton, Gruber and Gultekin [1981, 1982], and Coggin and Hunter [1982-1983].

(iii) Zacks Investment Research's *Icarus Service*. Started in the late 1970's, this service (in 1983) covers over 2500 stocks with forecasts contributed by more than 70 brokerage firms.

Several related questions arise when using one or more of the above sources:

(a) What is the incentive of the individual analyst to report earnings forecasts in an unbiased and timely fashion? For example, is there pressure on an analyst to make forecasts that do not diverge markedly from the current consensus, and do analysts trade on their information prior to publicly releasing their earnings forecasts?

(b) Given that an analyst has made a forecast revision, how quickly is that revision communicated to services such as The Earnings Forecaster, IBES, or

---

[3] Stewart [1973, pp. 119-126] describes a fourth "secondary source" [Casper] that was marketed by Catallactics. He noted that Casper "summarizes the forecasts of analysts working for a number of leading brokerage and institutional firms" (p. 122). We do not know whether this service still exists.

Icarus? For example, is there pressure from clients of the individual institution to have access to any forecast revisions before individuals who are not clients but who subscribe to The Earnings Forecaster, IBES, or Icarus?

When drawing inferences from research using security analyst forecast data, it is wise to recognize that incentive problems such as (a) or (b) may exist.[4]

Table A.2 contains a classified bibliography of studies in each of the areas listed in Table A.1 for the "Properties of Earnings Forecasts by Security Analysts" category of research. These areas are now discussed in sequence.

A. Security Analyst Forecast Errors: Statistics on Forecast Error Distributions and Their Determinants

This area has the largest number of single entries of the sub-categories in Table A.2. A variety of issues arise in this research:

(i) *What summary forecast error measures to examine?* It is well recognized in many studies that the decision context in which a security analyst forecast is used will influence how the magnitude of a forecast error (and other attributes such as its timeliness) will affect the decision maker's utility. It is also well recognized that we have limited knowledge of investor loss functions associated with the use of earnings forecasts in alternative decision contexts. For example,

> Since little is known about the nature of the loss function associated with earnings forecast errors the mean absolute error measure has been selected due to its simplicity and also to its use in previous studies of earnings forecast errors.
>
> Barefield and Comiskey [1975, p. 243]

The literature cited in Table A.2 contains a relatively standard set of error measures that may or may not relate to the loss function of a specific investor or other user of earnings forecasts, e.g., mean error, mean absolute error, and mean squared error. This same comment applies to the analysis in Chapter 3 of this monograph.

(ii) *What is the earnings concept being forecast by the security analyst?* There are several options here, e.g., (a) diluted versus non-diluted (primary) EPS, and (b) pre-extraordinary item versus post-extraordinary item EPS. Most authors assume (explicitly or implicitly) that analysts are forecasting primary pre-extraordinary item earnings – e.g.:

> The assumption is that security analysts attempt to predict a normalized

[4] Some insight into data collection procedures at "secondary source" institutions is provided by Imhoff and Pare [1982]. They report that "The Earnings Forecaster goes to press each Wednesday for release by Friday. Forecasts received on Tuesday are included in that week's issue. Most contributors, aware of these deadlines, plan to have final forecast revisions by Tuesday. According to Earnings Forecaster management at S & P, contributors feel a strong desire to compete with one another regarding the updating of forecasts and to reflect new information as soon as possible in most cases. When a contributor calls in a revised forecast for an entity that varies quite a bit from the other (older) forecasts, S & P will call these other contributors to notify them of the revision and, in many instances, authors of the older forecasts will ask to have their forecasts eliminated from the forthcoming issues of the Earnings Forecaster" (p. 434).

TABLE A.2

CLASSIFIED BIBLIOGRAPHY ON PROPERTIES OF EARNINGS FORECASTS BY SECURITY ANALYSTS

PANEL A. Security Analyst Forecast Errors: Statistics on Forecast Error Distributions and Their Determinants

Buckman 1963
Monteith 1966
Cragg and Malkiel 1968
Klepczynski 1971
Elton and Gruber 1972
Niederhoffer and Regan 1972
Stewart 1973
Gray 1974
Janell 1974
Stringer 1974
Barefield and Comiskey 1975
Barefield and Comiskey 1975a
Fraser and Richards 1975
Richards and Fraser 1975
Basi, Carey and Twark 1976
Richards 1976
Smith and Murphy 1976
Barefield and Comiskey 1976
Brandon and Jarrett 1977
Ferris and Hayes 1977
Richards, Benjamin and Strawser 1977
Richards and Fraser 1977
Richards and Fraser 1977a
Brown and Rozeff 1978
Crichfield, Dyckman and Lakonishok 1978
Fraser and Richards 1978
Fraser and Richards 1978a
Imhoff 1978
Jaggi 1978
Brown and Rozeff 1980
Collins and Hopwood 1980
Jaggi 1980
Branch and Berkowitz 1981
Finn 1981
Lees 1981
Cragg and Malkiel 1982
Elton, Gruber and Gultekin 1982
Fried and Givoly 1982
Imhoff and Pare 1982
Brown 1983
Givoly and Lakonishok 1983
Gultekin 1983
O'Brien 1983
Rozeff 1983
Baldwin 1984
Brown, Griffin, Hagerman and Zmijewski 1984
Hill and Schneeweis 1984
Schreuder and Klaassen 1984
Swanson, Shearon and Thomas 1984
Brown, Foster and Noreen 1985

PANEL B. Security Analyst Forecast Revisions: Statistics on Frequency of Forecast Revisions and Their Determinants

McEnally 1971
Abdel-khalik and Espejo 1978
Brown and Rozeff 1979a
Brown and Rozeff 1979b
Givoly and Lakonishok 1979
Richards and Martin 1979
Brown, Hughes, Rozeff and Vanderweide 1980
Givoly and Lakonishok 1980
Cragg and Malkiel 1982
Elton, Gruber and Gultekin 1982
Fried and Givoly 1982
Abdel-khalik 1983
Brown 1983a
Brown, Foster and Noreen 1985

PANEL C. Security Analyst Consensus Forecasts: Properties of and Issues in Aggregating Individual Analyst Forecasts

Griffin 1976	Coggin and Hunter 1982-1983
Richards and Fraser 1977a	O'Brien 1983
Givoly and Lakonishok 1979	Hill and Schneeweis 1984
Armstrong 1981	Brown, Foster and Noreen 1985

PANEL D. Divergence of Security Analyst Forecasts

Cragg and Malkiel 1968	Cragg and Malkiel 1982
Richards 1976	Coggin and Hunter 1982-1983
Richards and Fraser 1977a	Elton, Gruber and Gultekin 1982
Crichfield, Dyckman and Lakonishok 1978	Givoly and Lakonishok 1983
	Gultekin 1983
Finn 1981	Brown, Foster and Noreen 1985

PANEL E. Security Analyst Earnings Forecast Process: Experimental and Survey Research

Stewart 1973	Moizer and Arnold 1982
Report of the Advisory Committee 1977	Arnold, Moizer and Noreen 1983
Biggs 1979	Gibbs and Seward 1983
Lees 1981	Biggs 1984

> figure free from the impact of non-recurring factors and unaffected by company distributions.
>
> Crichfield, Dyckman and Lakonishok [1978, p. 652]

When the actual GAAP earnings number is used to compute the error measure, it is implicitly assumed that a one to one correspondence exists between what a security analyst calls an extraordinary (non-recurring, special, etc.) item and what GAAP classifies as an extraordinary item. No survey or other systematic evidence supports this assumption. One explanation for the results in Chapter 5 of this monograph is that when analysts forecast FY1 earnings, they attempt to focus on the actual GAAP-based earnings figure; however, when they forecast FY2 earnings, they attempt to focus on "permanent earnings." An alternative explanation for the Chapter 5 results is that analysts forecast the same earnings concept for FY1 and FY2, but that the FY1 forecast error has a higher transitory component than the FY2 forecast error.[5]

A related issue is whether analysts forecast earnings for the firm as it currently exists or for the firm as it will exist in the period being forecast, after, say, acquisitions or divestitures. This issue may be a relatively minor one for one year ahead forecasts but can be important when interpreting error measures for multi-year forecasts; acquisitions or divestitures not announced at the time of the forecast but consummated before the period being forecast can cause sizeable forecast errors when the GAAP-based number is used in the computation of the forecast error.

(iii) *What is the time horizon to compute forecast errors?* A one year ahead forecast horizon is the predominant choice in the research categorized in Table A.2. One exception is Brown and Rozeff [1978], who examined "quarterly earnings per share for forecast horizons of one to five quarters" (p. 3) as well as one year ahead forecasts. They noted they were investigating several horizons because "economic theory provides no guidance concerning the association of analyst superiority [over time-series models] with a particular forecast horizon" (p. 3). Another exception is Cragg and Malkiel [1968], who studied five-year earnings growth forecasts: "The growth rates were given as single numbers for each corporation.... Discussion with the suppliers of the data indicated that all firms were attempting to predict the same future figure, the long-run average ('normalized') earnings level, abstracting from cyclical or special circumstances" (pp. 68, 69). The research in this monograph focuses on (1) a data base with EPS forecast information for each year of a two-year forecast horizon, and (2) a data base with EPS forecast information for each year of a five-year forecast horizon. This multi-year focus enables us to address several important research issues not examined in detail before (see Chapter 1). Our rationale for analysis of a two-year and a five-year forecast horizon is data availability rather than any underlying theory specifying this as the appropriate time horizon for forecast evaluation. In a more complete analysis, the horizon period would be specified by the decision context in which the earnings forecast is used.

(iv) *How should forecast errors be pooled?* At least three levels of aggregation are possible: (a) by analyst, (b) by firm, and (c) by time. Research issues are faced in each of (a), (b), and (c).

---

[5] FY1 and FY2 is the notation used in this monograph for forecasts of one year ahead earnings (FY1) and two year ahead earnings (FY2).

Pooling Across Analysts: Most studies cited in Table A.2 have pooled across analysts when presenting forecast error summary statistics. Two studies adopting the individual analyst as the unit of analysis are Richards and Fraser [1977a] and Brown and Rozeff [1980]. Section A.2.C of this appendix contains a discussion of some aggregation issues in this area. These aggregation issues are attracting considerable attention in the forecasting literature in general and in the subset of that literature dealing with earnings forecasts.

One motivation for restricting the analysis to the individual security analyst level is that individuals with superior forecasting ability (if they exist) can be identified. This identification would permit investigation of issues such as: (i) the forecast procedures employed by superior analysts, and (ii) the timing of forecast revisions made by analysts with superior forecasting ability vis-a-vis revisions made by other analysts. Brown and Rozeff [1980] ranked the forecast errors made by 11 Value Line security analysts for each year of the 1973 to 1976 period. They reported the following:

> We correlated the analyst performance rankings of 1973 with those of 1974, those of 1974 with 1975, and those of 1975 with 1976. The resulting correlations of –0.27, –0.10 and –0.10, respectively, were insignificantly different from zero.... There is no evidence that good (bad) performance in one period is a harbinger of good (bad) performance in a subsequent period (p. 34).

Explanations that Brown and Rozeff discussed for this conclusion included: (i) "by selecting analysts who continuously covered firms [over the 1973-1976 period], we may have obtained a homogeneous group.... among whom skill differences are so muted that our methodology was not strong enough to uncover persistent differences," and (ii) "superior analysts are spotted by their superiors and by others in the organization. They are then promoted, given additional duties or used by others as internal consultants. Their total product rises, but their marginal product in forecasting earnings recedes to the level of other analysts" (p. 34). The 11 analysts in the Brown-Rozeff study covered different securities. An interesting issue would be to examine if their conclusion of inconsistent rankings of individual analysts over time holds for a group of analysts who all forecast earnings for the same securities.

Pooling Across Firms and Over Time: Two issues that arise in both contexts are (i) the effect of size or scale differences, and (ii) homogeneity of the observations. Consider (i). If firms differ in size (either at a point in time or over time), the forecast error of the larger firms can dominate summary statistics such as the mean forecast error or the mean squared error. Although the problem is well recognized, there has been limited analysis of how inferences drawn from a particular study may be affected by alternative approaches to the problem. These approaches include:

(i) deflating each firm's forecast error by a scale measure such as actual earnings, forecast earnings, total assets, market capitalization, or absolute magnitude of average earnings changes;[6] or

---

[6] The use of EPS forecast rather than earnings forecasts, in part, reduces the scale problem if there is a positive correlation between firm size and the number of shares outstanding.

(ii) focusing on error measures less affected by one or two large firms in the sample, e.g., focus on the fractiles of the distribution rather than the mean.

Related issues are (i) how to handle observations with negative denominators when the actual or expected earnings deflator is used, and (ii) how to handle outlier observations. Chapter 3 of this monograph explores these issues and presents evidence on the sensitivity of inferences drawn in that chapter to alternative deflators and to the existence of outlier observations.

The homogeneity problem in pooling across firms or over time comes in various forms, e.g.:

(i) Firms in different industries may differ in their underlying earnings variability; e.g., a 20 percent forecast error for a consumer food company may be extreme whereas the same error for a gold producing company may be average.

(ii) The distribution of earnings forecast errors may differ from one time period to another; e.g., banks in a period of high uncertainty over interest rates may have higher forecast errors than in a period of low uncertainty over interest rates.

These and other sources of non-homogeneity have been examined in the literature on the determinants of security analyst earnings forecast errors.

Determinants of the Distribution of Forecast Errors

The trend in the literature referenced in Panel A of Table A.2 is toward more explicit analysis of the determinants of forecast errors as opposed to just the presentation of descriptive statistics of forecast errors (e.g., the mean absolute error or the mean squared error). One model underlying the research issue raised in this literature is:[7]

$$FE_{it} = f(T, I, S, LOB, V, Y, A, F \ldots) \qquad \text{(Eqn. A.1)}$$

where FE_{it} = forecast error of ith firm in period t,

T = time yet to elapse before the earnings of firm i for the period being forecast is announced,

I = industry of firm i,

S = size of firm i,

LOB = number of lines of business of firm i,

V = variability measure of past earnings series of firm i,

Y = calendar year being forecast if firm i has a December 31 fiscal year (calendar year in which fiscal year being forecast has most number of days if non-December 31 fiscal year firm),

A = a coding of accounting method changes made by firm i during the forecast year, and

F = individual forecaster coding.

These (and other potential) variables do not come from any articulated theory; intuition and the results of prior research appear to be the most important motivations for studies examining one or more of the above.

---

[7] Albrecht, Johnson, Lookabill and Watson [1977] provide further discussion of this model.

A test of (Eqn. A.1) would require attention to both sample selection and variable measurement. For instance, a study that sampled only security analyst forecasts made in the same calendar month for firms with the same fiscal year would preclude examination of the importance of T as an independent variable. Similarly, a study that defined FE_{it} as [(Actual Earnings-Forecasted Earnings)/Standard Deviation of Earnings Change] would preclude examination of the importance of V as an independent variable. To date, few studies have been undertaken to empirically examine (Eqn. A.1). Most research in this area has examined a sequence of independent variables rather than simultaneously examining those variables in a multivariate design; interaction effects among the variables in (Eqn. A.1) have not been studied extensively. One limitation of examining a sequence of independent variables is that correlations between those variables are not taken into account. A study may report three correlated variables as individually significant determinants of security analyst forecast errors when in fact all three are proxying for the same underlying factor.

The most consistent finding in the literature is that the accuracy of a forecast increases as the time to the announcement of the earnings being forecast decreases. For instance, Elton, Gruber and Gultekin [1982] concluded the following for a sample of firms in the IBES data base over the 1976-1978 period:

> The most striking feature is the extreme regularity in the pattern of errors in earnings estimates. As successive forecasts are made over time the forecast error gets smaller (p. 6).

Results underlying this conclusion included:

	Month of the Earnings Forecast Relative to the Month of the Actual Earnings Announcement					
Month	**−10**	**−8**	**−6**	**−4**	**−2**	**0**
Absolute Percentage Error	19.0	16.3	14.0	11.1	8.0	5.3

The results in Chapter 3 of this monograph reinforce this finding and document that over the −22 month to −12 month period there is a similar progressive increase in forecast accuracy. Another finding in Chapter 3 is that over the −22 month to 0 month forecast horizon, the dispersion of forecast errors is reduced as the time to the announcement of the earnings being forecast decreases.

The null hypothesis that, holding the horizon period constant, all industries have the same distribution of security analyst forecast errors, has been rejected in many studies. For instance, Smith and Murphy [1976] present data on the ''average error coefficient'' (Σ (Actual-Forecast)^2/Σ (Forecast)^2) for security analysts at ''one of Canada's most prominent investment houses'' (p. 12):

- Forest Products .122
- Heavy Industry .119
- Mines and Metals .077
- Oil, Gas, and Pipelines .050
- Merchandising and Food .032
- Utilities .026

- Banks and Finance .025
- Brewing .016

Using an analysis of variance test, Smith and Murphy rejected the hypothesis that the "average error coefficient" of each industry was the same. However, after making pairwise comparisons among the eight industries they reported that "only a few industries exhibited significant differences..." (p. 19). Industry differences have also been reported in other studies, e.g., Barefield and Comiskey [1976]. Data reported in services such as IBES and Icarus also are consistent with industry differences in forecast accuracy.

Evidence about the relative importance of variables other than T and I as determinants of forecast accuracy is either less consistent across studies or based on less systematic research. In one of the few multivariate studies of (Eqn. A.1), Richards and Fraser [1975] examined the ability of 24 firm-specific independent variables (e.g., total debt/total assets, growth in sales, EPS variability, dividend payout ratio, and a beta estimate) to explain the 1973 forecast errors of security analysts for 100 companies. The conclusion was that "knowledge of the financial characteristics of the firm does not provide much information in explaining the forecast errors" (p. 11); T and I were not included as independent variables in this study.

Evidence of Bias in Forecast Errors[8]

Several studies have examined distribution properties of forecasts drawn over extended time periods. Fried and Givoly [1982] examined a sample of approximately 1200 forecasts made over the 1969 to 1979 period. Over this whole period, the mean percentage error was negative (–5.3%) and the percentage of observations where the actual earnings exceeded the forecast earnings was 48.8%; the conclusion was that "the bias appears to be quite small" (p. 92). Chapter 3 of this monograph reports that over the 1976-1980 period, the comparable mean percentage error was also negative (–3.8%). In contrast to Fried and Givoly [1982], we report that the percentage of observations where the actual earnings exceeded the forecast earnings was 58.3%; the negative mean percentage error arises in our sample due to the absolute value of the extreme forecast overestimates exceeding the absolute value of the extreme forecast underestimates. Different samples or time periods may well explain such differences; for example, Fried and Givoly [1982, Table 1] report that the negative bias was less marked in the 1976-1979 period. Elton, Gruber and Gultekin [1982] report that over the 1976-1978 period "bias is an extremely low source of error" (p.14).

At this stage, the overall impression from the literature is that when multiple forecasts are drawn over an extended time period, there is no evidence of a sizeable systematic bias in security analyst earnings forecasts. However, it should be recognized that even those studies using annual forecasts over an eleven-year period do not have a very large data base with which to make reliable inferences about the existence of systematic bias in forecasts. Moreover, few studies focus on individual forecasters; hence, most evidence cannot be used to infer that any individual analyst is sys-

---

[8] A forecast is unbiased (biased) if the expected value of the forecast error is zero (nonzero). We use the term to refer to a sample statistic (mean) summarizing one aspect of the empirical distribution of forecast errors.

tematically optimistic or pessimistic or is unbiased in his or her earnings forecasts.

Economy, Industry, and Company Factors

One classification of the determinants of forecast errors is (a) economy, (b) industry, and (c) individual company factors. An interesting research approach was used by Barefield and Comiskey [1975] who examined "the annual reports of sample companies which had forecast errors of at least 25 percent or twice the average for their industry.... In nearly all cases...large analyst-forecasting errors were accompanied by annual report commentary explaining the unusual performance" (p. 248). The explanations given were summarized as follows:

> General: increased foreign competition
> general economic turndown
> government spending cutbacks
> monetary policy
> foreign governmental policy changes
>
> Industry: strikes
> wage settlements
> price weakness due to excess industry capacity
> increased costs of industry's raw materials
>
> Company: strikes
> wage settlements
> start-up or break-in problems with new products or processes
> overestimation of new product demand
> cost overruns
> construction delays
>
> The error determinants which seemed to appear with greatest frequency were 'strike' and 'start-up or break-in problems with new products or processes' (pp. 248-249).

No analysis was made as to whether the same comments appeared in the Annual Reports of companies with smaller forecast errors.

Elton, Gruber and Gultekin [1982] examined for a sample of IBES firms (i) "how much of the forecast error is due to the inability of analysts in total to predict what earnings per share will be for the economy (actually for the total of firms in our sample)," (ii) "how much of the total error is due to the analysts misestimating the differential performance of individual industries," and (iii) "how much of the error is due to the inability to predict how each firm will differ from its industry average" (pp. 11-12). The percentage decomposition for forecasts made in selected months for a sample of December 31 fiscal year firms in the 1976-1978 period was:

Forecast Month	Economy Component	Industry Component	Firm Component
March	1.9%	35.6%	62.4%
June	2.7	31.8	65.6
September	3.0	28.2	68.9
December	1.9	17.6	80.5

The conclusion was that "the vast majority of forecast error arises from misestimates of industry performance and misestimates of company performance" (p. 14).

B. Security Analyst Forecast Revisions: Statistics on Frequency of Forecast Revisions and their Determinants

Research in this category can be divided into three areas: (i) descriptive statistics on the frequency with which analysts revise their forecasts and the magnitude of those revisions, (ii) analysis of systematic dependencies in forecast revisions over time, and (iii) examination of revisions made at the time of specific releases such as interim and annual earnings.

Studies reporting descriptive statistics on forecast revisions typically conduct this analysis as part of a larger research project. For instance, Givoly and Lakonishok [1979] examined the behavior of security returns at the time of and subsequent to analyst forecast revisions. As part of this project they reported (i) distribution statistics on forecast revisions; e.g., 19.8% of the upward revisions were increases of more than ten percent, and (ii) distribution statistics on the percentage of revisions per calendar month; e.g., June with 5.7% had the lowest percentage of revisions in the sample.

A small set of studies has examined whether consecutive revisions by security analysts are serially uncorrelated. Givoly and Lakonishok [1979] conducted a runs test on a sample of EPS forecasts for 49 companies that were made in the 1967 to 1974 period. The forecasts collected each year for a single company were those made by the individual analyst with the greatest number of revisions reported in *The Earnings Forecaster* of the prior year; over the entire 1967 to 1974 period, the same individual need not have been chosen. The conclusion was that there was some evidence of

> a positive dependence [in successive revisions over time]. However, this dependence is small. The computations show that the null hypothesis of independence cannot be rejected for most firms at the 5% significance level. The rejection rate is 13.5% when all revisions are considered and 5.8% when only revisions of over 5% are considered. It seems reasonable to conclude, therefore, that the sign of the revision is not highly autocorrelated over time (pp. 173-174).

The motivation for the above analysis was to examine if subsequent capital market research reported in their paper was subject to experimental design problems. (If forecast errors for the one firm are serially correlated over time, there can be less than random assignment of attributes other than those examined in the research.) Another rationale for examining autocorrelation statistics is to examine if the forecaster (or forecast model) is fully extracting all the information available in the past time series of the variable being forecast. This issue is related to Muth's [1961] concept of rational expectations.[9] One problem in using the above autocorrelations to examine the rationality issue is that they do not relate to forecasts by the same analyst over time;

[9] "In order to explain fairly simply how expectations are formed, we advance the hypothesis that they are essentially the same as the predictions of the relevant economic theory. In particular, the hypothesis asserts that the economy generally does not waste information and that expectations depend specifically on the structure of the entire system" [Muth, 1961, p. 315].

hence, one cannot use this evidence to make the inference that an individual forecaster is systematically ignoring time-series information. Chapter 2 of this monograph also presents autocorrelation evidence on analyst forecast revisions. As with Givoly and Lakonishok [1979], the motivation is capital market research design issues rather than to make inferences about the rationality of security analysts in their earnings forecasts.

Several studies have examined whether security analysts revise their forecasts in a manner consistent with the information released in successive interim or annual earnings releases. In an early study, McEnally [1971] used correlations between analyst earnings forecast errors and security returns to conclude the following: "short-term earnings expectations are heavily influenced by companies' historical earnings records and especially by their most recent annual earnings figures" (p. 704). More recent studies have used the adaptive expectations model in their research design. This model posits that forecasters (i) decompose their most recent forecast error into a permanent and a transitory component, and (ii) revise their expectations to incorporate fully the information contained in the permanent component. The following conclusion by Brown and Rozeff [1979a] is descriptive of the results of several studies:

> Adaptive expectations are a significant element in security analysts' revision of expectations of future quarterly earnings per share. In our sample, analysts responded to earnings forecast error as if they were behaving in an adaptive manner, raising (lowering) their forecasts of future quarterly earnings when they underpredicted (overpredicted) this quarter's earnings per share (p. 349).

Givoly and Lakonishok [1983a] provide a good overview of methodological issues with the use of the adaptive expectations model in earnings forecast research as well as a discussion of related research in economics on the formation of inflation expectations. They conclude that

> study on the formation of analyst forecasts is in its infant stages. The consistency that financial analyst forecast revisions show with a simple adaptive model, does not mean that the model is the most appropriate to describe the formation of analysts forecasts of earnings. More elaborate models may be examined.... There is a need for a theoretical framework.... Such a framework would consider elements such as the loss function of the individual analysts, the time-series behavior of earnings, the extent of exogenous information available to analysts, and its reliability (p. 30).

One issue unresolved by the existing research designs is how much of the revision can be attributed to the earnings release per se as opposed to other correlated information releases. Research designs that control for confounding releases exist and could be used in this area – see Foster [1980, Section 4]. In addition, survey research methods (interviews, questionnaires, etc.) could be used to strengthen the inferences drawn from studies examining forecast revision statistics in the period surrounding earnings releases. It is highly likely that earnings releases are but one of many sources analysts use in their forecast revision process. At present, our knowledge of the relative importance of dividend releases, stock split announcements, company visits, etc., is meager. One variable that the studies cited in Panel B of Table A.2 rarely mention as a determinant of security analyst forecast revisions is the direction and magnitude of prior security returns

– see Section 4.4 of Chapter 4 and Section A.3.B. of this Appendix for further discussion.

Another issue unresolved by the existing research is the timeliness of forecast revisions made by security analysts. The evidence in Chapters 4 and 5 of this monograph is consistent with security returns being a lead indicator of security analyst earnings forecast revisions. Research discriminating between competing explanations for this finding is of high interest. These explanations include: (i) security prices impound information to which analysts do not yet have access (insider trading by management is one mechanism by which information internal to the firm can be impounded into security prices), (ii) security analysts deliberately delay releasing an earnings forecast revision until they have used it to trade on their personal account, and (iii) security analysts are less efficient processors of information than is the aggregate capital market.

C. Consensus Forecasts: Properties of and Issues in Aggregating Individual Analyst Forecasts

In many of the papers cited in Table A.2, researchers had access to more than one security analyst (or institution) forecast for a given company. The approaches adopted in this situation include:

(i) Choose a single earnings forecast from one analyst/one institution. Gonedes, Dopuch and Penman [1976] used *The Earnings Forecaster* data base and chose the "forecasts of the first [source] listed" (p. 111). Givoly and Lakonishok [1979] used *The Earnings Forecaster* data base and selected "the revisions produced by the most active forecaster for each company (the one with the greatest number of revisions)" (p. 171).

(ii) Compute a forecast error for each analyst/institution and then average the forecast errors. Fraser and Richards [1978a] noted that in cases where "more than one forecast was available for a single firm – the forecast errors associated with the forecasts of the various analysts were averaged to provide a single forecast error for the firm in question" (p. 28).

(iii) Aggregate the individual forecasts to form a "consensus" forecast prior to computing forecast errors. Many studies using *The Earnings Forecaster* have used the mean of the individual forecasts as the forecast variable when computing error measures, e.g., McEnally [1971]; Barefield and Comiskey [1975, 1975a]; Basi, Carey and Twark [1976]; and Crichfield, Dyckman and Lakonishok [1978]. One motivation for using a consensus is that the forecast errors of individual analysts may not be perfectly cross-sectionally correlated. For instance, Zarnowitz [1979] noted that "while published forecasts [of macroeconomic variables] by ranking practitioners are often developed with particular skill and care, group average forecasts benefit over time greatly from cancellations of individual errors of opposite sign" (p. 8).

An important research issue is how the use of (i), (ii), and (iii) affects forecast error measures and inferences drawn from them. A small but growing literature exists on this issue, both as regards earnings forecasts in particular and as regards forecasting in general. For instance, Cogger and Hunter [1982-1983] used an IBES data base in a comparison of analyst consensus (arithmetic mean) forecasts, individual analyst forecasts, and the forecasts of three time-series models. For a sample of 149 firms in 1978 and 180 firms in 1979, the ranking in terms of total mean squared percentage error was:

	1978	**1979**
Analysts' Consensus	1	1
Individual Analyst	2	2
Linear Trend	3	4
Classical Exponential	5	5
Modified Exponential	4	3

The authors concluded that "the consensus was the best for one-year ahead EPS forecasts for both target years.... All pairwise difference of mean tests within each target year are significant [at the .05 level] , except the linear trend vs. modified exponential comparison for 1979" (p. 22). The literature on economists' forecasts of GNP, money supply, etc., also reports that consensus forecasts tend to be more accurate than the forecasts of the individual economists comprising the consensus – see Zarnowitz [1982].

Most of the literature using consensus earnings forecasts has used the mean as the proxy for the consensus forecast. The research in this monograph uses (i) the mean, (ii) the median, and (iii) a comparison of the individual revisions up versus down as proxies for the consensus forecast. On each of the major issues examined in Chapters 2 to 5, we report that the inferences drawn are unaffected by the choice of (i), (ii), or (iii) for the consensus proxy. Ideally, given a stationary set of data from N individual forecasters, a researcher could estimate the weights to apply to each individual forecast so as to maximize an objective function (e.g., minimize mean squared error). Figlewski and Urich [1983] discuss this weighting issue in a study of forecasts of the weekly changes in the money supply; they outline "aggregation methods which adjust for additive bias, differences in individual accuracy, and correlation among forecasts" (p. 695). However, they conclude that the more complex weighting schemes they examine "cannot improve on the accuracy of a simple average" (p. 695). Similar issues are important as regards aggregating security analyst earnings forecasts. The stationarity assumption underlying estimation of complex weighting schemes appears questionable at best for many series, especially given the high turnover in security analysts at some institutions. An additional factor is that the forecast from one institution may itself be a consensus of individual analysts; many of the gains from aggregating over diverse information sets may already be embedded in the forecast published by a single institution.

Several services such as IBES and Icarus publish their own consensus forecast measures that are derived from individual analyst information included in their data bases. Conversations with individuals at these services indicate that their "ideal" measure would access a data base that:

(i) included all analysts forecasting EPS for a specific company,

(ii) had each analyst instantaneously revising his or her forecast as new information becomes available,

(iii) had each analyst instantaneously reporting his or her revision to the service, and

(iv) had each analyst forecasting the same earnings variable, e.g., primary EPS before extraordinary items, where all analysts agree as to the meaning of an extraordinary item.

Clearly, this ideal world does not exist. However, we know little in a systematic way as to how (i) – (iv) are not descriptive, e.g., the nature of reporting lags between an analyst revising a forecast and its inclusion in the IBES system. Departures from conditions (i) – (iv) could well be another reason why complex weighting schemes to compute consensus earnings forecasts may not yield significant gains over the (apparent) simple weighting schemes used in current research.

D. Divergence of Security Analyst Forecasts

Research in this area has focused on (i) presenting descriptive statistics on the divergence across analysts in their forecasts or forecast errors, or (ii) using measures of security analyst divergence in capital market research. The latter research is discussed in Section A.3.C.

Representative studies on the correlation between analysts in their forecasts are:

- Richards and Fraser [1977a] examined the pairwise correlations among the 1973 earnings forecasts of nine analysts/institutions for 213 corporations. The lowest correlation was .8206 and the highest was .9992.
- Cragg and Malkiel [1968, Table 1] examined five-year EPS growth rate forecasts made by four different analysts in 1962 for 185 corporations. The correlation for pairwise combinations of the analysts ranged from .563 to .889.

An interesting issue yet to be explored is the reason(s) for the high correlations. Potential explanations include: (i) analysts use a common information set, (ii) analysts employ similar forecasting procedures, (iii) analysts share with each other information about their forecasts, and (iv) analysts have incentives to conform to the consensus forecast.

There is mixed evidence on whether analysts increase their agreement about the EPS that each firm will report as the time to the announcement is reduced. Crichfield, Dyckman and Lakonishok [1978] conclude that "while there is a tendency for the variation to decline, the decline [over the –13 to –1 month period] is uneven and often shows some increase in the middle month." (p. 665). Elton, Gruber and Gultekin [1982] conclude that "while there is some decline in the average dispersion as the estimates get closer to the end of the year, it is not uniform. Most of the decrease in dispersion across analysts occurs in the first four months of the year" (p. 18). In contrast, Chapter 3 of this monograph reports that the mean standard deviation of analysts' forecasts shows a systematic decrease in the –15 to –1 month period prior to the earnings announcement month. Most existing studies use the standard deviation as the measure of agreement among analysts. More extensive analysis in this area could be undertaken by focusing on subsets of analysts; e.g., is there a subset of analysts that consistently disagree with consensus revisions and what effect does inclusion of these analysts in the standard deviation measure have on inferences drawn from research in this area?

E. Security Analyst Earnings Forecast Process: Experimental and Survey Research

Although the activities and opinions of security analysts have been studied from many different directions,[10] very little detailed work appears to have been published on the earnings forecast processes used by security analysts. Interesting issues in this area include:

(i) The information sources used by security analysts. Chapter II of the *Report of the Advisory Committee on Corporate Disclosure to the Securities and Exchange Commission* presents the findings of one of the more detailed questionnaire studies on this topic. Stressed in this study was the importance analysts place on informal information sources, e.g., meetings with company officials and plant visits. Finn [1981] is one of the few studies that examined company visits by security analysts. For example, he reports that ''analysts tended to visit companies which had done well relative to the market, and not to visit those which had performed poorly'' (p. 26).

(ii) The approaches used when forecasting earnings. Approaches available include (a) statistical time-series modeling (e.g., Box-Jenkins analysis), (b) heuristic extrapolations of financial statement series, and (c) corporate strategy analysis incorporating information about the firm and its major competitors. There is little survey evidence available as to the relative use by security analysts of (a), (b), or (c).

(iii) The information processing behavior of analysts who adopt a non-mechanical approach. Biggs [1979] is one of the few studies in this area. Using a ''verbal protocol'' behavioral research design (analysts ''thought aloud'' when making decisions), Biggs studied 11 financial analysts who were given the task of choosing which one of five companies had the ''greatest earnings power.'' Earnings power was defined as ''the ability or potential of a company to generate earnings or income over a planning horizon of three to five years'' (p. 46). The focus of the research was on ''empirically examining the information processing assumptions of several models of individual choice behavior [additive compensatory, additive difference, conjunctive, and elimination by aspects] which have been proposed in the psychological literature'' (pp. 35-36). See also Biggs [1984].

(iv) The earnings forecast processes used by analysts with a superior forecasting record compared to those with an average or below average forecasting record. Superiority could be defined in several ways; e.g., (a) a forecast error measure such as mean absolute error, or (b) the ability of trading strategies using the earnings forecast to earn abnormal returns. Based on Zarnowitz's [1982] research on economic forecasters, it is likely that very few individuals would fall in the superior category for (a): ''No single

---

[10] Examples of research on the activities of or opinions of security analysts include:

(i) Attempts to model the decision process of a security analyst and predict the security selections that would be made, e.g., Clarkson [1962].

(ii) Human information processing based research on specific decisions made by analysts, e.g., Slovic [1972]; Slovic, Fleissner and Bauman [1972], and Ebert and Kruse [1978] examined man vs. linear model issues for analysts' predictions of stock price appreciation.

(iii) Opinions on corporate financial reporting objectives or corporate disclosure philosophy, e.g., Backer [1970] and *Report of the Advisory Committee* ...[1977, Chapter II].

(iv) Opinions on specific accounting controversies. Panel C of Table A-4 in this Appendix references many questionnaire and interview studies in which security analyst opinions on earnings forecasting by management are summarized.

forecaster has been observed to earn a long record of superior overall accuracy... But a small number of the more regular participants in the [annual survey of economists] did perform better in most respects than the composite forecasts from the same surveys'' (p. 21).

(v) The performance evaluation procedures used by institutions employing security analysts. For example: Is an examination of earnings forecasts included in salary decisions and promotions? Are comparisons of forecast accuracy made across analysts within the same institution or across analysts of different institutions who follow the same stocks? What penalties are imposed on an analyst who makes a forecast that diverges markedly from the consensus and (ex post) the consensus is more accurate?

A.3 Capital Markets and Security Analyst Earnings Forecasts

Given the capital market orientation of security analysts, it is not surprising that many empirical studies have linked security analyst earnings forecasts and capital market variables. Table A.3 contains a classified bibliography of studies in each of the four areas listed in Table A.1 for this category of research.

A. Announcement Effects of Security Analyst Forecasts

Very little research appears to have been done on the announcement effects of security analyst earnings forecasts. The most likely explanation is the difficulty of identifying when an analyst forecast becomes ''available'' to the capital market. The usual pattern is that analyst forecasts first are sent to a restricted client list and then to a broader set of clients and other external parties. The form of this broader circulation varies – e.g., (i) via services such as The Earnings Forecaster, IBES, or Icarus, or (ii) via publication in financial periodicals, e.g., the ''Heard on the Street'' column of *The Wall Street Journal*.

One study which has taken an announcement effect approach is Abdel-khalik and Ajinkya [1982]. The data source was earnings forecast revisions reported in *Options Alert*, a weekly publication of Merrill Lynch, Pierce, Fenner and Smith, Inc. The study focused on a nine-week event time period; weeks three and four were assumed to be the weeks ''that Merrill Lynch announced the revision internally'' and week five was ''the week these revisions were published in *Options Alert* and at which time they became public'' (p. 666). They noted that ''it was not possible to obtain the precise days on which forecasts were internally released'' (p. 679). The average abnormal returns were:

TABLE A.3

CLASSIFIED BIBLIOGRAPHY ON CAPITAL MARKETS AND SECURITY ANALYST EARNINGS FORECASTS

PANEL A. Announcement Effect of Security Analyst Forecasts

Abdel-khalik and Ajinkya 1982

PANEL B. Association Between Security Analyst Earnings Forecast Errors or Forecast Revisions and Security Returns

McEnally 1970
McEnally 1971
Niederhoffer and Regan 1972
Janell 1974
Gonedes, Dopuch and Penman 1976
Griffin 1976
Griffin and Ng 1978
Fraser 1979
Givoly and Lakonishok 1979
Richards and Martin 1979
Zacks 1979
Givoly and Lakonishok 1980
Elton, Gruber and Gultekin 1981
Finn 1981
Fried and Givoly 1982
Kross 1982
Givoly and Lakonishok 1983
Hawkins, Chamberlin and Daniel 1983
Imhoff and Lobo 1983
O'Brien 1983
Patell and Wolfson 1983
Pincus 1983
Brown, Foster and Noreen 1985

PANEL C. Association Between Security Analyst Earnings Forecast-Based Variables and Capital Market Risk or Return

Stewart 1973
Barefield and Comiskey 1975a
Friend, Westerfield and Granito 1978
Imhoff 1978
Barefield and Comiskey 1979
Malkiel 1981
Snyir 1981
Cragg and Malkiel 1982
Peterson and Peterson 1982
Peterson and Peterson 1982
Givoly and Lakonishok 1983
Farelly and Reichenstein 1984

PANEL D. Cross-Sectional Valuation: Role of Security Analyst Earnings Forecasts in Explaining Price, PE Ratios or in Active Equity Valuation Analysis

Cragg and Malkiel 1968
Malkiel and Cragg 1970
Malkiel 1970
Jahnke 1973
Jahnke 1975
Fouse 1976
Fouse 1977
Fouse 1978
Finn 1981
Cragg and Malkiel 1982
Michaud and Davis 1982
Hawkins, Chamberlin and Daniel 1983

Test Week	Upward Revision in Earnings Forecast Sample		Downward Revision in Earnings Forecast Sample	
	Abnormal Weekly Security Return	**t–Statistic**	**Abnormal Weekly Security Return**	**t–Statistic**
1	−0.00094	−0.31	−0.00489	−1.45
2	0.00260	0.94	−0.00316	−1.25
3	0.00908	2.79*	−0.00655	−1.89*
4	0.00578	1.95*	−0.00577	−2.12*
5	0.00235	0.88	−0.00694	−1.81*
6	0.00156	0.42	−0.00250	−0.77
7	0.00236	0.55	−0.00164	−0.19
8	0.00135	0.46	0.00015	−0.07
9	0.00618	2.06*	0.00144	−0.30

*indicates significant at the .05 level.

The authors concluded that "trading strategies could be formulated to earn significant abnormal returns on the basis of private knowledge of revisions of earnings forecasts by a select group of insiders" (i.e., Merrill Lynch analysts) and that "analysts' forecast revisions in this sample were prospective in the sense that they contained information that was not deducible from other publicly available information" (p. 678).

B. Association Between Security Analyst Earnings Forecast Errors or Forecast Revisions and Security Returns

Using expectations models based on the past reported earnings series of firms, Ball and Brown [1968] reported a positive association between the sign of a firm's earnings forecast error and the risk-adjusted security returns of that firm in the twelve-month period up to and including the earnings announcement month. Security analyst earnings forecasts represent an alternative expectations model that has several potentially appealing properties, e.g., (i) analysts can access a broader information set than just the past reported earnings series, and (ii) analysts can update their forecasts in a continuous manner whereas models based on the reported earnings series can update only every quarter or every year. Not surprisingly, many studies have employed variants of the Ball-Brown [1968] design with security analyst earnings forecasts as the expectations model.

An early example is McEnally [1971]. McEnally collected earnings forecasts from Standard and Poor's *The Earnings Forecaster* (during the July 1, 1968 to June 30, 1969 period); "the arithmetic mean of the analysts' estimates" was used in the research. Forecasts were selected for two dates:

(a) at the end of the week in which fiscal year t–1 ended (termed "end of year"), and

(b) at the end of the fourth week after earnings of year t–1 were announced (termed "after announcement week").

As part of the analysis, McEnally computed correlations between (i) the ratio of actual earnings to estimated earnings, and (ii) security returns in the 52 weeks up to and including the earnings announcement week. The measures of "estimated earnings" included security analyst forecasts (from (a) and (b) above) and the forecasts of 15 extrapolative or mechanical models; "the hypothesis underlying this test is that errors in the earnings expectation model that most closely approximates actual investor expectations will display the highest degree of association with security price changes'' (p. 697). The correlations for the security analyst forecasts and the three mechanical earnings forecast models with the highest correlations were:

	"End of Year" Sample (49 Companies)	"After Announcement Week" Sample (79 Companies)
Security Analyst Earnings Forecasts	.264	.487
Mechanical Models		
#1	.344	.336
#2	.333	.330
#3	.325	.328

The above design extends Ball and Brown [1968] to take account of both the sign and magnitude of earnings forecast errors. The results are consistent with security analyst forecasts made after the announcement of the prior year's earnings providing a better surrogate for investor expectations than any of the extrapolative models examined.

Fried and Givoly [1982] further examined this topic using a more extended time period (1969 to 1979) and additional mechanical forecasting models. The basic conclusion was the same: ''analyst forecasts are a better surrogate for market expectations of earnings than time-series models customarily used in the literature'' (pp. 103-104). This conclusion has relevance to many areas of capital market research, e.g., studies on the relative information content of alternative corporate releases such as earnings and dividends and studies on the effect of management earnings forecasts on security returns. The source of the superiority of analyst forecasts over time-series models is at present a disputed issue – see Section A.6.1 of this Appendix.

The focus of most capital market association studies has been on forecasts of one year ahead earnings. Elton, Gruber and Gultekin [1981] also reported results from ''a brief look at the excess returns associated with errors in two year forecasts'' (p. 977). Only firms with a December 31 fiscal year were included in the sample. Forecasts made in September of the current fiscal year (t) for

(i) the actual earnings of fiscal year t, and

(ii) the actual earnings of fiscal year t+1

were used to compute the percentage forecast errors for each year. Observations in each year were ranked and the average percentage forecast error for three portfolios computed:

Portfolio	Mean Forecast Error For Year t (One Year Ahead)	Mean Forecast Error For Year t+1 (Two Years Ahead)
Upper 30%	14.72%	26.74%
Middle 40%	–0.23%	–3.75%
Lower 30%	–94.01%	–155.29%

Cumulative abnormal returns over the seven-month period from October of year t to April of year t+1 were:

Portfolio	One Year Ahead Forecast Error Portfolios	Two Year Ahead Forecast Error Portfolios
Upper 30%	6.52%	7.92%
Middle 40%	–0.84%	–0.62%
Lower 30%	–5.4 %	–7.11%

The authors concluded that "the amount of excess returns that can be earned vary with the magnitude of the forecast error" (p. 985). There was no attempt to examine the incremental information content of the two year ahead forecast error given information about the one year ahead forecast error. Chapter 5 of this monograph examines this issue using several different research designs. The conclusion is that two year ahead earnings forecast errors have significant information content even after controlling for the magnitude of one year ahead forecast errors.

The practical investment implications of the above research have been noted in several studies: analysts can earn abnormal returns if they can make earnings forecasts that are more accurate than the earnings expectations currently impounded into security prices. Accuracy of forecasts per se is not a sufficient condition to earn abnormal returns. For example,

- These results present both challenge and opportunity for financial analysts. If their estimates are more accurate than the conventional published forecasts of the large institutions, there is ample opportunity for differentiating between the best and worst- performing companies.

  Niederhoffer and Regan [1972, p. 71]

- Excess returns are directly related to changes in earnings expectations. The results clearly confirm that an analyst able to forecast changes in expectations, rather than changes in earnings themselves, can achieve superior returns.

  Zacks [1979, p. 53]

Zacks recommended that analysts adopt a two-stage investment decision process: (1) make a preliminary independent earnings forecast and compare it to the consensus estimate, and (2) focus subsequent effort on refining forecasts that differ most from the consensus as these represent those "with the highest potential payoffs" (p. 55).

Forecast Revision Month as Event Month 0

A subset of studies has examined the behavior of security returns in the period surrounding security analyst earnings forecast revisions. There is consistency across the few studies examining the security return behavior in the pre-revision month period. For example, Finn [1981] reports that "both the direction and magnitude of the forecast [revisions] were positively related to excess return behaviour over the 12 month period up to month 0" (p. 29) where month 0 is the forecast revision month. The results in Chapter 4 of this monograph are similar to those in Finn [1981]. For instance, we report that stocks with upward (downward) revisions in earnings forecasts by security analysts had average cumulative abnormal security returns of +5.37% (–7.91%) in the –12 to –2 month period prior to month 0. An important but unresolved issue is the extent to which analysts use prior security returns as the basis for revising their earnings forecasts. It would be difficult to explain, from an economic survival perspective, the continued employment of analysts to forecast earnings if all they are doing is re-expressing, in an earnings forecast format, the information already available in a publicly observable datum such as a security price.

A less consistent result in the literature is the existence of systematic patterns in security returns in the period subsequent to the revision month. Elton, Gruber and Gultekin [1981] report finding "no discernible pattern in the cumulative [post-announcement] excess returns... This is what one would expect if expectations are incorporated into security price" (pp. 983, 984). Abdel-khalik and Ajinkya [1982] report that for a sample of "288 earnings forecast revisions... no abnormal returns could be earned after the week of public disclosure of the revisions" (p. 678). In contrast, Hawkins, Chamberlin and Daniel [1983] report that

> large positive revisions in earnings expectations do predict changes in stock prices. Over the period beginning March 1975 and ending December 1980, [investment in] 24 portfolios consisting of the 20 stocks with the largest one month increase in their mean, or consensus, estimate were initiated at quarterly intervals. The average twelve month total return for the test portfolio was 29.1%, compared to an average return for simultaneous investments in the S&P 500 of 12.0%. On a risk adjusted basis, the 24 test portfolios had an average twelve month alpha of 14.2% (p. 1).

Givoly and Lakonishok [1979, 1980] draw the same market inefficiency conclusions found in Hawkins, et al. [1983]. These studies are part of a larger literature reporting security pricing anomalies – see Foster [1984] for a review. Research is currently examining explanations other than market inefficiency for the above and similar results, e.g., experimental design problems, risk-misestimation, and asset pricing model misspecification.

C. Association Between Security Analyst Earnings Forecast Based-Variables and Capital Market Risk or Return

The two-parameter asset pricing model specifies beta or relative risk as the only firm-specific variable explaining differences across firms in their expected returns. One research direction in the literature has been to correlate security return estimates of beta (β_i) with financial statement variables – e.g., Ball and Brown [1969] and Beaver, Kettler and Scholes [1970]. Another research direction has been to correlate security return estimates of beta with either or both of the following two security analyst earnings forecast variables:

(i) D_i: the divergence across security analysts in their earnings forecasts.

(ii) P_i: the predictability of earnings as measured by the magnitude of forecast errors over time or the magnitude of forecast errors made by different analysts at a point in time.

An early example of the use of D_i is Stewart [1973] who, while conducting no formal tests, reported the security return estimates of beta and the maximum spread of forecasted earnings across analysts as a percent of actual earnings for a sample of 35 firms; he noted that "the same correlation exists between risk as measured by a high beta and the maximum spread of forecasted earnings as a per cent of actual earnings. The two highest beta groups show wider spreads while the two lower beta groups show narrower spreads'' (p. 125). An early example of the use of P_i is Barefield and Comiskey [1975a] who report a Spearman rank correlation of .513 between security return estimates of beta and the mean of the absolute forecast errors over the 1967-1972 period.

More extensive testing of the above issues is in Givoly and Lakonishok [1983]. The sample was 6,020 forecasts made for 424 companies over the 1969 to 1979 period. D_i was computed as the standard deviation of individual forecasts from the mean forecast. P_i was computed as the standard deviation of forecast errors across analysts. β_i was estimated using the market model with monthly data for the 48 months preceding the security analyst earning forecast month. The reported correlations between these variables were: β_i and D_i = 0.19 (t=4.50), β_i and P_i = 0.15 (t=4.97), and D_i and P_i = 0.48 (t=11.37).

Many of the initial tests of the two-parameter asset pricing models correlated security returns with security return estimates of beta (β_i) – see Jensen [1972]. In subsequent studies, a variable representing the divergence of earnings forecasts across analysts (D_i) was also correlated with R_i, e.g., Malkiel [1981], Cragg and Malkiel [1982], and Peterson and Peterson [1982, 1982a]. Malkiel [1981] reported the following:

Year	**Correlation Between R_i and β_i**	**Correlation Between R_i and D_i**
1962	.26	.44
1964	.13	.42
1966	.39	.22
1968	.27	.74
1980	.27	.31

The conclusion was that "the best single risk proxy appears to be the dispersion of analysts forecasts'' (p. 18). The above results and those from multiple regressions in the studies cited previously are consistent with at least two different hypotheses: (i) the two-parameter model is descriptively valid and D_i captures information pertinent to estimating the ex ante relative risk measure, or (ii) a multi-factor asset pricing model is descriptively valid with β_i and D_i representing different underlying factors.

D. Cross-Sectional Valuation: Role of Security Analyst Earnings Forecasts in Explaining Price (PE Ratios) or in Active Equity Valuation Analysis

The finance literature contains numerous articles reporting cross-sectional regressions with price as the dependent variable and earnings or earnings growth among the independent variables, e.g., Meader [1935] and Miller and Modigliani [1966]. A small subset of these articles has used security analyst earnings forecasts in estimating one or more of the independent variables. The inclusion of forecasts has much appeal as the equity valuation models examined in this literature are expressed in terms of expectations of earnings (dividends, etc.) and not in terms of past realizations of these series. One representative study is Malkiel and Cragg [1970]. The authors separately regressed price-to-earnings ratios on variables based on (i) the past earnings series and other historic variables, and (ii) security analyst earnings forecasts. The conclusion was that (ii) had considerably more explanatory power than (i). They noted the following with the use of (ii):

All coefficients have their expected signs. Moreover, the fits are very close

> for cross-sectional empirical work and are much better than those obtained with the historical data. About three quarters of the variability of price-earnings ratios is explained by the regressions. We should also mention that better fits were obtained by using the average growth rate of all predictors than by employing forecasts of a single analyst (p. 609).

An important concern when interpreting these results is the extent to which security analysts rely on P/E ratios themselves when forecasting earnings or whether they examine factors such as the strategies of competitors, the expected growth in consumer demand, etc. Exclusive reliance by security analysts on P/E ratios would make the regression exercise in Malkiel and Cragg [1970] circular.

In the 1970's there was an upsurge of interest in multi-period dividend discount models (DDM's) as part of investment strategies aimed at detecting under- or over-valued securities. Earnings forecasts only typically enter as a DDM input for those horizon years in which dividends are not directly forecasted; e.g., in the Wells Fargo model, analysts input dividend forecasts for the first five years and then input growth rate forecasts for earnings beyond year five and the associated payout ratio in those years – see Fouse [1976, 1977]. At present, published research has not examined the incremental contribution of security analyst earnings growth forecasts in DDM's relative to the use of forecasts from time-series models. One interesting aspect of several DDM's is that there is a mechanical relationship between model inputs and the model's predictions as to under- or over-valuation. Thus, it is possible to examine how different methods of estimating the inputs will map into different predictions as to under- or over-valuation. Given that the intent of DDM analysis is to detect mispriced securities, the incremental contribution of security analyst earnings forecasts could be measured by the abnormal returns resulting from its selections relative to the abnormal returns from the security selections made with the use of alternative forecasting models.[11]

A.4 Properties of Earnings Forecasts by Management

Data on earnings forecasts by management differ from data on earnings forecasts by security analysts on several dimensions:

a. Management forecasts are released by only a subset of firms whereas security analyst forecasts typically are available for a broad cross-section of firms. Some firms that are tracked by a large number of security analysts have an explicit policy of prohibiting the external release of management earnings forecasts.[12]

[11] A discussion of issues that arise in measuring the performance of DDM's is in Michaud and Davis [1982]. That paper argues that "consistent and significant ex ante anti-growth stock (high dividend yield, low P/E) bias 'explains' the forecasting performance of the model" (p. 563).

[12] A subset of studies has examined internal management earnings forecasts, e.g., Buckley [1973], Kodde and Schreuder [1983], and Schreuder and Klaassen [1984]. One issue that arises in generalizing from this research is whether firms that permit researchers access to their internal forecasts are a random sample. Buckley [1973] used a questionnaire to elicit internal management forecasts. He noted that "actual respondents are likely to have been companies that did well vis-a-vis their planning estimates ... Perusing the evidence indicate[s] that companies to whom questionnaires had been sent who had performed very badly compared with their earlier record tended more frequently to be non-respondents" (pp. 58-60).

b. Firms releasing management forecasts of earnings typically release only one forecast each year whereas security analysts publish revisions of their forecasts throughout the year.
c. Management forecasts are not always issued as point estimates. Phrases such as "earnings will be at least $X" and "earnings are expected to show adverse comparisons with the prior year," are used in some corporate releases.
d. Management forecasts are typically only for one year ahead earnings whereas security analysts' forecasts often cover both one year ahead and two years ahead earnings.

These differences between management and security analyst forecasts have led to less than complete overlap in the topics examined. For instance, research related to the properties of consensus forecasts and the properties of earnings forecast revisions has used security analyst forecast data rather than management forecast data. In contrast, research related to the motivations for issuing forecasts has used management forecast data. A classified bibliography of studies in this area is in Table A.4.

A. Management Earnings Forecast Errors: Statistics on Forecast Error Distributions and Their Determinants

Similar to the research on security analyst earnings forecasts, there is a trend in the literature referenced in Panel A of Table A.4 towards more explicit analysis of the determinants of forecast errors. The variable most consistently reported as a determinant of management forecast accuracy is the time yet to elapse before the end of the fiscal year of the period being forecast. For instance, Hagerman and Ruland [1979] examined management forecasts with horizons of eight to fourteen months: "... a Kendall rank order correlation test showed that forecast horizon and error are positively related at the one percent level. This finding indicates that the accuracy of management forecasts declines as the horizon is increased" (p. 175).

Although all the studies examining the industry membership variable do not show consistency, it appears that evidence of some industry differences in forecast error accuracy exists. In an early study, Dev and Webb [1972] reported that for a sample of U.K. earnings forecasts, two of the industry groups (building, timber, and roads; foods, groceries) had forecast errors significantly less than that of the complete sample. Jaggi [1980] reported the following industry breakdown for a sample of U.S. management forecasts:

Industry	**# of Firms**	**Mean Absolute Relative Prediction Error (Percentage)**
Manufacturing	82	30.4%
Chemicals	22	25.0
Utilities	22	24.8
Banking and Finance	12	21.8
Services (Transportation and Recreation)	18	21.8

The more interesting issue yet to be examined is ex ante predicting those industries for which management forecast errors are expected to be relatively low or high.

Inconsistent results exist for several other variables as determinants of management

TABLE A.4

CLASSIFIED BIBLIOGRAPHY ON PROPERTIES OF EARNINGS FORECASTS BY MANAGEMENT

PANEL A. Management Earnings Forecast Errors: Statistics on Forecast Error Distributions and Their Determinants

Green and Segall 1966
Green and Segall 1967
Daily 1971
Copeland and Marioni 1972
Dev 1972
Dev and Webb 1972
Westwick 1972
Buckley 1973
Dev 1973
McDonald 1973
Stewart 1973
Baker and Iralins 1974
Brandon and Jarrett 1974
Ferris 1975
Basi, Carey and Twark 1976
Ferris 1976
Lorek, McDonald and Patz 1976
Patell 1976a
Imhoff 1978
Jaggi 1978
Hagerman and Ruland 1979
Nichols and Groomer 1979
Platt 1979
Jaggi 1980
Beshera 1981
Pound 1981
Imhoff and Pare 1982
Porter 1982
Penman 1983
Schreuder and Klaasen 1984
Waymire 1984
Waymire 1984a

PANEL B. Management Earnings Forecast Process and Disclosure Decisions: Experimental and Survey Research

Daily 1971
Backer 1972
Kearney 1972
Skousen, Sharp and Tolman 1972
Asebrook and Carmichael 1973
Carmichael 1973
Keller 1973
McGrath and Walsh 1973
Miller 1973
Shank and Calfee 1973
Strawser and Benjamin 1973
Bedingfield and Lubell 1974
Carpenter and Daily 1974
Corless and Norgaard 1974
Corn 1974
Dev 1974
Hock 1974
Johnson 1974
Mautz 1974
Min 1974
Nickerson, Pointer and Strawser 1974
Poirier 1974
Burson-Marsteller 1975
Epstein 1975
Ferris 1975
Kidd 1976
Abdelsamad and Gilbreath 1978
Fuller and Metcalf 1978
Barnea, Sadan and Schiff 1979
Bart 1980
Reckers and Taylor 1980
Lees 1981
Danos and Imhoff 1982
Drury 1982
Danos and Imhoff 1983
Westwick (ed.) 1983

PANEL C. Characteristics of Firms with Voluntarily Disclosed Management Forecasts

Imhoff 1978
Hagerman and Ruland 1979
Ruland 1979
Jaggi and Grier 1980
Pound 1981
Waymire 1984a

forecast accuracy. For instance, Hagerman and Ruland [1979] report that "at the one percent level [using a Spearman rank test], the forecasts of large firms tend to be more accurate than those of smaller firms" (p. 176). Two rationales were given for this result: "Large firms are often more diversified and are thus better able to weather the effects of changing environmental conditions. In addition, large firms can commit more resources to forecasting and, consequently, can produce more accurate forecasts than smaller firms" (p. 175). In contrast to the Hagerman-Ruland result, Jaggi [1980] concluded that his "results do not indicate a trend of comparatively higher accuracy of management forecasts as the firm size becomes larger" (p. 100).

One issue not yet examined in detail is whether the distribution of management forecast errors depends on the context in which the forecast is released; e.g., are management forecasts issued at the time of a hostile takeover bid for the company more likely to be optimistic compared to forecasts issued at the annual company meeting?

One study (Porter [1982]) has employed the multivariate model in (Eqn. A.1) to examine the determinants of the accuracy of management earnings forecasts. The variables examined were firm earnings variability, firm leverage, firm relative risk (beta), year of forecast (1972, 1973, or 1974), and industry membership (manufacturing, utility, or other). The research used analysis of covariance. The main conclusions were: (i) earnings variability was a significant determinant of forecast accuracy (lower past variability meant less forecast error by management), (ii) utility firms had more accurate forecasts, (iii) the year of forecast was significant, and (iv) there was an interaction effect of (i), (ii), and (iii).

Research on the determinants of security analyst forecast accuracy and on the determinants of management forecast accuracy has substantial overlap. For example, many of the same variables are examined and the same methodologies often are employed. One area of difference is that only management has the ability to affect the reported earnings or earnings per share number; e.g., they can defer R&D expenditures, can increase year-end shipments, and can reduce the number of shares outstanding by share repurchases. In addition, they can reject projects that have (say) a positive net present value but which would cause reported earnings to differ from their forecast. At present, we know little about the extent to which managers take actions to improve the accuracy of their forecasts by means of affecting the actual earnings reported. In one of the few studies in this area, Ferris [1975] sent a questionnaire to British managers who had made earnings forecasts. Based on a sample of 31 responses, he concluded that "seventy-one percent indicated that their firm had utilized some type of discretionary action to reduce forecast deviations: (a) 22 firms manipulated their operating decisions and activities; (b) 16 firms pursued operating policies expressly directed at minimising expected forecast deviations; and (c) 16 firms attemped to suppress profits or avoid expenditures in order to reduce deviations" (p. 139). Such research faces the obvious problem of managers not always having the incentive to provide honest responses.

B. Management Earnings Forecast Process and Disclosure Decisions: Experimental and Survey Research

The literature cited in Panel B of Table A.4 covers experimental and survey research related to the earnings forecast procedures used by management or the factors associated with management's decision as to whether to publicly release their own internal earnings forecasts.[13]

The 1972-1973 deliberations by the Securities and Exchange Commission on whether to relax its policy of prohibiting firms from including earnings forecasts in their SEC filings generated much research activity.[14] Many questionnaire or interview studies about the pros and cons of management publicly releasing its own internal forecasts were conducted. Individuals surveyed typically included one or more of the following – accountants, corporate executives, investors, and security analysts. An illustrative set of responses from corporate executives is in Kearney [1972, pp. 72-74]:

- Do you take any action if earnings estimates prepared by the financial community differ substantially from your internal forecasts?

  51% Yes; 49% No

- Would the release of your internal profit forecasts along with their underlying assumptions aid the investing public in the evaluation of your company?

  36% Yes; 64% No

Lees [1981] found that 80 out of 123 security analysts surveyed opposed mandatory publication of management forecasts. Two reasons frequently given for this opposition were (i) "Analysts feel that forecasts prepared by members of their own profession are readily available to the public and that these projections adequately meet the needs of investors," and (ii) "Analysts have doubts about the reliability of company prepared forecasts" (p. 36). Note that security analysts have a vested interest in maintaining their own rationale for existence. It is not unlikely that their responses are influenced by self-preservation motives.

C. Characteristics of Firms with Voluntarily Disclosed Management Forecasts

Several studies have sought to isolate variables that discriminate voluntarily disclosing firms from non-disclosing firms (or voluntarily disclosing firms from a random sample of firms). Variables reported as significant include:

(i) Earnings Variability: "Forecast firms have significantly less variability in their time-series properties of earnings more frequently than the random sample," Imhoff [1978, p. 843]; and "Non-disclosing firms tend to have higher variability [of reported earnings] than disclosing firms," Jaggi and Grier [1980, p. 41].

(ii) Firm Size: "Firms in the forecast reporting sample tend to be larger than the average Compustat firm," Hagerman and Ruland [1979, p. 178].

(iii) Good News/Bad News: "It has been suggested that a company will only make a voluntary profit forecast disclosure... where an improved financial result is anticipated. A review of the firms in the sample provided some evidence in

---

[13] A detailed discussion of research issues in experimental and survey research is in Dyckman, Gibbins and Swieringa [1978].

[14] A good description of historical developments in the SEC's policy on forecasts is in Appendix X-A ("Evolution of SEC Policies and Practices Regarding Projections") of *Report of the Advisory Committee* ...[1977].

support of this proposition,'' Pound [1981, p. 519]. Results in Penman [1980] (see Section A.5.A of this Appendix) strongly support the good news-disclose/ bad news-not disclose hypothesis. Note that if firms systematically release formal forecasts only when there is good news, the very act of not releasing a forecast can be an implicit disclosure of bad news.

The literature currently lacks detailed theories of firm disclosure decisions – see Ball and Foster [1982]. Hence, it is not surprising that the choice of variables such as earnings variability and firm size in the above cited studies has been largely heuristic. The one research paradigm that has provided some underpinning to research in the corporate disclosure area is the stewardship or contract monitoring paradigm, e.g., Leftwich, Watts and Zimmerman [1981], and Chow [1982]. The existing studies on voluntary earnings forecasting by firms were not conducted using this paradigm.

A.5 Capital Markets and Management Earnings Forecasts

Table A.5 presents a classified bibliography of research on capital markets and earnings forecasts by management. Relative to the capital market/security analyst earnings forecast area, most of the research in Table A.5 focuses on announcement effect issues. In part, this appears attributable to researchers being able to identify more precisely the public release date of a management forecast than is the case with forecasts by security analysts. Potential legal penalties for differential disclosure create incentives for management to place an earnings forecast in the public domain via (say) a dated corporate news release or a formal statement at the annual meeting.

A. Announcement Effect of Management Forecasts

Penman [1980] provides detailed evidence on the behavior of daily security returns in the period immediately surrounding an annual earnings forecast announcement. An announcement was classified as a positive (negative) forecast error if the management forecast exceeded (did not exceed) the most recent annual earnings plus a drift factor. Out of a sample of 725 management forecasts made in the 1968 to 1973 period, 589 were positive and 136 were negative; this high percentage of positive forecast errors is consistent with management being more likely to release good news pubicly via a forecast than to release bad news via a forecast. The daily security returns surrounding the announcement date were:

	Positive Forecast Errors		**Negative Forecast Errors**	
Event Days	**Standardized Excess Returns**	**t–Statistic**	**Standardized Excess Returns**	**t–Statistic**
–5	.0900	1.89	–.0627	– .60
–4	.0469	1.01	–.0228	– .25
–3	.0581	1.28	–.0094	– .12
–2	.1722	3.45	.0319	.28
–1	.4650	7.35	–.1268	– .86
0	.1521	2.43	–.3209	–1.73
1	.1272	2.71	–.0270	– .23
2	.0262	.66	.0668	.66
3	.0171	.36	.1708	1.98
4	.1609	3.57	.1516	1.72
5	–.0345	–.80	.1095	1.32

TABLE A.5

CLASSIFIED BIBLIOGRAPHY ON CAPITAL MARKETS AND MANAGEMENT EARNINGS FORECASTS

PANEL A. Announcement Effect of Management Forecasts

Foster 1973	Nichols, Tsay and Larkin 1979
Cheever 1975	Penman 1980
Patell 1976	Beshara 1981
Jaggi 1978a	Morse 1982
Ruland 1978-1979	Penman 1982
Nichols and Tsay 1979	Waymire 1984

PANEL B. Association Between Management Earnings Forecasts and Security Returns

Patell 1976	Penman 1982
Nichols and Tsay 1979	Ajinkya and Gift 1983
Penman 1980	Gift 1983
Beshara 1981	Penman 1983
	Waymire 1984

Day 0 is the day the earnings forecast is reported in *The Wall Street Journal*. If the forecast is publicly released before (after) 3:00 p.m. of the prior day, the first trading time subsequent to the announcement would be event day –1 (event day 0). The above results are consistent with the capital market perceiving earnings forecasts by management to have significant security price revaluation implications.

The results for the positive forecast error group in Penman [1980] are consistent with those previously reported in Patell [1976]. However, using an earnings forecast model similar to Penman, Patell reported that firms in the bottom 25 percent of his sample (firms with forecasts furthest below expectation) had a positive standardized excess return in the announcement week. He hypothesized that the positive market reaction "may hinge on the imputed information content of the *act* of voluntary disclosure" (p. 273). Penman [1980], in contrast, reports that the 19 percent of his sample with a negative forecast error had a negative standardized residual on both days –1 and 0. Different samples, different time periods, etc., may well explain this difference between the two studies. One means of gaining more insight into whether "the act of management forecasting" conveys information would be to use a more timely expectations model to determine the surprise content of management's earnings forecasts. Security analyst forecasts issued immediately prior to the management forecast represent one means of gaining a more timely expectations model. Ajinkya and Gift [1983] use such an expectations model to conclude that "the capital market revises its expectations (and the equilibrium value of firms' common shares) in an unbiased fashion – i.e., a 'good news' forecast is associated with an upward price revision and a 'bad news' forecast with a downward revision" (p. 2). Waymire [1984] reports a similar result.

Penman's [1980] results are consistent with "good news" forecasts being released prior to the close of trading while "bad news" forecasts are more likely to be released after trading has closed. Morse [1982] reports a similar finding: the "good news" sample has the most significant reaction on day –1 while the "bad news" sample has the most significant reaction on day 0. Patell and Wolfson [1982] report a similar finding for the release of interim and annual earnings disclosures.

B. Association Between Management Earnings Forecasts and Security Returns

Several studies have examined the behavior of security returns in the period preceding the announcement of the management earnings forecasts. Patell [1976] and Nichols and Tsay [1979] examine an eight-week period up to the announcement week. Penman [1980] reports results for a 60 trading-day period preceding the day the management forecast is reported in *The Wall Street Journal*. A consistent result emerges from these studies: firms for which the management forecast exceeded that of a time-series model had positive security returns in the eight-week or 60 trading-day pre-announcement period while firms for which the forecast was less than that of the time-series model had negative security returns over the same period. For instance, Penman [1980] reports that over the [–60,0] trading day period, the "good news" management forecast sample had a cumulative abnormal return (CAR) of 2.55% while the "bad news" sample had a CAR of –0.94%. Explanations for this finding include: (i) investors revise their earnings expectations by relying on more timely non-earnings cues, (ii) management leaks part of the information contained in its forecasts to security analysts or others prior to their formal release, and (iii) management uses security returns as a prompt in deciding whether or not to forecast or in deciding the magnitude of the revision.

A.6 Benchmark Comparisons of Security Analyst, Management, and Mechanical Model Earnings Forecasts

Many studies have examined the relative ability of security analysts, management, and mechanical models to forecast earnings. The most common approach is to assess the relative accuracy of an earnings forecast using measures such as mean absolute error or mean squared error. A less common approach is to examine, via association measures, the ability of each earnings forecast to proxy for the capital market's expectations model. Table A.6 contains a classified bibliography of research in this area.

Most studies have posed the question as security analyst vs. mechanical models, security analyst vs. management, etc. An understanding of factors that could cause differences between forecasts of these three groups facilitates interpretation of individual studies. These factors include:

(a) Differences in the information set utilized in making the earnings forecasts (ID). Typically, the mechanical time-series models used as benchmarks have utilized only the past interim or annual earnings series. Security analyst forecasts presumably are based on a broader information set that includes macroeconomic forecasts, the competitive structure of a firm's industry, events such as acquisitions or divestitures, etc., as well as the past interim and annual earnings series. Management forecasts can incorporate internal information about future plans, cost structures, etc., as well as information that is in the public domain. (Note that, given the frequent interaction between management and security analysts, the latter may also be privy to some "confidential" information that management possesses but which is not publicly released.)

(b) Differences in the time at which forecasts are made (TD). Several studies of December 31 fiscal year firms have compared analyst (or management) forecasts made in March or April of the fiscal year being forecast with the random walk time-series model prediction. The random walk model uses last year's EPS which is, on average, publicly released by at least February 10th – see Givoly and Palmon [1982]. Hence, the analyst may have a 20- to 50-day advantage during which time more information about this year's annual EPS would be available. Indeed, by late April many companies have disclosed their first quarter results and the analyst would be predicting results for only the subsequent three quarters. Chapter 3 of this monograph documents the increase in forecast accuracy as the time to the announcement of the earnings being forecast is reduced. Chapter 4 illustrates, via a capital market association test, how use of a more timely expectations model can increase the observed association between earnings forecast errors and security price changes.

(c) Differences in the level of aggregation underlying the forecasts being compared (AD). The results of a study comparing security analyst forecasts with those of a mechanical model can be affected by whether individual analyst forecasts are used or whether a consensus of analyst forecasts is used – see Section A.2.C of this Appendix. One difficult problem in this area is assessing the degree to which the forecast of a security analyst (or manager) is already a consensus forecast of individuals within the security analyst's institution (or manager's firm). There may not be a stable relationship between individual forecasts and consensus forecasts because of differences across institutions or over time in the amount of "internal aggregation" underlying forecasts used in computing the consensus forecast.

TABLE A.6

CLASSIFIED BIBLIOGRAPHY ON BENCHMARK COMPARISONS OF SECURITY ANALYST, MANAGEMENT, AND MECHANICAL MODEL EARNINGS FORECASTS

PANEL A. Forecasts of Security Analysts vs. Forecasts of Mechanical Models

Monteith 1966
Cragg and Malkiel 1968
Klepczynski 1971
McEnally 1971
Elton and Gruber 1972
Janell 1974
Barefield and Comiskey 1975
Barefield and Comiskey 1976
Smith and Murphy 1976
Brandon and Jarrett 1977
Richards, Benjamin and Strawser 1977
Brown and Rozeff 1978
Ruland 1978
Brown and Rozeff 1980
Collins and Hopwood 1980
Branch and Berkowitz 1981
Finn 1981
Cragg and Malkiel 1982
Fried and Givoly 1982
Imhoff and Pare 1982
Coggin and Hunter 1982-1983
Kodde and Schreuder 1983
Rozeff 1983
Brown, Griffin, Hagerman and Zmijewski 1984
Hill and Schneeweis 1984
Swanson, Shearon and Thomas 1984

PANEL B. Forecasts of Security Analysts vs. Forecasts of Management

Basi, Carey and Twark 1976
Imhoff 1978
Jaggi 1978
Ruland 1978
Barefield, Comiskey and McDonald 1979
Jaggi 1980
Imhoff and Pare 1982
Kodde and Schreuder 1983
Schreuder and Klaassen 1984

PANEL C. Forecasts of Management vs. Forecasts of Mechanical Models

Green and Segall 1966
Green and Segall 1967
Copeland and Marioni 1972
Lorek, McDonald and Patz 1976
Ruland 1978
Hagerman and Ruland 1979
Nichols and Groomer 1979
Eckel 1982
Imhoff and Pare 1982
Kodde and Schreuder 1983

PANEL D. Composite Forecast Analysis

Cragg and Malkiel 1982
Fried and Givoly 1982
Imhoff and Pare 1983
Lobo and Nair 1983
Kodde and Schreuder 1984

(d) Differences in the efficiency with which the available information is utilized (ED). Analysts, management, or mechanical models may differ in the efficiency with which they use their respective information sets. Sections A.2.A and A.6.D discuss research on whether analysts exhibit any systematic bias or inefficiency in their forecasts. There is little related research on management forecasts, in part because of the absence of extended time series of management forecasts for individual firms.

The research referenced in Table 2.6 typically has not examined the importance of the above (and other) variables in a multivariate design, i.e.,

$$FE_i - FE_j = f\ (ID, TD, AD, ED, \ldots) \qquad \text{(Eqn. A.2)}$$

The approach in most studies has been to "control" for one or more of the above variables by precluding any sample variation in that variable, e.g., by sampling forecasts of analysts and management that are made in close proximity to each other. This approach precludes the researcher identifying interaction effects between the TD (timing difference) variable and the other variables as well as from estimating the importance of that variable itself.

A. Forecasts of Security Analysts vs. Forecasts of Mechanical Models

Two early studies reported little difference in the accuracy of the forecasts of analysts and those of mechanical models:

- The remarkable conclusion of the present study is that the careful estimates of the security analysts participating in our survey, the bases of which are not limited to public information, perform little better than these past growth rates. Cragg and Malkiel [1968, p. 83]
- Mechanical techniques do about as good a job of forecasting earnings as do security analysts. Elton and Gruber [1972, p. 423]

In contrast, the subsequent literature comes to the almost unanimous conclusion that security analysts outperform mechanical models, e.g.,

- Bank analysts produced better earnings forecasts than those achieved with two strictly mechanical forecasting rules.
Barefield and Comiskey [1976, p. 62]
- Value Line Investment Survey consistently makes better earnings forecasts than the Box Jenkins and naive time series models. The findings are in accord with rationality in the market for forecasts and the long-run equilibrium employment of analysts.
Brown and Rozeff [1978, p. 13]

Similar conclusions to the last two cited studies are in Smith and Murphy [1976], Brandon and Jarrett [1977], Richards, Benjamin and Strawser [1977], Brown and Rozeff [1980], Collins and Hopwood [1980], Branch and Berkowitz [1981], and Coggin and Hunter [1982-1983]. At this stage, explaining the conflict in conclusions between the early and subsequent studies is of low priority; the more important task is to structure research designs to make reliable inferences about the importance of factors such as information set differences (ID), timing differences (TD), aggregation differences (AD), and efficiency differences (ED).

The timing difference explanation has been probed in several studies with inconsistent results. Brown and Rozeff [1978] made a "brief investigation" (p. 12) of this explanation:

> During the period between the most recent quarterly earnings announcement and the subsequent Value Line prediction, Value Line acquires incremental information which, if an important part of its total information set, may explain Value Line's superiority. Information arising during this interval is likely to be most important for predicting next quarter's earnings. Assuming that the generation of this incremental information is positively related to the passage of time, earnings should be relatively easier to predict the further Value Line's prediction date is from the most recent earnings announcement date (pp. 12-13).

Brown and Rozeff [1978] correlated the Value Line forecast errors and the time interval since their most recent earnings announcement for the one quarter ahead forecasts in their study. They reported: "The insignificantly negative Spearman rho suggests that information obtained by Value Line during this interval has a negligible effect on its ability to predict next quarter's earnings" (p. 13). In contrast, Smith and Murphy [1976] reported the following for forecasts of the annual earnings of December 31 fiscal year firms made by Canadian security analysts: "The results [for forecasts published in May] indicate that the investment analysts did outperform each of the mechanical models.... Similar tests upon the forecasts [published in September] showed even more dramatic results in favour of the analysts" (p. 16).

One explanation for results showing the superiority of analyst forecasts over mechanical models is that the mechanical models examined did not make the most efficient use of the available data. Consider the Brown-Rozeff [1978] finding of analyst superiority. In a subsequent paper, Brown and Rozeff [1979] report that the "best" univariate model used in their earlier paper was "outperformed" by another Box-Jenkins univariate model. Collins and Hopwood [1980] reexamined the security analyst (Value Line) versus Box-Jenkins univariate model issue; the four Box-Jenkins models examined included the one proposed by Brown and Rozeff [1979]. The mean absolute percentage forecast error for security analysts and the four univariate Box-Jenkins models were:

Quarter in which Annual EPS Forecast Originated	**Security Analyst**	**Box-Jenkins Model #1**	**Box-Jenkins Model #2**	**Box-Jenkins Model #3**	**Box-Jenkins Model #4**
First	.3414	.5133	.6998	.6489	.5217
Second	.2806	.4009	.5469	.5035	.4257
Third	.2184	.2707	.3373	.3766	.3312
Fourth	.1003	.1538	.1776	.2318	.1629

The conclusion was that "the means and standard deviations of the forecast errors generated by the financial analysts were lower than those generated by each of the four univariate [Box-Jenkins] models" (p. 397).

The Collins-Hopwood [1980] study included two very interesting additions to the literature:

(i) An analysis of the effect of outliers on the above results. The conclusion was that the "analysts generated outliers that were lower both in number and degree than the univariate models. Investigation into the economic events that were the underlying causes of these outliers [e.g., a strike] generally indicated that [analysts were] more capable of incorporating the effects of these economic events as the events became known. The univariate models tended to lag in reaction until the effects of these economic events were incorporated in reported earnings" (p. 402).

(ii) Adoption of a multivariate research design that examined interactions between "the forecast model, the quarter from which the forecast is made and the year of the forecast" (pp. 395-396). The conclusion was that there was a "significant interaction between the quarter in which the annual forecast is made and the forecast method used. In particular, the advantage of the financial analysts over the [Box-Jenkins] models tended to decrease as the end of the year approached" (p. 403).

Insight into the aggregation difference explanation is provided in Coggin and Hunter [1982-1983]. This study reports that (i) consensus forecasts are significantly more accurate than individuals comprising the consensus, and (ii) consensus forecasts and individual analyst forecasts are each significantly more accurate than forecasts from three mechanical models.

Most studies of the security analyst vs. mechanical model issue have pooled across analysts when presenting their results (in part, because some sources disclose only the forecasting institution and not the analyst). As analysts can differ in the efficiency with which they utilize information (and in the information they can access), pooling across analysts can mask differences in samples as regards the security analyst vs. mechanical model result. Brown and Rozeff [1980] examined this topic for a subsample of the 50 firms in their [1978] study. These firms were those for which all 16 interim forecasts over the 1973-1976 period were made by the same Value Line analyst; 11 different analysts covering 17 firms satisfied this restriction. The conclusion was that "10 of the 11 analysts produced smaller forecast errors on average than did the corresponding [mechanical] benchmark models" (p. 33).

The development of data bases such as IBES and Icarus will make possible more extensive research into explanations for forecasting accuracy differences between security analysts and mechanical models. These services include monthly data on individual analyst forecasts (including the identity of the forecaster) and consensus forecasts; this facilitates tests of the differences in aggregation explanation and the differences in efficiency of information processing explanation. The data can be aligned in event time (see Chapter 3 of this monograph); this facilitates tests of the timing difference explanation. In addition, the data bases include forecasts for each year of a multi-year horizon; most existing tests of the superiority issue have focused on forecasts of one year ahead earnings.

One benchmark study examining a forecast horizon longer than one year ahead is Rozeff [1983]; forecasts of "long-term" (four to five years ahead) EPS growth rates were analyzed. Forecasts made by Value Line security analysts were compared to those made from mechanical time series models and those implicit in security prices (assuming a constant growth equity valuation model). Over both the 1967-1972 and 1972-1976 periods, Value Line forecasts had the lowest mean absolute error and the lowest mean square error. The sources of this superiority by Value Line over other long-term EPS growth forecasting approaches were not examined by Rozeff.

Analysts' Forecasts vs. Mechanical Model Forecasts in a Capital Market Context

A small subset of studies has compared the use of forecasts by analysts with forecasts of mechanical models in capital market association studies. McEnally [1971] probed the timing explanation for differences between the analyst and mechanical model forecasts. Forecasts were selected for two dates:

(i) at the end of the week in which fiscal year t–1 ended (termed "end of year"), and

(ii) at the end of the fourth week after earnings in year t–1 were announced (termed "after announcement week").

McEnally reported that the ranking of the correlation between security returns and earnings forecast errors, using security analyst forecasts as an expectations model relative to the use of 15 mechanical models, was affected by the time at which the security analyst forecast was made; for the "end of year sample" security analysts ranked ninth while in the "after announcement week" they ranked first.

In a more recent study, Fried and Givoly [1982] report that earnings forecast errors of security analysts have a higher association with security price changes than do the earnings forecast errors from mechanical models. Utilizing information in the magnitude of the earnings prediction errors, they reported the following abnormal returns for a strategy of investing long in firms with positive forecast errors and short in firms with negative forecast errors in the twelve months up to and including the earnings announcement month:

	Abnormal Return Using:		
Sample	**Security Analyst Forecast**	**Mechanical Forecasting Model #1**	**Mechanical Forecasting Model #2**
All Observations	14.12%	9.97%	9.45%
Positive Forecast Errors	7.45	2.73	3.32
Negative Forecast Errors	17.48	17.03	17.63

Only for the positive forecast error sample was the security analyst forecasting model superior. The timing explanation for the superiority of analysts' forecasts was examined by analyzing a subsample with analyst forecasts for the same company available both in (i) January and February *and* (ii) March and April. The conclusion was that "the timing advantage [of the March and April forecasts] does not result in a significant improvement in the association of financial analyst forecasts with stock price movements" (p. 102). In Chapter 4 of this monograph, a more powerful research design is used to examine the effect of the timing advantage of newly released forecasts over successively more dated analyst earnings forecasts. The conclusion is that the timeliness of the security analyst earnings forecast is a significant factor in explaining the observed association between earnings forecast errors and security returns.

B. Forecasts of Security Analysts vs. Forecasts of Management

The evidence on the relative accuracy of security analyst vs. management earnings forecasts is mixed. Many studies have reported finding no statistically significant difference, e.g., Imhoff [1978], Ruland [1978], and Imhoff and Pare [1982]. One interesting feature of Ruland [1978] was analysis of timing as a factor explaining differences in forecast accuracy.

Security analyst forecasts were collected both (i) immediately prior to and (ii) subsequent to the release of each management forecast examined. The conclusion was that although there was a decrease in management superiority over analysts from (i) to (ii), statistical testing did *not* indicate that "management forecast accuracy differs significantly from that of the analysts" (p. 444). The few studies that report significant differences find management to be the more accurate. For instance, Barefield, Comiskey and McDonald [1979] report that for a sample of 134 management forecasts matched with analyst forecasts, "management forecasting performance [is] superior to that of analysts at conventional significance levels" (p. 115). However, they caution against extrapolation of this result to all firms: "management may have provided forecasts only when they had greater than average confidence in the outcome" (p. 115).

Several difficult issues arise when making comparisons between security analyst forecasts and management forecasts:

(a) The loss functions facing management and security analysts when forecasting need not be the same.

(b) Management forecasts are not always issued in "point form." Some are issued with qualifications such as: "earnings per share will be at least $2.00" or "at a minimum, we are forecasting $2.00 per share." Inferences drawn about the relative accuracy of management forecasts using such inputs are ambiguous at best.

(c) Neither party typically discloses the assumptions underlying their forecasts. This non-disclosure makes it difficult to test the hypothesis that management can have a comparative advantage in forecasting the firm-specific component of the earnings forecast whereas analysts can have a comparative advantage in forecasting the industry- or economy-related components.

(d) Analysts and management derive reciprocal benefits from interacting with each other. There are incentives on both sides to communicate information, even when "insider trading" laws exist. The result is that an external researcher finds it difficult to discriminate among competing explanations for a finding of no difference in forecast errors; e.g., (i) neither management nor analysts have a comparative advantage in forecasting, or (ii) management has significant superiority in forecasting but it shares its forecasts (and possibly its assumptions) with analysts without "publicly" releasing those forecasts.

(e) Management has the ability to influence the variable being forecast via its financing, operating, or production decisions, and may have strong economic incentives (e.g., compensation plan effects) to have the firm report a particular level of earnings. In contrast, security analysts cannot take such actions to make their forecasts more accurate.

C. Forecasts of Management vs. Forecasts of Mechanical Models

The studies referenced in Panel C of Table A.6 differ in terms of sample selection, time period left in the fiscal year to forecast, the error measures used, and the mechanical models used as a benchmark. A consistent result does not emerge from this research:

- Lorek, McDonald and Patz [1976] concluded that "in cases in which management forecasts proved reasonably accurate, overall they were not more so than those generated from the time-series models. Where management forecasts proved to be relatively inaccurate, those from the Box-Jenkins models were significantly less so" (pp. 328-329).
- Nichols and Groomer [1979] – "the exponential smoothing model was found in general to produce forecasts as accurate as those disclosed by the executives" (p. 121).
- Hagerman and Ruland [1979] – "for the sample of forecasts as a whole, management forecasts are more accurate than those of the alternative models" (p. 178).

Many of the issues raised in Sections A.6.A and A.6.B of this Appendix apply to attempts to structure a research design that probes explanations for differences in accuracy between management forecasts and the forecasts of mechanical models.

D. Composite Forecast Analysis

A major limitation of the benchmark studies referenced in Panels A to C of Table A.6 is the narrowness of the question posed, i.e., forecast method A vs. forecast method B. The more interesting question is the relative improvement from combining A and B vs. method A alone vs. method B alone. Early work in this area focused on the forecasts of macroeconomic variables. For example, Cooper and Nelson [1975] illustrate how combining the forecasts of econometric models and Box-Jenkins time-series models can lead to improved forecasts of variables such as GNP and the unemployment rate. The conclusion was that "no single model or predictor can be said to dominate the others in the sense of subsuming their information content; rather each generally contains a marginal increment of information which may be usefully exploited" (p. 30). Other studies include Bates and Granger [1969], Newbold and Granger [1974], Granger and Newbold [1977, Chapter 8] and Makridakis and Winkler [1983]. The last study noted:

> Unless an adequate theory exists concerning the data-generating process or strong evidence is available indicating that a particular forecasting method is better than other methods for a given situation, it might be desirable to consider several methods.... The results reported here suggest that using averages of forecasts provides considerable practical benefits in terms of improved forecasting accuracy and decreased variability of accuracy (p. 995).

The research in this area is related to the consensus forecast literature – see Section A.2.C of this Appendix.

When the earnings forecasts of an individual security analyst are combined with the forecasts of a mechanical model, the comparison of predictions of the composite model with the individual analyst predictions will provide insight into whether that analyst is systematically ignoring information in the public domain (i.e., whether he or she is being "rational" in the Muth [1961] sense of the word). Cragg and Malkiel [1982] report evidence on this topic, although they stress that "the tests [they] conduct are at best only slightly indicative of whether the rational-expectations hypothesis is appropriate" (p. 83). Their tests include examination of whether "there was some combination of historical information and analysts' forecasts that together might be better than using any individual piece of information alone" (p. 94). They reported that "there is no combination of analysts' forecasts and historical information that could be used to make better predictions on a consistent basis.... We found no consistent or coherent pattern indicating that readily available information is not efficiently incorporated in the forecasts" (p. 96). Fried and Givoly [1982] report a similar finding based on partial correlations between the forecast errors made by security analysts and two mechanical models: "The coefficients of the partial correlation between realization and time-series predictions, given financial analyst forecasts, are generally very small and close to zero. This means that, in addition to the utilization of autonomous information, analysts also fully exploit the time-series and cross-sectional properties of the earnings series that are captured by the [two mechanical] models of earnings" (p. 100).

One information set not examined in current research on composite forecasts is the time-series and cross-sectional properties of the security return series. The results in Chapter 4 of the monograph are consistent with security returns being a lead indicator of security analyst earnings forecast revisions. These results raise the issue of whether analysts could make more timely forecast revisions by more explicitly incorporating security return information into their forecasting procedures (or at least by using in a timely fashion the information the capital market is using in its security price revaluation process).

The use of composite forecasts (or partial correlations) to make inferences about security analyst rationality requires that all the analyst forecasts examined be made by the one individual. Where this condition is not met, the analysis of composite earnings forecasts is better motivated strictly as a search for a model with improved forecasting accuracy or decreased variability of accuracy. When management and security analysts' forecasts are combined, one rationale for predicting composite forecasts to be superior would be that there is less than perfect overlap in the information sets each accesses. For example, management has access to its own internal strategic plans and forecasts while security analysts have access to industry information based on company visits to each firm in the industry.

REFERENCES

Abdel-khalik, A.R., "Three Generations of Research on Quarterly Reports: Some Thoughts on the Research Process," in R.D. Nair and T.H. Williams, *Perspectives on Research* (Madison: University of Wisconsin, 1980), pp. 60-106.

———, "Overfitting Bias in the Models Assessing the Predictive Power of Quarterly Reports," *Journal of Accounting Research* (Spring 1983), pp. 293-296.

——— and B.B. Ajinkya, "Returns to Informational Advantages: The Case of Analysts' Forecast Revisions," *The Accounting Review* (October 1982), pp. 661-680.

——— and J. Espejo, "Expectations Data and the Predictive Value of Interim Reporting," *Journal of Accounting Research* (Spring 1978), pp. 1-13.

——— and R.B. Thompson, "Research on Earnings Forecasts: The State of the Art," *The Accounting Journal* (Winter 1977-78), pp. 180-209.

Abdelsamad, M.H. and G.H. Gilbreath, "Publication of Earnings Forecasts: A Report of Financial Executives' Opinions," *Management Planning* (January/February 1978), pp. 26-30.

Ajinkya, B.B. and M.J. Gift, "Corporate Managers' Earnings Forecasts and Symmetrical Adjustments of Market Expectations," Working paper, University of Florida, 1983.

Albrecht, W.S., O. Johnson, L.L. Lookabill and D.J.H. Watson, "A Comparison of the Accuracy of Corporate and Security Analysts' Forecasts of Earnings: A Comment," *The Accounting Review* (July 1977), pp. 736-740.

Armstrong, J.S., "Relative Accuracy of Methods Used to Forecast Annual Earnings: A Quantitative Review," Working paper, IMEDE (April 1981).

———, "Relative Accuracy of Judgemental and Extrapolative Methods in Forecasting Annual Earnings," *Journal of Forecasting* (October-December 1983), pp. 437-447.

Arnold, J., P. Moizer and E. Noreen, "Investment Appraisal Methods of Financial Analysts: A Comparative Survey of U.S. and U.K. Practices," Working paper, University of Manchester, 1983.

Asebrook, R.J. and D.R. Carmichael, "Reporting on Forecasts: A Survey of Attitudes," *The Journal of Accountancy* (August 1973), pp. 38-48.

Backer, M., *Financial Reporting for Security Investment and Credit Decisions* (New York: National Association of Accountants, 1970).

Backer, M., "Reporting Profit Expectations," *Management Accounting* (February 1972), pp. 33-37.

Baker, H.K. and S.M. Iralins, "An Analysis of Published Financial Forecasts," *Atlantic Economic Review* (No. 4, 1976), pp. 42-46.

Baldwin, B., "Segment Earnings Disclosure and the Ability of Security Analysts to Forecast Earnings Per Share," *The Accounting Review* (July 1984), pp. 376-389.

Ball, R., "Anomalies in Relationships Between Securities' Yields and Yield-Surrogates," *Journal of Financial Economics* (June/September 1978), pp. 103-126.

——— and P. Brown, "An Empirical Evaluation of Accounting Income Numbers," *Journal of Accounting Research* (Autumn 1968), pp. 159-178.

——— and ———, "Portfolio Theory and Accounting," *Journal of Accounting Research* (Autumn 1969), pp. 300-323.

——— and G. Foster, "Corporate Financial Reporting: A Methodological Review of Empirical Research," *Studies on Current Research Methodologies in Accounting: A Critical Evaluation,* Supplement to *Journal of Accounting Research* (1982), pp. 161-234.

Barefied, R.M. and E.E. Comiskey, "The Accuracy of Analysts' Forecasts of Earnings per Share," *Journal of Business Research* (July 1975), pp. 241-251.

——— and ———, "The Association of Forecast Error with Other Risk Measures," *Journal of Business Finance and Accounting* (Autumn 1975a), pp. 315-325.

——— and ———, "The Accuracy of Bank Earnings Forecasts," *Business Economics* (May 1976), pp. 59-63.

——— and ———, "The Differential Association of Forecast Error and Earnings Variability With Systematic Risk," *Journal of Business Finance and Accounting* (Spring 1979), pp. 1-8.

———, ——— and C.L. McDonald, "Accuracy of Management and Security Analysts' Forecasts: Additional Evidence," *Journal of Business Research* (August 1979), pp. 109-115.

Barnea, A., S. Sadan and M. Schiff, *Publishing Earnings Forecasts* (New York: Vincent C. Ross Institute of Accounting Research, 1979).

Bart, J.T., "Single vs. Multiple-Value Earnings Forecasts – One or the Others?" *CA Magazine (Canada)* (March 1980), pp. 50-53.

Basi, B.A., K.J. Carey and R.D. Twark, "A Comparison of the Accuracy of Corporate and Security Analysts' Forecasts of Earnings," *The Accounting Review* (April 1976), pp. 244-254; see also "A Reply," *The Accounting Review* (July 1977), pp. 741-745.

Bates, J.M. and C.W.J. Granger, "The Combination of Forecasts," *Operations Research Quarterly* (December 1979), pp. 451-468.

Beaver, W.H., R. Clarke and W.F. Wright, "The Association Between Unsystematic Security Returns and the Magnitude of Earnings Forecast Errors," *Journal of Accounting Research* (Autumn 1979), pp. 316-340.

———, P. Kettler and M. Scholes, "The Association Between Market-Determined and Accounting-Determined Risk Measures," *The Accounting Review* (October 1970), pp. 654-682.

———, R. Lambert and D. Morse, "The Information Content of Security Prices," *Journal of Accounting and Economics* (March 1980), pp. 3-28.

——— and D. Morse, "What Determines Price Earnings Ratios?" *Financial Analysts Journal* (July/August 1978), pp. 65-76.

Bedingfield, J.P. and M.S. Lubell, "Extension of the Attest Function to Published Forecasts – An Opinion Survey," *CPA* (January 1974), pp. 40-45.

Beshara, R.L., "Newness and Imputed Accuracy of Management Forecasts: An Empirical Investigation," Ph.D. dissertation, University of Florida, 1981.

Biggs, S.F., "An Empirical Investigation of the Information Processes Underlying Four Models of Choice Behavior," in T.J. Burns (ed.), *Behavioral Experiments in Accounting II* (Columbus: College of Administrative Science, Ohio State University, 1979), pp. 35-81.

———, "Financial Analysts' Information Search in the Assessment of Corporate Earning Power," *Accounting, Organizations and Society* (Vol. 9, Number 3/4, 1984), pp. 313-323.

Bowen, R.M., "Valuation of Earnings Components in the Electric Utility Industry," *The Accounting Review* (January 1981), pp. 1-22.

———, J.M. Lacey and E.W. Noreen, "Determinants of the Corporate Decision to Capitalize Interest," *Journal of Accounting and Economics* (August 1981), pp. 151-179.

Branch, B. and B. Berkowitz, "The Predictive Accuracy of the Business Week Earnings Forecasts," *Journal of Accounting, Auditing and Finance* (Spring 1981), pp. 215-219.

Brandon, C.H. and J. Jarrett, "Accuracy of Forecasts in Annual Reports," *The Financial Review* (1974), pp. 29-45.

——— and ———, "Accuracy of Externally Prepared Forecasts," *Review of Business and Economic Research* (Fall 1977), pp. 35-45.

——— and ———, "Revising Earnings Per Share Forecasts: An Empirical Test," *Management Science* (March 1979), pp. 211-220.

Brown, L.D., "Accounting Changes and the Accuracy of Analysts' Earnings Forecasts," *Journal of Accounting Research* (Autumn 1983), pp. 432-443.

———, "Financial Information and the Formation of Analyst Expectations," Working paper, SUNY at Buffalo, April 1983a.

———, P. Griffin, R. Hagerman and M. Zmijewski, "A Comprehensive Analysis of the Predictability of Analysts' and Time-Series Model Forecasts of Earnings Per Share," Working paper, SUNY at Buffalo, 1984.

———, J.S. Hughes, M.S. Rozeff and J.H. Vanderweide, "Expectations Data and the Predictive Value of Interim Reporting: A Comment," *Journal of Accounting Research* (Spring 1980), pp. 278-288.

——— and M.S. Rozeff, "The Superiority of Analyst Forecasts as Measures of Expectations: Evidence from Earnings," *The Journal of Finance* (March 1978), pp. 1-16.

——— and ———, "Univariate Time-Series Models of Quarterly Accounting Earnings per Share: A Proposed Model," *Journal of Accounting Research* (Spring 1979), pp. 179-189.

——— and ———, "The Predictive Values of Interim Reports for Improving Forecasts of Future Quarterly Earnings," *The Accounting Review* (July 1979a), pp. 585-591.

——— and ———, "Adaptive Expectations, Time-Series Models, and Analyst Forecast Revision," *Journal of Accounting Research* (Autumn 1979b), pp. 341-351.

——— and ———, "Analysts Can Forecast Accurately!" *The Journal of Portfolio Management* (Spring 1980), pp. 31-34.

Brown, P., F.J. Finn and P. Hancock, "Dividend Changes, Earnings Reports, and Share Prices: Some Australian Findings," *Australian Journal of Management* (October 1977), pp. 127-147.

——— and J. Kennelly, "The Information Content of Quarterly Earnings: An Extension and Some Further Evidence," *The Journal of Business* (July 1972), pp. 403-415.

Buckley, A., "Planning Estimates – A Survey Of Their Accuracy," *Accountancy* (June 1973), pp. 56-60.

Buckman, J.W., "The Reliability of Earnings Forecasts," Prepared for the Trust Investment Committee of the Continental Illinois National Bank and Trust Company of Chicago (Chicago: September 13, 1963).

Burson-Marsteller, "Corporate Financial Officers and Security Analysts on the Disclosure of Projections of Future Economic Performance" (New York: Burson-Marsteller, 1975).

Carmichael, D.R., "Reporting on Forecasts: A U.K. Perspective," *The Journal of Accountancy* (January 1973), pp. 36-47.

Carpenter, C.G. and R.A. Daily, "Controllers and CPAs: Two Views of Published Forecasts," *Business Horizons* (August 1974), pp. 73-78.

Cheever, J.K., "Forecasted Earnings in an Efficient Market," Unpublished paper, California State Polytechnic University, 1975.

Chow, C.W., "The Demand for External Auditing: Size, Debt and Ownership Influences," *The Accounting Review* (April 1982), pp. 272-291.

Clarkson, G.P.E., *Portfolio Selection: A Simulation of Trust Investment* (Englewood Cliffs, N.J.: Prentice-Hall, 1962).

Coggin, T.D. and J.E. Hunter, "Analysts' EPS Forecasts Nearer Actual Than Statistical Models," *The Journal of Business Forecasting* (Winter 1982-1983), pp. 20-23.

Collins, W.A. and W.S. Hopwood, "A Multivariate Analysis of Annual Earnings Forecasts Generated from Quarterly Forecasts of Financial Analysts and Univariate Time-Series Models," *Journal of Accounting Research* (Autumn 1980), pp. 390-406.

Cooper, J.P. and C.R. Nelson, "The Ex Ante Prediction Performance of the St. Louis and FRB-MIT-PENN Econometric Models and Some Results on Composite Predictors," *Journal of Money, Credit and Banking* (March 1975), pp. 1-32.

Copeland, R.M. and R.J. Marioni, "Executives' Forecasts of Earnings per Share versus Forecasts of Naive Models," *The Journal of Business* (October 1972), pp. 497-512.

Corless, J.C. and C.T. Norgaard, "User Reactions to CPA Reports on Forecasts," *The Journal of Accountancy* (August 1974), pp. 46-54.

Corn, I.G., "The Case Against Forecasting Earnings," *MSU Business Topics* (Summer 1974), pp. 11-16.

Cox, D.R. and D.V. Hinkley, *Theoretical Statistics* (London: Chapman and Hall, 1974).

Cragg, J.G. and B.G. Malkiel, "The Consensus and Accuracy of Some Predictions of the Growth of Corporate Earnings," *The Journal of Finance* (March 1968), pp. 67-84.

——— and ———, *Expectations and the Structure of Share Prices* (Chicago: The University of Chicago Press, 1982).

Crichfield, T., T. Dyckman and J. Lakonishok, "An Evaluation of Security Analysts' Forecasts," *The Accounting Review* (July 1978), pp. 651-668.

Daily, R.A., "The Feasibility of Reporting Forecasted Information," *The Accounting Review* (October 1971), pp. 686-692.

Danos, P. and E.A. Imhoff, "Auditor Review of Financial Forecasts: An Analysis of Factors Affecting Reasonableness Judgments," *The Accounting Review* (January 1982), pp. 39-54.

——— and ———, "Factors Affecting Auditors' Evaluation of Forecasts," *Journal of Accounting Research* (Autumn 1983), pp. 473-494.

Dev, S., "Mergers and Shareholders," in J. M. Samuels (ed.), *Readings on Mergers and Takeovers* (London: Paul Elek Books, 1972), pp. 163-198.

———, "Problems in Interpreting Prospectus Profit Forecasts," *Accounting and Business Research* (Spring 1973), pp. 110-116.

———, "Statements of Company Prospects," *Accounting and Business Research* (Autumn 1974), pp. 270-274.

——— and M. Webb, "The Accuracy of Company Profit Forecasts," *Journal of Business Finance* (Vol. 4, No. 3, 1972), pp. 26-39.

Dimson, E., "Risk Measurement When Shares Are Subject To Infrequent Trading," *Journal of Financial Economics* (June 1979), pp. 197-226.

Dreman, D., "Tricky Forecasts: Nearly Everyone's Crystal Ball is Clouded," *Barron's* (July 24, 1978).

———, "Hard to Forecast: Even the Most Careful Earnings Projections Often Go Awry," *Barron's* (March 3, 1980).

Drury, D.H., *Management Forecasts of Earnings: Issues and Practices* (Hamilton, Ontario: The Society of Management Accountants of Canada, 1982).

Dyckman, T.R., M. Gibbins and R.J. Swieringa, "Experimental and Survey Research in Financial Accounting: A Review and Evaluation," in A.R. Abdel-khalik and T.F. Keller (eds.), *The Impact of Accounting Research on Practice and Disclosure* (Durham: Duke University Press, 1978), pp. 48-105.

Ebert, R.J. and T.E. Kruse, "Bootstrapping the Security Analyst," *Journal of Applied Psychology* (February 1978), pp. 110-119.

Eckel, N., "An EPS Forecasting Model Utilizing Macroeconomic Performance Expectations," *Financial Analysts Journal* (May-June 1982), pp. 68-77.

Elton, E.J. and M.J. Gruber, "Earnings Estimates and the Accuracy of Expectational Data," *Management Science* (April 1972), pp. B409-B424.

———, ———, and M. Gultekin, "Expectations and Share Prices," *Management Science* (September 1981), pp. 975-987.

———, ——— and ———, "Professional Expectations: Accuracy and Diagnosis of Errors," Working paper, New York University, 1982.

Epstein, M.J., "The Shareholder's View of Earnings Forecasts," *Managerial Planning* (November-December 1975), pp. 33-36.

Farrelly, G.E. and W.R. Reichenstein, "Risk Perceptions of Institutional Investors," *Journal of Portfolio Management* (Summer 1984), pp. 5-12.

Ferris, K.R., "Profit Forecast Disclosure: The Effect on Managerial Behavior," *Accounting and Business Research* (Spring 1975), pp. 133-139.

———, "The Apparent Effects of Profit Forecast Disclosure on Managerial Behaviour: An Empirical Examination," *Journal of Business Finance and Accounting* (Autumn 1976), pp. 53-66.

——— and D.C. Hayes, "Some Evidence on the Determinants of Profit Forecast Accuracy in the United Kingdom," *The International Journal of Accounting Education and Research* (Spring 1977), pp. 27-36.

Figlewski, S. and T. Urich, "Optimal Aggregation of Money Supply Forecasts: Accuracy, Profitability and Market Efficiency," *The Journal of Finance* (June 1983), pp. 695-710.

Financial Executives Institute, "How Accurate Are Forecasts?" *Financial Executive* (February 1973), pp. 26-32.

Finn, F.J., "The Internal Investment Performance Evaluation of Managed Investment Funds," Working paper, University of Queensland, March 1981.

———, *Evaluation of the Internal Processes of Managed Investment Funds* (Greenwich, Conn.: JAI Press, 1984).

Foster, G., "Stock Market Reaction to Estimates of Earnings per Share by Company Officials," *Journal of Accounting Research* (Spring 1973), pp. 25-37.

———, "Security Price Revaluation Implications of Sub-Earnings Disclosure," *Journal of Accounting Research* (Autumn 1975), pp. 283-292.

———, "Quarterly Accounting Data: Time-Series Properties and Predictive-Ability Results," *The Accounting Review* (January 1977), pp. 1-21.

———, *Financial Statement Analysis* (Englewood Cliffs, N.J.: Prentice-Hall, 1978).

———, "Accounting Policy Decisions and Capital Market Research," *Journal of Accounting and Economics* (March 1980), pp. 29-62.

———, "Capital Market Efficiency: Definitions, Testing Issues and Anomalies" in M.J. Gaffikin (ed.), *Contemporary Accounting Thought* (Melbourne, Australia: Prentice-Hall, 1984), pp. 151-180.

———, C. Olsen and T. Shevlin, "Earnings Releases, Anomalies and the Behavior of Security Returns," *The Accounting Review* (October 1984), pp. 574-603.

Fouse, W.L., "Risk and Liquidity: The Keys to Stock Price Behavior," *Financial Analysts Journal* (May-June 1976), pp. 35-45.

———, "Risk and Liquidity Revisited," *Financial Analysts Journal* (January-February 1977), pp. 40-45.

———, "Common Stock Evaluation," *Seminar on the Analysis of Security Prices* (The University of Chicago, November 2, 1978).

Fraser, D.R., "Do Analysts' Forecasts Matter?" *University of Michigan Business Review* (September 1979), pp. 15-19.

——— and R.M. Richards, "Forecasting Bank Earnings," *Magazine of Bank Administration* (August 1975), pp. 40-45.

——— and ———, "Forecasting Earnings for Insurance Companies" *Best's Review* (April 1978), pp. 20-22, 86.

——— and ———, "The Accuracy of Earnings Forecasts for Public Utilities," *Public Utilities Fortnightly* (November 23, 1978a), pp. 27-30.

Fried, D. and D. Givoly, "Financial Analysts' Forecasts of Earnings: A Better Surrogate for Market Expectations," *Journal of Accounting and Economics* (October 1982), pp. 85-107.

Friend, I., R. Westerfield and M. Granito, "New Evidence On The Capital Asset Pricing Model," *The Journal of Finance* (June 1978), pp. 903-917.

Fuller, R.J. and R.W. Metcalf, "Management Disclosures: Analysts Prefer Facts to Management's Predictions," *Financial Analysts Journal* (March-April 1978), pp. 55-57.

Gibbs, P.M.D. and W.T. Seward, "How An Investment Analyst Uses A Profit Forecast and Makes His Own," in Westwick [1983], pp. 134-147.

Gift, M.J., "Information Content of Management Forecasts: Risk Shift and Mean Earnings Shift Effects on Equilibrium Security Prices," Ph.D. dissertation, University of Florida, 1983.

Givoly, D. and J. Lakonishok, "The Information Content of Financial Analysts' Forecasts of Earnings," *Journal of Accounting and Economics* (Winter 1979), pp. 165-185.

——— and ———, "Financial Analysts' Forecasts of Earnings: Their Value to Investors," *Journal of Banking and Finance* (September 1980), pp. 221-233.

——— and ———, "Divergence of Earnings Expectations: The Effect on Market Response to Earnings Signals," Working paper, Tel Aviv University, February 1983.

——— and ———, "Properties of Analysts' Forecasts of Earnings: A Review and Analysis of the Research," Working paper, Tel Aviv University, April 1983a – forthcoming in *Journal of Accounting Literature*.

——— and D. Palmon, "Timeliness of Annual Earnings Announcements: Some Empirical Evidence," *The Accounting Review* (July 1982), pp. 486-508.

Gonedes, N.J., "Capital Market Equilibrium and Annual Accounting Numbers: Empirical Evidence," *Journal of Accounting Research* (Spring 1974), pp. 26-62.

———, N.J., N. Dopuch and S.H. Penman, "Disclosure Rules, Information-Production and Capital Market Equilibrium: The Case of Forecast Disclosure Rules," *Journal of Accounting Research* (Spring 1976), pp. 89-137.

Granger, C.W.J. and P. Newbold, *Forecasting Economic Time Series* (New York: Academic Press, 1977).

Gray, W.S., "The Role of Forecast Information in Investment Decisions," in Prakash and Rappaport [1974], pp. 47-79.

Green, D. and J. Segall, "The Predictive Power of First-Quarter Earnings Reports: A Replication," *Empirical Research in Accounting: Selected Studies 1966,* Supplement to *Journal of Accounting Research,* pp. 21-36.

——— and ———, "The Predictive Power of First-Quarter Earnings Reports," *The Journal of Business* (January 1967), pp. 44-55.

Griffin, P.A., "Competitive Information in the Stock Market: An Empirical Study of Earnings, Dividends and Analysts' Forecasts," *The Journal of Finance* (May 1976), pp. 631-650.

——— and D.S. Ng, "Competitive Information Sources and Capital Market Behavior: Theory and Empirical Tests," Working paper, Stanford University, July 1978.

Grimm, W.T., *Mergerstat Review 1982* (Chicago: W.T. Grimm & Co., 1983).

Gultekin, M.N., "Formation of Earnings Estimates," Working paper, New York University, June 1983.

Hagerman, R.L. and W. Ruland, "The Accuracy of Management Forecasts and Forecasts of Simple Alternative Models," *Journal of Economics and Business* (Spring 1979), pp. 172-179.

Hawkins, E.H., S.C. Chamberlin and W.E. Daniel, "Earnings Expectations and Security Prices," Working paper, Lynch, Jones and Ryan, November 1983; forthcoming in *Financial Analysts Journal*.

Hill, J. and T. Schneeweis, "Accuracy and Consistency of Analyst and Time Series Forecasts of Earnings Per Share," Working paper, Brown Brothers Harriman, 1984.

Hitschler, W.A., "To Know What We Don't Know or The Caribou Weren't In The Estimates," *Financial Analysts Journal* (January-February 1980), pp. 28-32.

Hock, C.A., "Earnings Per Share Forecast Accuracy and the Use of Two Discretionary Accounting Variables: A Study of Possible Income Manipulation," Ph.D. dissertation, Pennsylvania State University, 1974.

Imhoff, E.A., "The Representativeness of Management Earnings Forecasts," *The Accounting Review* (October 1978), pp. 836-850.

———, "A Closer Look at Management Forecasts," *Management Accounting* (May 1980), pp. 18-23, 30.

——— and G.J. Lobo, "Information Content of Analysts' Composite Forecast Revisions," Working paper, University of Michigan, September 1983; forthcoming in *Journal of Accounting Research.*

——— and P.V. Pare, "Analysis and Comparison of Earnings Forecast Agents," *Journal of Accounting Research* (Autumn 1982), pp. 429-439.

——— and ———, "Composite Predictors of Accounting Data," Working paper, University of Michigan, November 1983.

Jaggi, B., "Comparative Accuracy of Management's Annual Earnings Forecasts," *Financial Management* (Winter 1978), pp. 24-32.

———, "A Note on the Information Content of Corporate Annual Earnings Forecasts," *The Accounting Review* (October 1978a), pp. 961-967.

———, "Further Evidence on the Accuracy of Management Forecasts Vis-a-Vis Analysts' Forecasts," *The Accounting Review* (January 1980), pp. 96-101.

——— and P. Grier, "A Comparative Analysis of Forecast Disclosing and Non-Disclosing Firms," *Financial Management* (Summer 1980), pp. 38-43.

Jahnke, W.W., "The Growth Stock Mania," *Financial Analysts Journal* (May-June 1973), pp. 65-68.

———, "The Growth Stock Mania Revisited," *Financial Analysts Journal* (January-February 1975), pp. 42-44, 69.

Janell, P.A., "An Empirical Evaluation of the Relationship Between Errors in Analysts' Forecasts of Earnings Per Share and Stock Prices," Ph.D. dissertation, Michigan State University, 1974.

Jensen, M.C., "Capital Markets: Theory and Evidence," *The Bell Journal of Economics and Management Science* (Autumn 1972), pp. 357-398.

Jensen, R.E., *Review of Forecasts: Scaling and Analysis of Expert Judgments Regarding Cross-Impacts of Assumptions on Business Forecasts and Accounting Measures* (Sarasota, Florida: American Accounting Association, 1983).

Johnson, K., "One Company's Forecasting," *CPA Journal* (September 1974), pp. 47-49.

Kearney, A.T., "Public Disclosure of Business Forecasts," Part I of *Public Disclosure of Business Forecasts* (New York: Financial Executives Research Foundation, 1972), pp. 1-76.

Keller, R.J., "Disclosure of Projected Financial Information in Corporate Annual Reports," Ph.D. dissertation, Louisiana State University, 1973.

Kidd, R.H., *Earnings Forecasts: A Research Study* (Toronto: The Canadian Institute of Chartered Accountants, 1976).

Klepczynski, C.H., "Analysis of the Forecasting Ability of Investment Services and Simplistic Models," MBA paper, Pennsylvania State University, December 1971; results summarized in Basi, Carey and Twark [1976].

Kodde, D.A. and H. Schreuder, "Forecasting Corporate Revenue and Profit: Time-Series Models versus Management and Analysts," Working paper, Catholic University of Nijmegen, Netherlands, 1983 (forthcoming in *Journal of Business Finance and Accounting).*

——— and ———, "Optimal Combination Forecasts: Method and Application," Working paper, University of Nijmegen, 1984.

Kross, W., "Profitability, Earnings Announcement Time Lags, and Stock Prices," *Journal of Business Finance and Accounting* (Autumn 1982), pp. 313-328.

Lees, F.A., *Public Disclosure of Corporate Earnings Forecasts* (New York: The Conference Board, 1981).

Leftwich, R., R.L. Watts and J.L. Zimmerman, "Voluntary Corporate Disclosure: The Case of Interim Reporting" in *Studies on Standardization of Accounting Practices: An Assessment of Alternative Institutional Arrangements,* Supplement to *Journal of Accounting Research,* 1981, pp. 50-77.

Lobo, G.J. and R.D. Nair, "Combinations of Forecasts of Accounting Earnings," Working paper, University of Wisconsin-Madison, September 1983.

Lorek, K.S., "Critique; A Commentary on Research on Earnings Forecasts; The State of the Art," *The Accounting Journal* (Winter 1977-1978), pp. 210-217.

———, C.L. McDonald and D.H. Patz, "A Comparative Examination of Management Forecasts and Box-Jenkins Forecasts of Earnings," *The Accounting Review* (April 1976), pp. 321-330.

McDonald, C.L., "An Empirical Examination of the Reliability of Published Predictions of Future Earnings," *The Accounting Review* (January 1973), pp. 502-510.

McEnally, R.W., "Using Earnings Estimates In Selecting Common Stocks," *Trusts and Estates* (January 1970), pp. 35-38.

———, "An Investigation of the Extrapolative Determinants of Short-Run Earnings Expectations," *Journal of Financial and Quantitative Analysis* (March 1971), pp. 687-706.

McGrath, P.S. and F.J. Walsh, *Disclosure of Financial Forecasts to Security Analysts and the Public* (New York: The Conference Board, 1973).

Makridakis, S. and R.L. Winkler, "Averages of Forecasts: Some Empirical Results," *Management Science* (September 1983), pp. 987-996.

Malkiel, B.G., "The Valuation of Public Utility Equities," *The Bell Journal of Economics and Management Science* (Spring 1970), pp. 143-160.

———, "Risk and Return: A New Look," Working paper, Lynch, Jones and Ryan, April 1981.

——— and J.G. Cragg, "Expectations and the Structure of Share Prices," *American Economic Review* (September 1970), pp. 601-617.

Marais, M.L., "An Application of the Bootstrap Method to the Analysis of Squared, Standardized Market Model Prediction Errors," Working paper, University of Chicago, May 1984.

Mautz, R.K., "A View From The Public Accounting Profession" in Prakash and Rappaport [1974], pp. 99-127.

Meader, J.W., "A Formula for Determining Basic Values Underlying Common Stock Prices," *The Annalist* (November 29, 1935), p. 749.

Michaud, R.O. and P.L. Davis, "Valuation Model Bias and the Scale Structure of Dividend Discount Returns," *The Journal of Finance* (May 1982), pp. 563-573.

Miller, M.H. and F. Modigliani, "Some Estimates of the Cost of Capital to the Electric Utility Industry," *American Economic Review* (June 1966), pp. 334-391.

Miller, T.I., "An Inquiry Into the Feasibility of External Reporting of Forecasted Financial Information," Ph.D. dissertation, University of Arkansas, 1973.

Min, H.K., "A Theoretical and Empirical Investigation into Publication of Forecasts," Ph.D. dissertation, University of Oklahoma, 1974.

Moizer, P. and J. Arnold, "A Survey of the Methods Used by U.K. Investment Analysts to Appraise Investments in Ordinary Shares," Working paper, University of Manchester, 1982.

Monteith, D., "An Evaluation of Earnings Per Share Forecasts as Made by Four Financial Institutions," Paper prepared for the Trust Investment Committee of Continental Illinois National Bank and Trust Company of Chicago, March 3, 1966.

Morse, D., "Wall Street Journal Announcements and the Securities Markets," *Financial Analysts Journal* (March-April 1982), pp. 69-76.

Muth, J.F., "Rational Expectations and the Theory of Price Movements," *Econometrica* (July 1961), pp. 315-335.

Newbold, P. and C.W.J. Granger, "Experience with Forecasting Univariate Time Series and the Combination of Forecasts," *Journal of the Royal Statistical Society,* Series A (Vol. 137, 1974), pp. 131-146.

Nichols, D.R. and S.M. Groomer, "A Study of the Relative Accuracy of Executives' Estimates of Earnings," *Abacus* (December 1979), pp. 113-127.

——— and J.J. Tsay, "Security Price Reactions to Long-Range Executive Earnings Forecasts," *Journal of Accounting Research* (Spring 1979), pp. 140-155.

———, ——— and P.D. Larkin, "Investor Trading Responses to Differing Characteristics of Voluntarily Disclosed Earnings Forecasts," *The Accounting Review* (April 1979), pp. 376-382.

Nickerson, C.A., L.G. Pointer and R.H. Strawser, "Published Forecasts: Choice or Obligation?" *Financial Executive* (February 1974), pp. 70-73.

Niederhoffer, V. and P.J. Regan, "Earnings Changes, Analysts' Forecasts and Stock Prices," *Financial Analysts Journal* (May-June 1972), pp. 65-71.

Noreen, E. and J. Sepe, "Market Reactions to Accounting Policy Deliberations: The Inflation Accounting Case," *The Accounting Review* (April 1981), pp. 253-269.

O'Brien, P.C., "Analysts' Forecasts of Earnings Per Share: A Preliminary Investigation," Working paper, University of Chicago, March 1983.

Patell, J.M., "Corporate Forecasts of Earnings per Share and Stock Price Behavior: Empirical Tests," *Journal of Accounting Research* (Autumn 1976), pp. 246-276.

———, "Corporate Earnings Forecasts: Empirical Tests and a Consumption-Investment Model," Ph.D. dissertation, Carnegie-Mellon University, 1976a.

——— and M.A. Wolfson, "Good News, Bad News, and the Intraday Timing of Corporate Disclosures," *The Accounting Review* (July 1982), pp. 509-527.

——— and ———, "The Intraday Speed of Adjustment of Stock Prices to Earnings and Dividend Announcements," Working paper, Stanford University, December 1983, forthcoming in *Journal of Financial Economics*.

Penman, S.H., "An Empirical Investigation of the Voluntary Disclosure of Corporate Earnings Forecasts," *Journal of Accounting Research* (Spring 1980), pp. 132-160.

———, "Insider Trading and the Dissemination of Firms' Forecast Information," *The Journal of Business* (October 1982), pp. 479-503.

———, "The Predictive Content of Earnings Forecasts and Dividends," *The Journal of Finance* (September 1983), pp. 1181-1199.

Peterson, D. and P. Peterson, "The Effect of Changing Expectations upon Stock Returns," *Journal of Financial and Quantitative Analysis* (December 1982), pp. 799-813.

Peterson, P.P. and D.R. Peterson, "Divergence of Opinion and Return," *The Journal of Financial Research* (Summer 1982), pp. 125-134.

Pincus, M., "Information Characteristics of Earnings Announcements and Stock Market Behavior," *Journal of Accounting Research* (Spring 1983), pp. 155-183.

Platt, C.J., "How Reliable Are Profit Forecasts?" *Accountancy* (April 1979), pp. 95-97.

Poirier, R.D., "Financial Forecasts – To Disclose or Not to Disclose," *Magazine of Bank Administration* (March 1974), pp. 26-31.

Porter, G.A., "Determinants of the Accuracy of Management Forecasts of Earnings," *Review of Business and Economic Research* (Spring 1982), pp. 1-13.

Pound, G.D., "Profit Forecast Disclosure in Australia," *The Australian Accountant* (August 1981).

Prakash, P. and A. Rappaport (eds.), *Public Reporting of Corporate Forecasts* (Chicago: Commerce Clearing House, 1974).

Rappaport, A., "Don't Sell Stock Market Horizons Short," *The Wall Street Journal* (June 27, 1983).

Reckers, P.M.J. and M.E. Taylor, "The U.S. Takes a New Look at Financial Forecasts," *Cost and Management* (Canada) (March/April 1980), pp. 26-30.

Report of the Advisory Committee on Corporate Disclosure to the Securities and Exchange Commission (Washington: U.S. Government Printing Office, 1977).

Richards, R.M., "Analysts' Performance and the Accuracy of Corporate Earnings Forecasts," *The Journal of Business* (July 1976), pp. 350-357.

———, J.J. Benjamin and R.H. Strawser, "An Examination of the Accuracy of Earnings Forecasts," *Financial Management* (Fall 1977), pp. 78-86.

——— and D.R. Fraser, "Further Evidence on the Random Nature of the Errors Associated with Corporate Earnings Forecasts," Paper presented at Annual Meeting of Western Finance Association, June 1975.

——— and ———, "Management's Role in Profit Forecasting," *Review of Business and Economic Research* (Spring 1977), pp. 34-41.

——— and ———, "Further Evidence on the Accuracy of Analysts' Earnings Forecasts: A Comparison Among Analysts," *Journal of Economics and Business* (Spring/Summer 1977a), pp. 193-197.

——— and ———, "The Predictability of Corporate Earnings," *Atlantic Economic Review* (March-April 1978), pp. 43-47.

———, and J.D. Martin, "Revisions in Earnings Forecasts: How Much Response?" *The Journal of Portfolio Management* (Summer 1979), pp. 47-52.

Ross, S.A., "The Arbitrage Theory of Capital Asset Pricing," *Journal of Economic Theory* (December 1976), pp. 341-360.

Rozeff, M.S., "Predicting Long-Term Earnings Growth," *Journal of Forecasting* (October-December 1983), pp. 425-435.

Ruland, W., "The Accuracy of Forecasts by Management and by Financial Analysts," *The Accounting Review* (April 1978), pp. 439-447.

———, "Management Forecasts, Stock Prices, and Public Policy," *Review of Business and Economic Research* (Winter 1978-1979), pp. 16-29.

———, "The Time Series of Earnings for Forecast Reporting and Nonreporting Firms," *Journal of Business Finance and Accounting* (Summer 1979), pp. 187-201.

Scholes, M. and J. Williams, "Estimating Betas from Nonsynchronous Data," *Journal of Financial Economics* (December 1977), pp. 309-327.

Schreuder, H. and J. Klaassen, "Confidential Revenue and Profit Forecasts by Management and Financial Analysts: Evidence From The Netherlands," *The Accounting Review* (January 1984), pp. 64-77.

Shank, J.K. and J.B. Calfee, "Case of the Fuqua Forecast," *Harvard Business Review* (November-December 1973), pp. 34-54, 176-178.

Siegel, S., *Nonparametric Statistics* (New York: McGraw-Hill, 1956).

Skousen, K.F., R.A. Sharp and R.K. Tolman, "Corporate Disclosure of Budgetary Data," *The Journal of Accountancy* (May 1972), pp. 50-57.

Slovic, P., "Psychological Study of Human Judgment: Implications for Decision Making," *The Journal of Finance* (September 1972), pp. 779-799.

———, D.A. Fleissner and W.S. Bauman, "Analyzing the Use of Information in Investment Decision Making: A Methodological Proposal," *The Journal of Business* (April 1972), pp. 283-301.

Smith, L.D. and G.J. Murphy, "Earnings Forecasting – Investment Analysts Versus Exponential Smoothing Models," *Journal of Business Administration* (Fall 1976), pp. 11-21.

Snyir, A.G., "The Economic Implications of a Decomposition Analysis of the Risk Characteristics of Selected Properties of Earnings Forecasts and Forecast Errors," Ph.D. dissertation, Purdue University, 1981.

Stewart, S.S., "Research Report on Corporate Forecasts," in *Disclosure Of Corporate Forecasts To The Investor* (The Financial Analysts Federation, 1973), pp. 75-203.

Strawser, R.H. and J.J. Benjamin, "Should Forecasts be Included in Financial Statements?" *The Magazine of Bank Administration* (August 1973), pp. 42-45.

——— and ———, "Proposed Objectives of Financial Statements," *Managerial Planning* (March-April 1976), pp. 31-37, 41.

Stringer, K.W., "Forecasts of Economic Performance," in Prakash and Rappaport [1974], pp. 243-250.

Swanson, E.P., W.T. Shearon and L.R. Thomas, "Predicting Current Cost Operating Profit Using Component Models Incorporating Analysts' Forecasts," Working paper, Texas A & M University, 1984.

Swidler, S. and P. Vanderheiden, "Another Opinion Regarding Divergence of Opinion and Return," *The Journal of Financial Research* (Spring 1983), pp. 47-50.

Waymire, G., "Additional Evidence on the Information Content of Management Earnings Forecasts," Working paper, Washington University – St. Louis, 1984.

———, "Some Evidence on the Association Between Earnings Volatility and Frequency of Voluntary Management Earnings Forecast Disclosure," Working paper, Washington University – St. Louis, 1984a.

Westwick, C.A., "Profit Forecast in Bid Situations," *Accountancy* (July 1972), pp. 10-16.

———, "How Accurate Are Profit Forecasts?" in Westwick [1983], pp. 148-183.

———, (ed.), *Profit Forecasts: How They Are Made, Reviewed and Used* (Aldershot, England: Gower Publishing, 1983).

Zacks, L., "EPS Forecasts – Accuracy Is Not Enough," *Financial Analysts Journal* (March-April 1979), pp. 53-55.

Zarnowitz, V., "An Analysis of Annual and Multiperiod Quarterly Forecasts of Aggregate Income, Output and the Price Level," *The Journal of Business* (January 1979), pp. 1-33.

———, "The Accuracy of Individual and Group Forecasts from Business Outlook Surveys," NBER Working paper No. 1053 (December 1982).